FESO-The first published "Rhodesian" novel in first English translation and 25 Zezuru (Zimbabwen) poems in Zezuru and English texts.

FESO—The setting of the story is the region roughly stretching from the Mazoe Valley to Dande in the fertile Zambezi Valley and vaguely in the mid-17th century, a period witnessing the restless migrations of the "Vatapa" people during the golden era of the Rozvi Empire of Mambo (King) Changamire.

ZEZURU POEMS (the first major Englishing of a rich, traditional poetry now being recast in written form by new poets)—The hills and birds and people of Zimbabwe-land live again in these verses of love, nostalgia, and nature.

AN ORIGINAL BY THREE CONTINENTS PRESS
Washington D.C.

OTHER THREE CONTINENTS TITLES:

BESIDE THE FIRE, by Obioma I. Eligwe, two allegorical Nigerian tales recreated in the style of the traditional night stories.

DEREK WALCOTT: Contemporary West Indian Poet and Playwright, by Umberto Bonsignori, the first critical study of this major Caribbean writer's dramas.

A CRITICAL GUIDE TO ANTHOLOGIES OF CARIBBEAN LITERATURE, by Donald Herdeck and David Ganz, covering some fifty collections of writings in English, French, Spanish, Portuguese, and Dutch.

USHABA: The Hurtle to Blood River, by Jordan K. Ngubane, a Zulu Umlando, the classical history of the Zulu peoples. Africans, English and Boers wrestle together in the coils of *apartheid,* falling ever closer to the brink of catastrophe.

CRITICAL PERSPECTIVES ON AMOS TUTUOLA, collected and edited by Bernth Lindfors, editor of *Research in African Literatures,* University of Texas at Austin. Book reviews and critical essays on Nigeria's first great novelist from 1952 to 1974 cover in detail *The Palm-Wine Drinkard* and all subsequent works.

ZIMBABWE

PROSE and POETRY

The Dawn of the Monomotapa Kingdom—an historical essay, by S. M. Mutswairo

FESO, a novel by Solomon M. Mutswairo

and

Twenty-five Zezuru (Zimbabwen) Poems, by Mutswairo, Chidavaenzi, Kousu, and Chitepo

*Translations and English version of FESO and poetry by
S. M. Mutswairo and D. E. Herdeck except Chitepo's
"Soko Risina Musoro" which is by H. Carter*

Three Continents Press
4201 Cathedral Avenue N.W.
Washington, D. C. 20016

FIRST ENGLISH EDITION:
Three Continents Press
4201 Cathedral Ave., N.W.
Washington, D.C. 20016

©Three Continents Press 1974

FESO was originally published in Zezuru (1957) by the Rhodesian Literature Bureau and Oxford University Press, Cape Town, South Africa. (For poems see special verse title page.)

ISBN 0914478001 (Hardcover)
ISBN 0914478028 (Paper)

Oct. 6, 1975

Library of Congress catalog Number: 74-7822

Library of Congress Cataloging in Publication Data

Mutswairo, Solomon M. 1924—
  Zimbabwe: Prose and Poetry

Front cover and verse "cover" by H. S. Clapp
as well as drawing (from historic photograph)
of Nehanda and Kagubi.

For my wife, Victoria Vuyelwa
a wonderful wife, mother, and teacher

Asi parainge makomo rakwira zuva,
Vafambi romanikidza kutiva mimvuri

Now, my mind calls back the high noon fire
All blazing the bronzed sky—everyone
                        fleeing to shadow

ZIMBABWE

**Prose and poetry in English:
with original Zezuru (Zimbabwen)
texts of the verse**

TABLE OF CONTENTS

Acknowledgments

In the preparation of the manuscript of this book I am particularly indebted to Miss Ida W. Currie, an elder at The Presbyterian Church of The Pilgrims, Washington, D.C., and to Kay D. Backman, M.D., by whose generous contributions the arrangement and typing of the manuscript was made possible. I am also particularly indebted to Dr. Backman for her generous help in many ways during my stay in Washington, D.C.

My dear wife, Victoria Vuyelwa, also deserves my special debt of gratitude for her indefatigable encouragement in the need for the English translations of this and other works.

The fine cooperation of Oxford University Press, Cape Town, for allowing me to translate my novel from the original Zezuru (Shona) version is also hereby acknowledged with thanks, and to the Rhodesia Literature Bureau who acted as publishers of the original text. I am also thankful to so many people for their advice, suggestions, and encouragement in the English version of the book that it is not possible to name them all here. Also I wish to thank Dr. George Fortune for his friendship and interest in my language and its oral literature.

I also gratefully acknowledge permission to reproduce the poems given by Longmans, Green and Company, Cape Town, in whose book they first appeared, and again to the Rhodesia Literature Bureau under the directorship of Mr. E. W. Krog for its permission on the same poems.

I wish to express my appreciation to Herbert Chitepo as well as to The School of African and Oriental Studies, University of London, for permission to include the first epic poem "Soko Risina Musoro" in this volume. Luke Chidavaenzi also gave approval to my translating and publishing his two poems in this collection.

I hope the new edition delights the reader and does not disappoint old friends who have read *FESO* and my poetry and that of the others in the original Zimbabwen.

S. M. Mutswairo
Washington, D.C.
U.S.A.

The Dawn of the Monomotapa Kingdom

The Monomotapa Kingdom. By the mid-14th century A.D., long before writers left any imprint of their activities, the Kingdom of Monomotapa was flourishing in a vast region south of the Zambezi River, with Zimbabwe as its nucleus and focal point of development. Ancient maps of Monomotapa show that the kingdom was so vast that it extended northwestwards as far as Zambia's Barotseland, west into the land of the Batswana, east to the Indian Seaboard of Mozambique, south to much of the region extending south of the Limpopo River now known as the Transvaal in the present-day Republic of South Africa.

One of the most ancient maps of Monomotapa is dated 1528, "Hieronymus Verrazani faciebat,"[1] which records numerous names in Portuguese along the east, west, and southern coasts of Africa. Monomotapa Kingdom, as well as that of Monoemugi to the north, are clearly shown richly traversed by numerous rivers. An Italian map by Malleo di Benigna, dated 3rd April, 1503, and many others by Dutch cartographers, are of great interest to us in our understanding of the ancient Kingdom of Monomotapa. But the best one given in *Monomotapa* was compiled by an Italian and published in 1623. The original copy is to be found deposited in the Archives of the Vatican in Rome. This map shows quite clearly that Monomotapa dominated the whole of Southern Africa, including all of the regions which were ruled by vassal kings such as Manyika, Kitebe, Sedanda, Chikanga, and Sofala, bordering on the Indian Ocean.

A nation is born. In this region which was comparatively secluded from much of the ravages of war by hordes of invading tribes, a nation was born. The people were, by and large, descendants of the Great Monomotapa himself and were called the Makaranga. As a matter of fact, they proudly called themselves the "Children of the Sun," believing their king to have been God-appointed to rule over them. Since the Makaranga were well organized in primitive family units of tribes and clans, they quickly absorbed into their society other smaller tribes to become a large nation. We will, therefore, call this nation of extended tribal units the Vatapa. In

1

this context, the name Vatapa can be regarded much in the same light as the name Anglo-Saxon was used to refer to all the English-speaking peoples of Saxon descent.

The Vatapa were intelligent, diligent, innovative, intrepid, and well organized people who carried on their humble activities of development in a relatively peaceful land, at least, for several centuries. They had progressed far beyond the bronze age, and had mastered the art of smelting iron-ore, copper, and even gold which abounded within the confines of their land. They had, therefore, advanced far into the Iron-Age "A" culture which remained the basic material culture of the Zimbabwen plateau.

Being, thus, freed from constant interference by external forces, the Vatapa became skilled craftsmen in the art of forging iron implements, for example, axes, hoes, adzes, knives, and spearheads. They were also highly regarded in the art of making gold bracelets, bangles, earrings, wire, as well as pottery, basketry, and the weaving of cloth from cotton, and wood bark. Some of their weapons and instruments often showed great artistry and remarkable skill and dexterity. Their search for minerals is clearly manifest in numerous shallow mines and ancient diggings scattered throughout the length and breadth of ancient Monomotapa.

The Vatapa—master builders. The Vatapa were a remarkably accomplished people. They had such skilled men in stone masonry that they built edifices of stone whose relics are still to be seen scattered throughout the ancient boundaries of Monomotapa. Much as we wonder how the ancient Egyptians built the colossal pyramids and sphinxes in Egypt, so likewise, we marvel just how the Vatapa built the numerous structures of which the most spectacular are the Great Zimbabwe Ruins still preserved as a marvellous relic some few miles away from the modern town of Fort Victoria. Other structures included aqueducts, and water canals and sluices, which were designed to lead water to irrigated lands. Such relics are still to be seen in the Chipinga, Melsetter, and Umtali districts. Indeed, these are among the great wonders of Africa today. These aqueducts are reminders of a people who must have practised some horticultural industries and, possibly, grew rice, fruits, and other cultigens of their day by irrigation.

They worshipped no idols. Like so many other peoples of the world, the Vatapa had the knowledge of a deity—*Mwari*, whom they worshipped through the mediation of their departed spirits called *midzimu*.[3] It is remarkable that they worshipped no idols, either of wood, stone, iron, silver, or gold, or fetishes of any kind. It is probable that, apart from the worship being conducted in private closets, or in caves, or Mwari Shrines, such as was carried on by the Varozvi at Njelele, Matojeni, and Mangwe in the Matopos Hills, and at Ntaba dzika Mambo (Manyanga), special public worship was conducted in places like the Great Temples of Zimbabwe where religious festivities were conducted annually on a nation-wide scale. The people were monotheistic in their religious belief (in common with many other African people). There, at Zimbabwe, they offered animal sacrifices to their ancestral spirits to appease them in times of epidemics, disaster, or calamity threatening their existence. However, notwithstanding all this, the Vatapa remained highly superstitious. Magic and religious rites were often undifferentiated and, these, together with their superstitions, governed the life of every man among them. Religion thus welded the people together into a powerful nation, and there were no agnostics, atheists, or dissenters. Any such would-be deviates were well aware of the serious consequences that might befall them through the wrath of ancestral spirits.

Several missionaries working among the present-day Vatapa have arrived at the conclusion that, ". . . the notion of the Supreme Being among the Tonga and Zulu, for instance, is much more dim and obscure, hidden, and mysterious than among the Ba-Ila (Zambia), or the Mashona (present-day Vatapa)."[4] To God—*Mwari*—the Vatapa ascribed various names, viz.: *Nyadenga* (The Heavenly One), *Wokumusoro* (The One Above), *Musiki* (The Creator), *Chipindikure* (One Who Enters from afar), *Chirozvamauya* (The Destroyer of the good, and the bad), *Muumbi* (The Moulder), *Chidzivachepo* (The Great Pool—The Rain Giver), *Mutangikugara* (The Earliest Settler), *Muwanikwa* (The Eternal Present), *Samasimba* (The Almighty), *Runji* (The Lightning)—as in:

Runji rusingapfumi (rusingasoni) nguwo,
   rwaivetera (rwaivenekera) kupfuma (kusona) pasi,
meaning,

3

The needle which does not sew cloth,
but shines to sew the earth.

The Vatapa—an old nation. The Vatapa were (and still are), practically speaking, monolingual, i.e., they spoke more or less the same language, shared the same customs and traditions, and paid homage to God with the same religious rituals and beliefs—a particularly homogeneous people. As a nation, they are probably the oldest south of the Zambezi River, barring the Bushmen and Hottentots who comprised the earliest arrivals in that region. The Vatapa lived in a clearly delineated territory and had a powerful centralised form of government under an emperor. For many centuries they had successfully defended their territory against outside invasion, as well as against internal disintegration. They have, therefore, been a nation for centuries, either *de jure*, or *de facto*.

The origin of the Vatapa. No one knows precisely who the first king of the Vatapa (Makaranga) was to arrive in the land that later became Monomotapa, possibly some 1000 years ago. In point of fact, the country apparently was not even known by this name, nor by any name known to us today. Also, no one knows just when the history of Monomotapa "begins." Though some scholars have denied the very existence of the Kingdom of Monomotapa, recent historians have begun to probe into the living past of the Vatapa and their work is turning up important information. Accordingly, I shall assert that there is overwhelming evidence to prove and to strengthen the argument for the existence of this kingdom many centuries ago. Briefly, one can say the following.

At the beginning, Monomotapa (as the monarch later came to be known) was the King of the Vakaranga. As his kingdom expanded through annexation of neighbouring territories, he became the emperor of all the tribes who were now confined within his empire. Although the name Karanga seems to fit in so well with the idea of the "Children of the Sun," as the Vakaranga proudly called themselves (seemingly from Nguni—"ilanga," the sun), it does not, however, seem correct to attribute the origin of this name to Nguni derivation. Nguni interpretation was merely coincidental and is of recent time (19th C).

Probably the Karangas came from Uranga in the

region of Unyamwezi, east of Lake Tanganyika in present-day Tanzania (see Map on p.273). This is seemingly the true homeland of the Karangas. From here we seem to have a true derivation of the name "Karanga," from "Uranga," with the Karanga prefix chi-Karanga—meaning the Karanga language, or ways of the Karangas. Many people of Karanga origin can still be traced in Tanzania and Malawi even unto this day, although they have lost the use of their language over the passage of many centuries. However, this is only a hypothesis but it seems to tie in well with the probable homeland of the black Africans from the Cameroon through the southern borderland of the Katanga region of Zaïre.

The name "Monomotapa." The name Monomotapa[5] has been written in various ways: Mwenemutapa, Manamutapa, Mwenemotapa, Benemotapa, Mwanamutapa, Motapa, Mutapa, etc. Some writers think Mwanamatapa was the King's name, meaning "the owner"—mwene, of the mines which were found scattered throughout his kingdom. It is not surprising to find that this same error has cropped up in the names of places in Zimbabwe today as the result of distortion by Europeans and Ngunis alike. For example: Chinhoya (Sinoia), Mhanyami (Hunyani), Katoma (Gatooma), Shurugwe (Selukwe), Marondera (Marandellas), Kariva (Kariba), Gweru (Gwelo), Hwehwe (Que Que), etc., have all been distorted to a point of no easy recognition. The author thinks, however, that the true and correct name of Monomotapa is "Mwene Mutapwa," meaning that the foreigner has become the owner. As a foreigner, Monomotapa had taken possession of the land by conquest. Another interpretation might be "Munhu Mutapwa," meaning one who adopts people, or one who "enslaves" the people, in the sense that the people became the king's subjects, though not literally his slaves in the strictest sense of the word. A third suggestion is "Mwene Motapa," meaning the owner (mwene) of Motapaland.

P. P. Schebesta and G. Spannaus have both suggested that the Karanga came from the so-called Hamitic stock in Ethiopia, or the Sudan. This suggestion is questionable and does not seem to agree with the above suggestion regarding the original home land of the Vakaranga in Uranga. The Vakaranga belong to a common stalk of the so-called Bantu.

For simplicity's sake, then, and for increasingly good historic reasons, the name or term Monomotapa used to indicate both the empire and the person of the Monomotapa is correctly employed when discussing the peoples and their culture in Zimbabwe, or, in the modern cartography, Rhodesia. The peoples of this area are long-time residents and their roots deep in the soil which gave birth to a rich and complex culture centuries before European intrusion.

Taken from S. M. Mutswairo's unpublished work, *The Zimbabwe Epic,* and here altered slightly for this volume.

1. A. Wilmot, *Monomotapa (Rhodesia). Its monuments and its history from the most ancient times to the present century,* London, Fisher Unwin, 1896.

2. D.W.T. Shropshire, *The Church and Primitive Peoples,* London, MacMillan, 1938, p. 265.

3. Michael Gelfand, *Shona Ritual,* Cape Town, Juta and Co., 1959, pp. 74-89; and Gelfand's *Shona Religion,* Cape Town, Juta, 1962.

4. Shropshire, p. 301.

5. D.P. Abraham, "The Monomotapa Dynasty," *NADA,* 36 (1959), 59-86. See also "The Early Political History of the Kingdom of Mwene Mutapa (850-1589)" in *Historians in Tropical Africa, Proceedings of the Leverhulme Inter-Collegiate History Conference* (Salisbury, 1962), 61-91; also see "Maramuca: an exercise in the combined use of Portuguese records and oral tradition," in *Journal of African History,* II, No. 2 (1961), 211-25.

Preface to FESO

FESO has come into the English-speaking world through the encouragement of many of my own people who had read over the past two decades the original Zezuru version or of those who had read the English-language summary of it in E. W. Krog's *African Literature in Rhodesia* (Gwelo, Mambo Press, 1966).

In fact, as early as 1957, an American missionary working in Zimbabwe (Rhodesia) expressed an interest in translating the novel into English. This proved impossible, but recently I have had the encouragement and collaboration of Dr. Donald Herdeck, and the result is this volume which also contains many Zezuru poems. Accordingly, I want to express my sincere thanks to him for his long hours of help and patience in the creation of a contemporary and, I believe, lively version in English of the originals—yet faithful to the spirit of Zimbabwe.

Our translation attempts two, sometimes quite difficult, things at the same time. First, we have sought to present an accurate rendering of the original text. Second, I have amplified the dialogue as well as the descriptions of Zimbabwen customs, ideas, and characteristic speech patterns, etc. in order to make clear the roots of the actions and the context of continuum in which the narrative takes its course. Here Prof. Herdeck has been most stimulating in suggesting a detail, a touch, the use of an interesting local term, or a briefly expanded speech or authorial comment where a "cut-and-dried" literal translation of the original was opaque or would even be confusing to the non-Zimbabwen cultured individual. In a few cases we have also tried to reflect the relative solemnity or sprightliness or whatever of a speech by king, councillor, or herdboy, by different vocabularies and rhythms, even to the inclusion of modern slang where appropriate.

In short, we wished to reflect the original text as closely as possible but have felt not only free, but obliged, to

7

enrich the text at certain places so as to offer the reader a more immediately comprehensive and dramatic world—one, though imagined in part, yet quite obviously is still alive in the hearts of all Zimbabwens.

Solomon M. Mutswairo
Washington D.C.
December 31, 1973

Introduction

  FESO was the first book to be sponsored by the Rhodesia Literature Bureau. The manuscript of this historical novel, set in the pre-colonial world of the Zezuru (Shona) speaking people descended from the builders of the famous city of Zimbabwe, was approved in 1956 and published the following year in Cape Town by Oxford University Press. It thus became the first novel in Zezuru and the first creative work of literature in that language by a modern author except for a random religious poem or two. (Only the day book of Peter P.P. Patsanza entitled *Kare, Nhasi Mangwana* [The Past, Today and Tomorrow], used as a school reader and published in the early 1940s, seems to have been in print any earlier.) Also published in 1957 were two other narrative works: *Nzvengamutsvairo* (Watch Out for the Broom!) by Dr. Bernard T.G. Chidzero, and *Umthwakazi* (The Land's Master) by Peter S. Mahlangu, the former in Zezuru and the latter in Ndebele, a northern Zulu dialect.

  Mutswairo's *FESO* became at once the most popular novel and a bestseller, capturing the imagination of many students in Zimbabwe from grammar school to the university. The Rhodesian Ministry of Education as well as the University of South Africa prescribed it for their students who were studying the Zimbabwen language.

  The setting of the novel is the rural past of several centuries ago when the rituals and customs of the good old days and the wars of kings were the daily fabric of life and legend. Ancient Zimbabwe, the land of proud towns and free people, of wide and grassy plains filled with the almighty cattle, is evoked in nostalgia and in excitement for the modern reader. And the figures of sorcerers and soothsayers, and the memory and love of Nehanda, add pepper and mystery to the narrative. Nehanda, whose origin stems back to the ancient dynasty of the King of Monomotapa itself, the realm that created the great fortress-city of Zimbabwe, sings in this work. The hymn about and to her became particularly popular and subsequently was widely anthologized in Zezuru texts. The fact that a recent Nehanda had actually been hanged by the British during the rebellions of 1896-97 has no doubt added some salt to her namesake's appearance in the

9

novel. (And see the poem "The Picture of Nehanda and Kagubi," p. 151.) All of the various poems which appear in *FESO* invoke, then, the spirit of the ancestral Nehanda who speaks for the oppressed of all times and places.

Some years after *FESO's* publication, the African National Congress was revived in Rhodesia (later to evolve into ZANU, the Zimbabwe African National Union, and ZAPU, the Zimbabwe African People's Union) and the more militant nationalists seized upon *FESO* as a subtle tract of protest and call for liberation. The resulting fame, or notoriety, added to the attention the work had already received from its literary success, turned the novel into a "classic" of rebellion and nationalism. The more zealous often recited the work's poems or paragraphs of the prose in public gatherings to the weeping of the women and the groans and teeth-gnashing of the deeply moved men. A particularly lively reading even led to the arrest of the militant reciting the poem "Nehanda" and *FESO* quickly became a *cause célèbre.*

Accordingly, the Rhodesian authorities decided to move against this dangerous work which they had "stupidly" been unwise enough to publish and no further printing was allowed nor the use of the text in schools continued. Though no official explanation has ever been given, it is clear the work is still seen as an articulator of the inchoate national dreams of the African citizens of white-dominated Rhodesia.

FESO was first handwritten as a simple exercise in 1946-47 when the author was a student at Adams College, Natal, South Africa. Solomon had studied, among other works, the Zulu-language novel *U-Shaka* (1936) by R.R.R. Dhlomo and he decided to write a sizable work in his own mother-tongue, Zezuru, one of the so-called Shona dialects of Zimbabwe. There was not then any intention to write a political tract, however veiled, but Solomon's natural sympathies for his people, his love of their past, both the heroic and the routine, and his personal experiences in the modern world of apartheid could but give expression, willed or unwilled, to the long mute feelings of an entire nation.

The eventual "discovery" of hidden meanings and undercurrents of significance in the work not only surprised, but pleased, the author. A terrain he had entered as a linguistic pioneer employing a loose, novelistic structure borrowed from the West, but full of the texture of African thought and emotion, easily became a mysterious landscape where chimeras and ghosts whispered of the never-dying past, and where events of the sunny days of long ago had secret meanings for the cloudy present. Perhaps the novel is more than one man's imaginings after all, and, rather, the evocation of the time-spirit or culture-soul of a troubled, silenced people. A "Daniel" then is still needed to unravel further the allegory of *FESO* not only for Zimbabwe but all of Africa.

The setting is the region roughly stretching from the Mazoe Valley to Dande in the Zambezi plain and vaguely in the mid-17th century, a period witnessing the restless migrations of the "Vatapa" people during the golden era of the Rozvi Empire of Mambo (King) Changamire.

The characters in *FESO* are all "imagined"- and so is the narrative line. However, the names used are true Zezuru names—borrowed from various of Solomon's relatives or from elsewhere in Vatapa legend. Such names as Pfumojena (White Spear) was the author's distant great-grandfather's sobriquet; Nyan'ombe (Cattle Owner), his maternal grandfather's; Feso came from the author's uncle; and Chipo (Vachapo) from his grandmother. Chokumarara and Manzira, the herdboys in the novel who begin and end the story, take their names from two playmates of Solomon's from happier times. To a certain extent the qualities and experiences of all these people find space and psychic reality in the tale, but the mythical world of an innocent and bolder past is the subject, and the object.

Fictitious then are the major figures of Pfumojena and Nyan'ombe, the rival kings, and so is the lovely Chipo, the "Helen of Troy" of the novel (though Homer's epic was unknown to Solomon when he wrote the work). Current political events and pressures have, however, intertwined themsleves in the destinies of these characters—so their fates can now be read as portents or hopes for the better future of the peoples of Zimbabwe— when wars and the threats of war and defeat and occupation are but legends of a dimly-remembered cruel past.

It is therefore a most important task of the author and publisher to ensure that old Zimbabwe speak to all of us, this time to the world entire, if only in the borrowed feathers of William Shakespeare, modernized.

D.E. Herdeck
(based on discussions with the
author and on other sources)

FESO

Original in Zezuru (Zimbabwen)
translated
by the author, Solomon M. Mutswairo,
and Donald E. Herdeck
1973

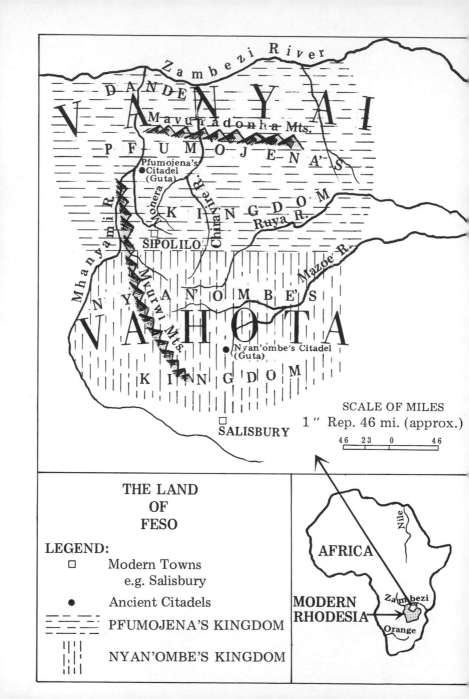

THE LAND
OF
FESO

LEGEND:

☐   Modern Towns
     e.g. Salisbury

●   Ancient Citadels

–═–═:   PFUMOJENA'S KINGDOM

|¦|¦| NYAN'OMBE'S KINGDOM

TABLE OF CONTENTS
FESO

Chapter I

The Vahota Invasion of Mazoe

Many centuries ago there lived in Mazoe district, far-renowned farmers. Their harvests—stored in log barns, rock-footed—lasted a good, long time, keeping food safe for all the people of the district.

In those days, tall trees—with crowns of leaves at their top, suitable for roofing houses and other simple domestic works—abounded in the virgin forests of Mazoe. The abundance of forests also made it easy for the inhabitants to put up their houses and to construct their cattle kraals and other enclosures, such as pallisades, for enclosing their fields. Building logs and sticks and branches were so freely available that the people lacked nothing in wood products.

Then the people built huts of logs, with rounded roofs decorated with circular grass caps at the top. Such huts today are still to be seen in the villages of many of the Zezurus who still do not have modern houses because of their lack of money for modern materials.

In that beautiful, grassy plain extending as far as the eye can see, and overlooking the range of hills—Nyamuhumbe, Manangate, Mbeve, Musekure, and Mushande (where we find today the small settlement of Glendale), the simple folk of the district grazed their cattle and other domestic beasts. The entire plain, well watered by the Mazoe river, extending as far as the site of the Mazoe Dam now used for watering citrus fruits, was then the grazing ground for the animals of the ancients. The goats skipped and frolicked and scaled the rocky surfaces of the hills, while the herders enjoyed the quiet, serene atmosphere of the open land.

It is in this land that we find a tribal clan of the Vahota people under their chief, Nyan'ombe—the Cattle Owner. Still other clans were scattered in numerous surrounding regions of the country. This section of the people goes under the clan name Tembo—the Zebra, and the laudatory praise name, Mazvimbakupa—Those-Who-Long-to-Give! They comprise only a small part of the larger group of the Vahota in Marandellas District in the now-so-called Chihota

17

Tribal Trust Land, but who consider themselves the descendants of that great and powerful Paramount Chief, Mutasa, of the Manyika tribal group inhabiting the region around Umtali. Their great-grandfather, they say, sitting by the fires at night, was Makombe of the Vabarwe, and his wife, Mureche—the daughter of Matope Nyanhehwe Monomotapa, the original king of the Vakaranga and, later, of all the Vatapa of ancient Zimbabwe.

The formidable, aggressive neighbours of the Vahota were the Vanyai, who inhabited a near-by region to the north of the Vahota kingdom, under the Mambo, Pfumojena—the White Spear. They also claimed direct descendance from the great King Matope Nyanhehwe Monomotapa. Fierce warriors, these very proud people looked down on every tribe around them.

The Vahota who invaded Mazoe were great warriors, too. They had easily conquered the inhabitants of the land and settled here to found new homes for themselves. At the death of Paramount Chief Gombekombe, Nyan'ombe, his first-born son, was installed chief in his place. To mark his chieftaincy he wore a white chief's pendant around his neck. He grew up to become a man full of courage, knowledge and wisdom, respected and loved by all his people.

Chapter II

The Dialogue of Chokumarara and Manzira

It is here in this wide plain of Mazoe that we meet two herdboys of Paramount Chief Nyan'ombe: Chokumarara and Manzira guarding their cattle.

Chokumarara is only seventeen years old, but with a very alert mind. He is brown-skinned, slightly built, long faced, with black, glittering eyelids. He is wearing a skin head cover of a leopard that his father killed a year before. His mouth is seemingly always agape, thus exposing his teeth and his lungs to the dust and other unsavoury products of the dry season. As a result, his teeth are dirty looking, almost as dark as one who has spent the whole day eating the fruit of the tsubvu wild plum. His large, flat nose resembles the buttocks of a frog; his breathing is laboured as of one with a clogged nose, or, as of one who has a bad cold, and must breathe heavily through the mouth.

His hands are wiry, though, with veins large and distended beneath the skin. He has well built legs with well formed calves. His apparel is a mere loincloth passed between the legs and tied securely to his waist with a leather strap. Beside him, high up on a large boulder where he is sitting, is his dog—Kugarahunzwana. With this dog he hunts hares in the bush and cane rats in the swampy marsh.

His friend, Manzira, is younger by about a year. Though a mere sixteen years old, his mind is much more mature than one might expect and he often talks like a grownup man. He is a very handsome looking lad, with small eyes—resembling the black-eyed peas that are used in playing the nyimo game. He wears a bushy-looking mop of hair which seemingly has not been barbed in a long time. He is well built, obviously well fed by a loving mother, and his large arms are fat and round like those of a rich girl who does not engage in hard work. His legs are large, too, with well formed calves—not shapeless like an elephant's legs. Manzira has a sharp and alert countenance, with a fine white set of teeth. He is of middle height, not as tall as Chokumarara, but one can feel he will rise tall like the fast growing *mushori-wondo* tree as his years of manhood come.

In his right hand Manzira holds a bundle of arrows and in his left he has a bow made from the soft but supple wood of the *munyani* tree. With these weapons held tightly, he watches some birds in a nearby tree, half hidden in the branches. His favorite kills are doves and black-eyed bulbul which he enthusiastically tells everyone are juicier than any other bird. So, perched in a fig tree, waiting for a shot, he calmly munches a few juicy figs, comfortable in his loin covering of fawn buckskin, his shining legs hanging down.

"Friend Chokumarara!" shouts Manzira dangling-legged on his branch, "Never in my life have I tasted such juicy and delicious figs."

"A rotten fig to you! You make even the dead laugh, oh, my father Tembo! Don't bother me with such fool things!" Chokumarara snorted as he absent-mindedly stroked the back of his dog.

"I wonder," Manzira persisted, "why the figs at the Chief's Court aren't as nice as these! Those at home are as tasteless as a watermelon grown on a dry piece of land. I eat 'em only when I'm starving to death."

"When the sadza meal is late?"

"Yes!" he grunted.

"Or when the women are away in the fields?"

"Yes!"

"Or when the chow from the little mother's house is not so tasty? When there's no meat to snap your teeth on?"

"Yes!"

"Everything to you is 'yes'!" observed Chokumarara.

"But why, then, are those home figs so tasteless?"

Chokumarara hesitated awhile and then said in a whisper, "Haven't you heard that those fig trees are under the spell of witches who own them? The witches have sent out owls that hoot in their branches at night, cursing their fruits and rendering them tasteless. At least, that is what my grandmother told me," ended up Chokumarara, defensively, fidgeting and scratching himself like someone bitten by lice or red ants at night.

"Ha! Ha!" laughed Manzira, "I don't believe that! And where have you ever heard such nonsense—that witches can send their spells even against trees? Of course I know that

20

witches can bewitch people at night, or cast bad luck for their victims at crossroads. Look, Chokumarara! Watch out for the . . . !' He didn't finish what he wanted to say, for Chokumarara broke in:

"I know what's on your mind," he said, "you're worrying about the cattle going astray! Don't worry! Sitting up here on this rock I can see them grazing in the reeds near the river. But listen," he insisted, his interest in conversation rising like a flooded river. "Have you heard of the recent doings at the Chief's Court?"

"Ha! What did you say? What? You mean about Feso returning wobbling after a big drinking party at the kraal of Chogugudza?" Manzira replied, not giving much thought to what his friend had insinuated.

"Why be so smart about nothing? You dummy! No one cares about a little drinking now and then, and besides, everyone gets potted some time," Chokumarara protested. But he continued, "Don't you know the chief wants to get married? Has that ever crossed your mind, you bumpkin? Haven't you heard that the chief has asked his council to help him end his bachelor days?"

"Certainly I have," replied Manzira, rather bashful about such things, and looking down in his embarrassment. "It's interesting gossip," he muttered, "but I don't pay much attention to the old boys' stories, though I'd be happy in the celebration that'd come with a royal wedding. I'm sure that men like Feso who delight in long snorts of the hard stuff will be only too glad of such a chance. Of course I wouldn't want to libel the good reputation of so great an Army Commander," he mock apologized, "but he was really crocked that day." Looking up to Chokumarara he said, "So? Tell me where you first heard this rumour."

At this point Chokumarara slid down from the stony outcropping, his dog scrambling down with him. Looking squarely at his mate, he half whispered, "Last night, after you had gone to sleep, I overheard the chief confiding with his two Army Commanders—Feso and Mapondera— saying he desired to end his celibacy and that he was looking around for a good looking woman, one who would fill completely the position of chief's wife. The Commanders and now the other members of his council have agreed he should go ahead.

21

And, since this is a matter for the whole nation of the Vahota to decide, they all suggested that it was their responsibility to seek a suitable woman, no matter where such a paragon might be found."

"Don't tell me that they could even consider getting a wife from the Vanyai who live far to the north of us in the Zambezi valley?"

"Why not?" retorted Chokumarara.

"Why? Because they are such a proud people, and we've fought them in lots of battles and always lost."

"We've won some, too!" rejoined Chokumarara.

' Well, maybe—even so—they look down upon us, sneering at our pride in being the 'great' Vahota people. So, why go so far to seek a wife? Why not one of our women here? Are they not as good as any, if not better?" demanded Manzira.

"Because the good and the inspiring often come from afar. They'd do it just for the kicks! Isn't it more fun to grab what's hard to get?"

"Sure, why not? Let's break the barrier of pride and prejudice of the Vanyai," Manzira snickered.

But Chokumarara was serious: "The council is resolved to go to any length to find a beautiful and suitable woman for the chief. Besides, it's not really the Vanyai that matter. Rather, it's the woman. If the chief wants her, I mean, if he *really* wants her, then all that's left is her own personal decision. That's what really matters." He added, "After all, every detail of what the prospective woman should be has already been decided: for instance—she has to have a beautiful set of teeth, as shining as the moonlight; and she's got to have a glamorous face—and eyes piercing as the rays of the sun. Anyway, that's how Feso described this dream woman." Finished, Chokumarara grabbed up his spear alongside the alert-eyed Kugarahunzwana to start off after the now distant cattle.

"Well, it's hopeless!" Manzira laughed. "No such woman in all this country." But he shrugged, "So what, all's in the mind of the lover." Wise beyond his years, or so he believed, he went on—"I remember once meeting in Zambara a young woman carrying a bundle of wood. She was so ugly looking that we nicknamed her 'The-Hyena-Is-Better-

Looking'—an unfair description though, I guess, not knowing what her heart and personality were like," he quickly qualified. But to make his point he had to argue, "For someone, she was probably wonderful."

"I wonder where such a model can be found?" he exclaimed, "And models don't make good wives, anyway."

Chokumarara had nothing more to say, and raced away with his dog towards the moving herd. The sun was setting and it was time to round up the restive cattle and go home.

But, once caught up, walking just behind the dust of the rumbling, bellowing, spotted beasts, Chokumarara couldn't let the matter drop. "Since the chief made public his desire to marry a woman meeting all those descriptions of perfection, he has made a proclamation to be sent throughout the land of the Vahota calling together at his town all the prominent people. He'll tell them all his wish and he'll ask for ideas from them."

But by this time Manzira was more interested in keeping his eye out for evening doves than in listening to more old men's concerns. When the doves he had spotted flew away at their noisy approach, Manzira blamed his friend for the mishap. But Chokumarara was a quiet lad and only replied, sarcastically, "My friend, it was your heavy-footed breaking of the small twigs that scared the birds away. The poor birds have only saved their lives, like rabbits escaping a wild forest fire. There should be more just across the next ford of the stream." And then he went on with his story.

"Tomorrow—and this should interest you—tomorrow's the day when the people gather. This conference will nominate those suitable to go around looking for the wonderful girl who will be the Chief's bride." By this time, they had tailed the cattle into the kraal and slammed shut the gate with logs.

Now piqued, Manzira drew closer and whispered, "Hey, what about Mapondera's daughter? Isn't she a good prospect for the chief's bride?"

"What? Her? Well, I don't know—maybe somebody likes her looks—but as for me she isn't as beautiful as she should be. Just think of her deep, sunken eyes; they're like a monkey's, and besides, she's so dark it's as if her mother had eaten the fruit of the *mutsubvu* tree while she was pregnant with her. Anyway, when this matter was being discussed, I saw Mapondera stroking his long beard as if the matter wasn't of any interest to him. And why should it be? It's probably a cinch that either Feso or Mapondera himself will be nominated for the espionage job to a far off land, so he'll have to give up any personal hopes," Chokumarara concluded.

Manzira thought it over but only said, "Well, maybe; we'll see." But the whole night through Manzira pondered over these things as if he were personally involved—losing sleep and rest over the matter of the chief's bride, like everybody else in the village that night—except the snoring Chokumarara who had started the whole thing in the first place.

Chapter III

Nyan'ombe Faces The Nation

It is not unusual for excessive happiness or sorrow to rob one of his sleep. Sometimes when a man is obsessed with a particular thing, he turns it over and over in his mind, hence being robbed of his vitally needed rest. He may dread the approaching day, or he may wish that a particular thing would not happen, or vice versa. So it was with Manzira. He became obsessed with the expected happiness whose advent he wished he could hasten.

The next day dawned with a lovely, cloudless sky. There was hardly any breeze to sway the trees in the hills. It was quiet, serene, and peaceful. The silence was only occasionally broken by the cooing of the dove, or the chirping of the shrine-bird, or the chaunting of the black-eyed bulbul-birds which always frequented the fig tree near the *dare*—the men's meeting place, in the early hours of the day.

The chief's entire village yet lay quiet and still. The only thing that seemed to disturb the peace was two figures lighting the fire at the men's place and causing a pillar of smoke to rise. The entire village, including the gateway keepers of the stone wall fortification surrounding the village, was still at peace with itself.

In days gone by, some village enclosures were built of large stones. They were built surrounding king's, paramount's or chief's dwellings and used for protection against their enemies in times of war. But ordinary people's villages did not have such enclosures.

Today there are hardly any villages at all with such enclosures among the Zezuru people. But a sketchy idea of such an enclosure is afforded today by the wooden enclosures protecting corn fields from the pigs, cattle, sheep and goats which otherwise would enter to destroy them. But there is a difference between these two kinds of protection. The former walls were naturally much stronger than the latter because, like the ones built in England by the ancient Romans, or the one spanning hundreds of miles in northern China, these were built of stone and afforded much better and stronger protection, and they had to be high to keep out clever enemies—far craftier than even the hungriest of goats.

In this village, now, Chief Nyan'ombe's royal house was situated in the heart of the town. His uncles' houses, his councillors, and his army generals stood some little distance away from the big house.

The royal dwelling was large and spacious. A verandah surrounded it completely, built of strong wooden poles tied securely together. The roof was so low, however, that in order to get into the house, one had to bend down way low, being careful not to hit his head on the upper entrance post above him. Inside, the house had a raised platform immediately to the right of the door. This provided a sitting place for all visitors to the royal house. The chief's seat was a built-in earthen structure permanently moored to the ground. It was kept well plastered with red mud by the women and shone with the reflection of whatever light diffused through the open doorway. It glowed like polished stone. Over the throne was spread a lion's skin and a leopard's, too, to give it a regal look.

Hanging from the wall were shields and spears, bows and arrows, axes and battle-axes, the *mashave* spirit dancing axes, game and fighting sticks, and a host of other accoutrements. Food calabashes, and all kinds of leather sacks hung on pegs, just barely visible on the dark wall. Some of these had been inherited from Nyan'ombe's father, and even from his grandfather, things they themselves had often used during their days on earth. Very worn they were; therefore, more of sentimental value than of practical use.

Seated now in the royal seat is Nyan'ombe himself. He wears a leopard's skin and looks young and handsome. With him are his councillors and army commanders. In their midst stand tall the two prominent Army Commanders—Feso and Mapondera. These two, the mambo's closest advisors, always suggest important directions to be taken in the affairs of the nation. They await the great council of the people.

As the sun rises in degrees above the horizon, the quietness and serenity of the village is turned into a din as crowds pour into the village, throwing up dust like herds of cattle as they shamble in from all directions. They push and jostle through the great stone gateway leading into the heart of the village. Men, proud of their past battles, stalk in carrying their shields and glittering spears as if going to war. Men and boys, well fed and confident, come sauntering into the chief's village.

Although they strutted proudly into chief Nyan'ombe's village, they nevertheless approached the royal residence solemnly, with dignity and respect, for they all loved and honoured their young chief. Some had travelled long distances and had come panting, dreading to be late for the occasion, only to find that the meeting had not yet started. From far or near, old or young, seasoned veterans or unscarred youths, they pressed toward the ancient meeting place. Soon there was quiet, and decorum and order reigned once more in the capital village. All spears and shields were laid down on the ground. Everyone present on this day deeply sensed the gravity of the occasion, for a king's bride would be mother to them all and give them their future king.

At the appointed time, the sun centered in the sky, Nyan'ombe left the royal house and headed for the men's place—the dare—an open space with a pavilion and graced by a large fig-tree with hanging branches almost touching the ground. The procession, headed by two of his army commanders, and Nyan'ombe himself, confidently stepped toward the multitude, while the rest of the retinue trailed behind them. Then the gathered men started to clap in unison amid the women's ululations and dancing, springing up at the sight of their chief. Then, when all again was quiet, and the body guard stood with the men's spears pointing up as if in an array for battle itself, Nyan'ombe stood up and strongly addressed the congregation thus:

"Ndinokukwazisai mose!" ("I greet you, my people!")

"Greetings to you, Changamire, Mazvimbakupa!" they shout back.

They stare at their handsome prince—at the leopard crown on his head and, adorning it, the ring of ostrich feathers fluttering in the breeze and glittering in the sun.

"You have all been invited to this council because it is the desire of your leaders that as many of you as possible should take part in the deliberations. We solicit your ideas and suggestions."

"Changamire. We hear you!" the men enthusiastically rumble out.

27

Continuing, the chief speaks loudly:"We have desired to follow our tradition in which everybody concerned with the welfare of our nation should understand and participate in weighty decisions. I, as your national father and chief, desire to share my secret thoughts with you, my children—my people."

A roar of applause from the crowd, clapping and whistling and in every way the people show their approval of Nyan'ombe's remarks.

"As some of you might know already, this matter closely concerns me—your chief. My council has decreed that the chief should end his bachelorhood and seek a new mother of the nation and a helpmate in ruling the Vahota nation."

Again, a roaring and thunderous applause from the crowd, some nodding and some talking to one another in an act of approval, while the women a second time ululate wildly with their shrill voices. Then there was silence, as if the people were now digesting in their minds what Nyan'ombe had said.

Continuing, Nyan'ombe said, "In accordance with our tradition and custom, it's been suggested that the chief's wife should be of a royal house, or the daughter of noble birth of a distinguished family brought up in the nature and nurture of nobility, or of such a noble quality as to be able to serve the nation's needs as its mother. This matter has not been resolved, and we sincerely hope that you can help us solve the problem. 'Two heads are better than one,' the old ones say. For this reason you have all been invited here today to prove your heads."

A roar of laughter pervaded the audience, followed immediately by a roar of applause; the women wildly screaming and dancing and the men clapping their hands in unison, while the older folks nodded their heads in an act of approval. Nyan'ombe, though still a young man, commanded respect among his people. He spoke with courage, determination, and showed wisdom and a concern for his people's welfare. He loved his people and wanted them to participate and feel an important part of the entire nation. For a royal marriage, he well knew, was not a private concern between two people which could be dealt with casually and egotistically. Rather, it was a bond which included first the immediate members of the family, then the extended family, and, finally, the whole nation given to the prince's charge. Nyan'ombe was making a good beginning by taking his people into his confidence and trust and getting everybody involved.

Feso who was sitting next to Nyan'ombe, and whose big, brown penetrating eyes had been peering over the crowd, now stood up and, first, addressing the chief while clapping his hands, said, "Changamire! Tembo Mazvimbakupa!"

The crowd responded by clapping their hands in unison.

"Greetings to you all," he says, turning to the crowd. In the silence that follows, he continues thus, "The chief has already outlined the intention of this Court and, indeed, of our nation—namely, the marriage of the chief. We are all agreed that there can be no real home for a man who has no wife. She is not only a wife, but a companion, a helpmate, a co-councillor, a stabilizer of a man's character—yea, but above all—a mother! A mother of Nyan'ombe, and a mother of us all!" And many more eloquent embroideries on these themes. At this point the crowd roars out an ovation. But he, he beckons with his hand, implores them to return to silence.

"This task is not the doing of us mortal men alone, but the desire and expectation of Nehanda Nyakasikana—our great and noble spirit—medium well known to all of us, and whose wisdom and guidance have been the mainstay of this nation against our foes of the Pfumojena."

Moving like a giant back and forth in front of the emotional mass of his countrymen, Feso begins to chant the famous lines they all knew—had known for generations back to first time, the song to Mhondoro—the Lion Spirit:

"NEHANDA! You great earthly spirit!
A mighty Lioness! Oh Great One of ancient times!
With fear, they quaked hearing your voice
In the Pande tree near a flat rock.
You ordered, 'Go, Warriors! and destroy
Those Vanyai gathered in the north.
Fight, my heroes! But stretch not
Your hands to seize booty from them.'
At Nehanda's command, together they gathered
Legions of men who headed for the lowlands.
Indeed, devastating battles they fought!
Though they obeyed not the entire command.

Yet, nevertheless, the land they took:
Nehanda! I say, 'Arise! And help us!' "

Ending his half-chant, Feso finishes, "I cannot over-
state the importance of this matter. I urge you all to take
time to consider the best possible way of meeting this chal-
lenge." The people moved by the old anthem studied Feso
and their chief—and, after all—Feso was one of the Army
Commanders of Nyan'ombe's several regiments, and much
older than Nyan'ombe himself, commanding great respect
among the people. He not only commanded his regiment
with his wisdom, but also with his great stature, standing
more than six feet tall, and being large-limbed, and a phy-
sique well seasoned by his life of hardship and warrior disci-
pline. While talking he used his arms liberally and his head
turned in all directions as if to make sure he observed what
was happening all around him every moment.

Beneath his strangely thin hair, he wears a sable antelope's skin strung above his shoulder on one side and tied in
the waist with a leather belt. Ah, yes, an impressive figure he
is, with a beard like a patriarch's.

When Feso had concluded his remarks, Jeranyama, a
tall, clever-looking commander, stood up and addressing the
crowd says: "Changamire! Our Chief Nyan'ombe! Mazvimbakupa! I'm just like a little dog barking at its master."

"Bark on!" the crowd roars.

The chief nods, amused.

"This is a matter of great concern to all of us. Since
this matter has been presented to the general public, it is like
our old saw which says, 'He who kills a goat in a public place
desires to share its blood with those present.' Now, I, your
servant, Jeranyama, propose that this court send messengers
throughout this wide land in an effort to feel out all the
scattered nations' branches for this desired pangolin-
armadillo—the chief's cherished dish! Nyan'ombe as our
chief, once we've found the very best virgins, must exercise
his own prerogative to pick and choose the very best that this
whole broad expanse of land and sky can give." Pleased with
these expressions, the people applauded heartily, some nodding and some jesting in admiration, calling out comments,
ideas, even names of those girls they thought beautiful.

Among the most distinguished commanders of

Nyan'ombe was Mapondera, sitting there quietly beside the king, pondering over what the people were saying. He, too, was a man regarded with the highest esteem, feared and revered by the young and the old alike because of his undaunted leadership in previous wars under Chief Gombekombe—Nyan'ombe's late father. Though much older than Nyan'ombe, he still keeps his great physical strength born of arduous and rigorous life in the battles. He wears a beard and a leopard skin girt about his shoulder, and always carries with him a spear and a knobkerry club wherever he goes. He is even reputed by some to be possessed of magical powers to rise into the air in combat and to remain invisible in the face of danger. By such means, fair and foul, he is believed to have inflicted many casualties on the enemy in numerous battles. Standing up at last, he addresses the chief and the quieted crowd, thus, "Chirombowe!" then turning to the chief, to the mambo: "There is no great impediment here that cannot be surmounted."

The crowd awaits expectantly in a tense atmosphere. Now the difficulties will be enumerated by this experienced fighter.

"I see no great problem that we, the Vahota, cannot overcome. Most fortunately there is a chief of a nation adjacent to our own kingdom who is reputed to have an extremely lovely daughter—the only daughter he has. Never has such beauty been seen anywhere in this land—the beauty of both body and character, I'm told." His voice is buoyant—but still serious.

Continuing, he half-cries, "The mambo, father of this wonderous woman, rules a tribe of people we all know as the Vanyai—of the totem Nzou—the Elephant, and of the laudatory praise-name, Samanyanga—meaning the one possessing tusks. A great people, and proud people, they are. But," and here his wise speaker's voice falls, "alas, such beauty is being forcibly made to waste its loveliness in lonely solitude. Kept in a dark dungeon of a hut, this noble princess is doomed to spend her days in isolation—like a calf in a far away place tied down to a peg by a string. Such surprising and cruel treatment has arisen from the belief that her beauty, so great is it," and here his drum-rumbling voice, shakes, "is a gift from the ancestral spirits and, as such, a living symbol of the beauty of the entire Vanyai people themselves. The people have been driven to worship her as if she were an immortal goddess.

"No man—let alone one of us, of the Vahota—is ever to be permitted to look right at her, or think of her as a mortal woman of flesh and blood. Even though they be of the most exalted rank, to court her, even through the most circumspect intermediaries for matrimony, is forbidden. Many there have been, however, who despite these barriers," and his bass-voice falls even deeper, "so splendid is her shining beauty that many have lost their lives-so wild are their dreams of her magnificence. She has become the embodiment of all that the Vanyai live for—a tragic symbol for us who can see it, of the narrowed and superstitious minds—of a people for whom the word freedom is unknown, though they mouth the word often, and who reject for others—and, hear this, even to closing their eyes to the lovely, if mortal, glory of their own chief's daughter." These eloquent words expressed, the calm general gazes out at the nervous crowd, confused at this unheard of beauty, trapped in such toils of insane love and pride.

Continuing then, he says, "This treatment of the girl is believed by the Vanyai to have come from the ruling of the ancestral spirits—whom they worship—that such unearthly beauty should not be sacrificed to mundane matrimony. Hence, her father, Pfumojena, named her Chipochedenga, meaning the Gift of Heaven! There she sits on a royal stool with a noble woman's fur cap on her head and strange dances are performed before her while all can only view her if at all, sideways looking—and from afar. I suggest, accordingly," and here he coughs, "that Mambo Nyan'ombe send a shrewd and cunning man as a spy to find out ways and means of encouraging her to flee her golden prison. However," and, Mapondera pauses most dramatically, "we must understand that this intended beguilement of the Vanyai princess is fraught with danger and bloodshed to the nation and we ought to be prepared for any eventuality. The Vanyai may well never forgive us for that sacrilege as they would term it. But our chief deserves the finest mortal woman in the world." So spoke the great warrior Mapondera.

"We are not afraid!" shouts the crowd, "Yes, yes, only the best is good enough for our nation!"

"But it won't come so long as you sit on your hunkers here," Mapondera grunts dryly above the shouted oaths.

Whereupon, in no time at all, the people chose Feso to undertake this fateful task, he agreeing to risk his life for the sake of his chief and his country.

All at last settled, at least as far as they were concerned, the crowd starts to disperse. Here and there a few wild cries and boastful epithets were directed at the Vanyai, and some of the women cried noisily, half in excitement, half in imagined terror of what might come of all this. But soon the people's cries are only distant humming echoes dying away, away in the distance, as the evening sun stood down in the west.

"I predicted, didn't I?" triumphantly crowed Manzira, the young herdboy, to his friend. "Didn't I say that if Mapondera was not appointed they would have to choose Feso?"

"Indeed, you were right, my comrade," replied Chokumarara, as the two herders were fitting in the wooden guard poles in the paddock gate, securing their cattle kraal's entrance for the night.

"We'll see, if we're lucky, where the whole affair will end," concluded Manzira as he turned home after another long day.

Chapter IV

Nyan'ombe and Feso

Towards the latter part of the evening when all the crowds had dispersed, and the noise and din had died down, and when the village had regained its tranquility, Nyan'ombe sent for Feso to come to the *imbahuru*. In haste Feso hurried to the palace, a little anxious to know what further matter was upon the chief's mind.

"Chirombowe! I am Feso, come at your bidding," so he announced his presence according to custom.

"Draw near, Commander. Sit yourself over there and make yourself at home," Nyan'ombe replied warmly. As he sat his young niece handed both men a gourd of beer.

In the dark inner room lit from the diffused light of the fire on the stone hearth, Nyan'ombe sat composedly and rather in a contemplative mood. Finally he found the right words.

"I have desired to be with you alone and to thank you for accepting the great task the people have placed on you. It is a heavy work you have accepted, but my confidence in your capability equals the joy I have in you. And the people, too, wisely believe you will serve us well," Nyan'ombe said.

"Changamire! Mazvimbakupa!" Feso replied, clapping his hands.

"The burden has been lifted off my mind because I know the nation could not have made a better choice, and you go to the country of the Vanyai with my blessings and those of the Vahota ancestral spirits."

"I'm grateful for the opportunity and privilege of being able to serve my chief and country in this way, my Lord, and I am not too proud to hope I can be worthy of your confidence."

"I do not doubt it. Not for one moment!"

"We'll rise and fall together," Feso assured him.

"Our task is a formidable one knowing, as we all do, how the Vanyai look down on us and regard us as a weaker nation. But one way, Feso, in breaking down the pride of a

34

nation is through their women folk. Weakening this bond or link automatically weakens the nation, and it is our desire to start with the weakest link—much as the Varozvi of old broke the stronghold of the Vambire under Chihunduro by giving the latter a Murozvi woman for a bait. Remember that! There was a sad outcome—all caused by a woman!"

"Yes, Changamire! Mazvimbakupa! I heard the story as a youth. Your memory is wonderful, my Lord!"

"Indeed, Feso, there are very few people that I have as much confidence in as I have in you. I have known you since I was a youth in the days of my late gallant father. I know your feeling towards me and your devotion to our nation. I cannot doubt but that you will acquit yourself like a man."

Nyan'ombe ordered that more drink be given his commander. The chief was now extraordinarily lively with joy and gladness this evening. His praise for Feso seemed infinite and it seemed to be a genuine outpouring from his deepest and innermost feelings toward his Army Commander. Possibly, too, his lonely years, with no wife, made him feel ardent this night.

"These many years I have lived and known you, I have not detected any disloyalty to the Nyan'ombe throne." He, too, took up his cup and took another long draught, then lifting his hands, he pointed up at the flickering shadows on the ceiling for emphasis and said, "I know you are a man of principles, of courage and fortitude, and that you will carry out this mission to the best of your ability." He had said this many times now—but what of that?

"Changamire! Whatever you say shall be done!" Feso said, lowering his head once more, if proudly, in obeisance to his superior.

"When do you depart?"

"Tomorrow, my Lord!"

"But you won't have much time to prepare, will you?"

"It's the mind that needs preparation, not the body, and besides, it has already received such preparation. My eyes and hands and feet will get me there—and our ancestors—if they love us—will get me back with your wife."

"Anything else you need?"

"Nothing, Mazvimbakupa! Nothing else. Your trust is

all I need carry."

"Very well, then, farewell, noble Commander! Farewell!" The chief stood.

"May the spirits of our fathers look with favour on you," and he waved with a brotherly gesture his general on to his mission.

Chapter V

Pfumojena and the Vanyai

The Vanyai lived in a far off land to the north of the Vahota country. Their Chief, Pfumojena—the White Spear (so named by the people because he wielded a white spear whithersoever he went, and his rule being fierce, and dictatorial) proudly ruled over them.

Pfumojena was highly superstitious, and the entire legal and religious code of the land centered mainly on what he felt were the dictates of his ancestral spirits. His judgments and powers were, accordingly, a reflection of such convictions and upon them depended the life and death of his people. As a result, many of his people had lost their lives over trivial matters. Most men dreaded and hated him, but were careful to order their lives in such a way as not to cause his displeasure which, too often, resulted in execution, or, as a less harsh punishment, expatriation.

Many of Pfumojena's victims had been caught in the unwitting toils of Chipochedenga—the Vanyai princess. Chipo's beauty and growing fame could hardly fail to attract the attention of many a man who felt himself rich enough—or brave enough—to court her. Buzz, buzz they hummed around her father's house—and their eyes followed her lithesome steps when she went to the river with the other maidens to bathe—or draw water. The mere expression of desire on the part of an admirer, or, horrible sacrilege, the playful attempt to touch her body, was punishable by a severe sentence, if not death. Some, so convicted, had their hands cut off, or their eyes put out, or executed with only a summary trial before the court called *dare*. Pfumojena insisted on each such occasion in the sanctity of his daughter as a gift from heaven. He again would proclaim her a holy, pure, and untouchable woman—a joy for the gods and not of men—let alone commoners or, unthinkable, men from the other tribal groups around whom he regarded with contempt. So, poor, sweet, sanctified Chipochedenga became an exalted figure only to be seen, never to be touched or sung to, to be admired only from afar, to be yearned for, not possessed; oh oh—she was green pastures to be seen, not to be grazed upon.

The Vanyai who, at one time in the past, had been vassals of the great King Monomotapa, had lived side by side with the Vatapa of Monomotapa in the great valley of the Zambezi river in the north. They had, therefore, imbibed the civilization and cultural heritage of their former masters and were now become, thanks to their undoubted courage and hardihood in battle, a proud and powerful nation. They regarded all others as decadent and treated them as their underdogs. Little would they consider intermarriage with their neighbours. Vanyai blood was better blood. It must never be defiled by servile stuff. And their king, tough master, manipulated their legal system as it pleased him and profitted him, and his friends. The people were expected to obey him implicitly, without question. In the main the Vanyai prospered. Success makes one forget freedom—or personal dignity. So, there were those who liked him and favoured his rule because he exalted their nation and made the Vanyai a unique and envied people.

Pfumojena's large country spanned hundreds of square miles of fertile land and bright water, and, very happily, huge tracts of forest land. In this land flourished all kinds of game and wild animals—the lion, the elephant, the buck, the deer,—numerous species of birds, and an abundance of wild fruit trees. Fish, too, swam in the many rivers and streams. It was a land richly endowed with good things for man's joy, a coveted land, beautiful and attractive in many ways.

An old tradition, perhaps better regarded as a religious ritual, was observed at Pfumojena's royal village. The people observed a harvest-season festival at which time all family heads were expected to bring a basketful of the year's harvest—be it maize, fingermillet, or black-eyed peas—as a kind of tax to the Mambo's court. Once given freely, the tribute now was expected. Failure to bring in a share of one's harvest was an offense and punishable by a severe court sentence, even to the seizure of the family lands or, if mambo had special antipathies that day, expulsion from the land.

So it happened that because some men prefer freedom to a selfish and narrowly imposed law and order, and despite stringent security measures, there were many families and sometimes single farmers who did not bring tribute to

the royal court but who fled the bountiful Vanyai territories—to seek to make homes elsewhere. One dissident group
was led by Mutowembwa and Musarapasi who proclaimed
themselves outside the law and defied mambo and his court.
Chief outlaw was Mutowembwa—so named because he said,
"I've become like the dog's soup," meaning—"I'm hunted by
Pfumojena like a dog hunts a rabbit."

These outlaws lived in caves hidden in the forest
called *Mudzimundiringe*—meaning, "my ancestral spirit watch
over me and protect me," and here they preferred to live a
life without a government rather than giving in to an evil and
corrupt and wicked rule of a mad and puritanical king. High
jagged rocks, sudden pits and steep cliffs, treacherous water
courses and briary forests, were terrors to strangers and any
would-be pursuer was sure to go in there at his own risk, for
it was difficult, if not impossible, to hunt anyone in such
thickets. Perhaps worse were scorpions, snakes, sting-beetles,
gnats, green flies, and poison thousand-leggers.

Well rubbed down with powerful ointments to drive
off the crawling and flying insects, and well content behind
their tiny fires kindled far back in their snug caves, sat Mu-
towemba and his exiled band. They spoke softly then of their
lost ones—and their eyes glittered when talk turned to their
hated king.

One ritual they had dreaded most was the one in
which a diviner—a mambo appointed medicine man—
"scrutinized" bones, sometimes he could see the culprit's
face in the medicine bowls—to read out who was plotting
against the mambo. But most important in his divination
were the *hakata*—a set of six or eight wooden sticks. Throwing them on the hard-packed earth before his leaning hut at
the edge of the forest, he would peer and peer, studying them
with his hard eyes, seeking out the tell-tale counters, sniffing
out his victims. Then, satisfied, he would indicate them as
witches and wizards. Exhausted by tension were those he
freed from blame.

But, wiser, if quiet men noted those whom Pfumojena had denied the right to court his daughter, or even those
whom he had merely suspected, were the most hard hit. Dying at the cruel thrust of the spear was most often the verdict. But those, lesser men mostly, no real threats, to whom
the mambo granted clemency, served at Pfumojena's village

tending his cattle and accomplishing the chores of the royal house.

Almost slaves they were. Confiscation of the latters' possessions—mainly cattle and other domestic animals—was a common practice, hence, the numerous lerds of cattle that Pfumojena had all over his dominion. To stifle protest, crying aloud and wailing for executed relatives was prohibited at the mambo's village. The belief was, and Mambo's diviners were quick to echo their master, that such plaints would arouse the anger of the ancestral spirits and bring evil on the village. Hence, the people's name for him "Pfumojena—The White Spear," was doubly-frightful, for the death colour of his everready spear, so sharp in war and the hunt, had drunk the warm blood of many of mambo's own people.

But, life in Pfumojena's dominion was not always riddled with gloom and despondency. Once every year at the end of the harvest season, the chief held a great festival in honour of Chipo—his daughter. The people would gather at the royal village to eat, drink, and to dance to the throbbing drums of the Vanyai. Seated royally on a stool, and covered with a leopard skin, and beautifully adorned with intricate beadwork necklaces, and hand and foot bangles, was Chipo, her face shining in the bright sunlight from the oily ointment made from peanut butter and fat churned from milk. These fatty aromas did not fail to attract swarms of flies and other flying creatures to the feast of the Vanyai "goddess" who, perched there, became a symbol of adoration more than a symbol of enjoyment. She, herself, looked out through heavy lids and allowed no one, least of all her father, to see her thoughts.

On this particular annual celebration, thousands of men, women and children gathered for the occasion. Pfumojena, with great shouting, has ordered the slaughter of scores of his herds of cattle to feed the crowds. Numerous, huge earthen caldrons everywhere are boiling with chunks of stewed beef and the women are busy stirring their pots of *sadza*—thick porridge made from maize-flour, rice-flour, finger-millet, or African corn. Some are seen helping themselves to the large hunks of meat in the simmering caldrons, paying little heed to traditional decorum.

The people sit in groups according to their home villages, their proud women serving their men-folks with food and drinks made of the *rupoko-millet* seeds. The Vanyai, excellent beer brewers of both the intoxicating *doro*, a white liquor smelling like fermented fruit, and the sweet *maburo*, the mild drink, quaff and guzzle the brews. Some, seated outside in the open air, more inside the huts, drink and swallow, gorging the steaming meat, loud and full mouthed, happy, rushing toward delirium. Strong souls, young legs, dance and sing within and without the houses, for is not this a day of rejoicing and overeating and surfeiting? Who worries about tomorrow? Noisiest and gayest of all are the poor and the beggars who are eating as if it were their first and last day for soup and beer and cow-flesh.

Beneath the shade of a tree whose branches sprawl over a large space, Pfumojena and his councillors sit, eating and swilling like the rest, telling each other tales of the great past, sometimes bragging of victories of their own days. Although Pfumojena is in his late fifties, he still shows a manly form; past prowess and vigour mark him the biggest man of all. But his face, so wrinkled, showing folds, tells of a life riddled with problems of state, and, perhaps, a few too many wives. Weather beaten, his visage glares at the world, a soldier-face that has endured and weathered, burned and arrow pocked, in many a cruel season.

This is the stern one, unrelenting, cruel, rarely merciful in war or peace—though now he laughs at a bawdy retort, and the beer is streaming over his broken teeth. He stands now, stretching his bulk, six feet tall, and something, rather handsome in a ferocious way, broad his shoulders, long his mighty back. He pulls at his moustache, yanks at his goaty beard, yawns and grins to his henchman, a real patriarch of the nation.

Despite their fears, his warriors recognize his commanding dignity, respect him. Wearing his royal gown, sewn of a giant spotted leopard skin, his head-piece, tassels dangling, a fibered crown, Pfumojena is a king. He roars a lion's roar—all eyes turn toward him—will he speak? No. He had no words, only a great man's joy of good-eating, the maw jammed with meat, warning off the craven jackals. Greasy-jawed, his councillors and army commanders leap up, grin and roar back at him. Foremost are Sariramba and Zambara, the former a short, almost stunted man, a barrel-drum hulk, with blood-shot eyes, and a shiny face. Wary, quick-spoken, and wise, he follows the mambo, agrees with his decrees, his words screen what his true thoughts may be. Zambara, Pfumojena's closest councillor, long-legged, long-armed, he, too, is a wise man and of long experience at the Mambo's Court. Both are veterans of the untold battles of Pfumojena and his father, their blood has spotted the plains and forests with their men's—no cowards they—but they loll in the shade of the mambo—no action taking unless he first moves—or wills.

Now, relaxed, the three great ones are seated again, close hunched, cracking good beef bones together, enjoying a pot of beer set before them. Sariramba, as the junior, pours the foaming liquor from pot to tankard, serving his comrades from a fire-burned gourd designed for the chief's special use.

"There we were, caught almost in a dead-end canyon, a damned dangerous spot for a man with human skin," started up Sariramba, again, picking up his interrupted soldier's yarn. "Escape was out, only those whose ancestors heard their prayers could ever hope to leave this place unharmed. Only stabbing, shouting, pushing, could get a man home free to embrace his wife!"

The old battle gleaming in his eyes! Sariramba continued in his proud narration of his past, "In the heat of the fight, I saw Mungate drop dead from a stab wound in the side, blood gushing like a red spring of deadly water, bubbling and frothing, I cried out, overwrought, maddened by the outrage, 'My father Chironga! My father Chironga! Whose blood is this to be so spilt by these primitive barbarians?' So, crazy with fury, I stood up and, quitting myself like a man, stabbed back at the fool, raking him right in the armpit, deep inside the chest, down he tumbled, a thrown rock to the ground. Then I jumped up and down in jubilation, howling like a wild man, screaming, 'My spear! My spear! My spear has got him—I mean the spear of the child of Mushora has felled him!' "

"What was the age, or size of the man you were fighting with, you boastful one?" asked Mhingapinge, a senior prince, quaffing his bright black gourd of beer.

"Age? Size? that's irrelevant! A foe is a foe whether he is young or old, big or small. Never despise any man until he is trampled under your feet, for it is the small things he despises that a man often succumbs to rather than the big things he can handle and see more clearly." And he pointed to Mhingapinge—"Remember the old saying: 'A man who has just eaten a dove is fuller than one only dreaming of a wild bull feast.' But I was young then, ready to battle, as I still am," he shouted, "Indeed, I gave thanks to my ancestors who have driven so many foes into my hands. I held steadfast, then, just three years past circumcision, and slew the enemy."

Pfumojena, amused at his army general's half-defensive remarks, said, "How many men have fallen at your hand, great commander? It seems from your tale you slew only one man that horrible day." At this the gathered chiefs all laughed and jeered the boasting Sariramba.

With a smile on his face, he turned slowly to face Chief Pfumojena and, then, like a man thinking of the best way to present his case, turned back to and pointed at Mhingapinge, accused him by saying in a mock-rage: "My story has been interrupted by this impostor of a councillor, Nzou Samanyanga," he declared, looking at the chief. "I meant to proceed further with my story. My Lord, with your permission, I shall go on—not just about my own deeds—but those of all the brave men of those days." Here, he seemed saddened, for, after all, most of those scarred farmer-soldiers were down in the dark earth many years now.

Pfumojena nodded. "Proceed."

So, Sariramba picked up the thread. "Now it happened that when the shades of evening were beginning to close in upon the earth, we felt the premonition of defeat by the Vahota under their leader Mugandani, and hard pressed we were, I've already told you; we then had to stab and push more fiercely than ever before. Dead and groaning men tripped our feet, dying men all over the field, ours and theirs, called out for help—but we could not stop. One moment's halt and we would join them on the gore-drenched grass. Certainly we were engaged in battle with one of the strongest and fiercest regiments of the Vahota—indeed those were good fighters. They had learned their art from the great chief, Gombekombe, mysterious hero from a far off land in the south. But, believe me, Oh Great One with Elephant Tusks!" and the wily general ducked his head at the mambo, " we finally routed the entire regiment in the plains of the

Mhanyami river south of Harare. Corpses lay scattered all over the valley and, what a feast it was for the vultures and other creatures of the air and forests! And so, when Mhingapinge arrived with his reinforcements, the great task had already been done. No Vahota escaped that day, because we slaughtered them to the last man. Not a single Muhota escaped. Because they never admitted defeat, we must admit they were great, brave men; yes, we slaughtered them to the last man."

Those were the battles that Sariramba fought during the reign of Pfumojena's father, when the mambo here was but a young boy. Thus, aging Sariramba liked to recount such stories, gladly, fully, singing praises of the greatness of the Vanyai people, and the royal line of Pfumojena.

The festival of Chipo—the Princess, was drawing to a close. The people had surfeited their stomachs with so much food, and the beer drinkers had filled their bellies with drinks, while the dancers had danced their emotions away—but everyone knew, not quite forgetting in all the dust and smells of beer and urine, and the screams of lost babies, that the end of the festival would be marked by sorrow and suffering for some. For, the crowds could not go home until the diviner had made his ablutions of the nation, freeing from the charge of witchcraft and sorcery most, but possibly finding some out to destroy their mambo. This ritual of cleansing the nation of its evil and setting it on a new and clean path for the new year was both longed for—and dreaded.

While Sariramba had recounted the heroic deeds of by-gone days, and attempted to quicken the hearts of his hearers to the glory of the nation, Pfumojena listened, seemingly interested enough in the discourse, but all the while his mind was pre-occupied with the state of the nation, and when Sariramba was off on a new tale of the old days, he shouted, "Enough! Enough of that! We must now turn our minds to the present affairs." So saying, he pulled his winebright commander aside to begin a serious talk with him.

"Tell me, great commander, What is the state of the Mudzimundiringe Forest Region where we sent a detachment of men a few months ago?"

"Your Highness," replied Sariramba, "the messengers have informed us that the outlaws are increasing in leaps and bounds, in numbers and in courage."

"I was afraid of that." Pfumojena ground his heavy teeth, "We will send more men, an entire regiment if you agree, to breach the hide-out, to break their bones. We cannot encourage our people to flee our commands—and our taxes—by their example of defiance."

"Last time we sent our men into the forest, they returned empty-handed after a long, and fruitless hunt," said Sariramba.

Pfumojena glared at him, agreeing angrily, "Yes, and we lost many of our best men in the hunt."

"Yes, Changamire, we did. Not any fault of ours, but they are not stupid boars in there—but real men—and they hate us."

"How do you account for that, Sariramba?" Why can't we wipe them out as we have our other foes?"

"For many reasons, Changamire. First, it is hard to track down the outlaws. They hide like jackals and rabbits in the thickets. No doubt they have learned well the nature of the jungles, all the paths, where there are streams and cliffs and fallen trees. So well do they know every hole in the ground, and every crevice in the hills, that they can hide and ambush our men and then steal off, laughing, when we send in more of our stumbling men. Second, they do not submit themselves to an open battle, always resorting to the cowardly tactics of hit and run as each opportune moment comes; we may call it cowardice, but it's good tactics all the same," the grizzled fighter admitted.

"We must get rid of such serpents, Sariramba. We must exterminate these rebels," groaned Pfumojena. "Already I sweat in my bed, even with my newest wife, hating these men I cannot reach!"

"Changamire, we know their number grows all the time, either our regiment will sweep them out or we must reconcile them—we must offer them reasons to return—and guarantees for their safety." Here the councillor moved on dangerous turf, and his voice shook a little as he offered a small piece of what he had long been thinking.

But Pfumojena hardly noticed. War was in his mind. "Yes, yes, our leopard regiment will take the field! but first—send out spies."

"I agree," replied Sariramba, "first our spies will slip

into the forest, then we can know where they hide—who leads them—where their capital is. There we will put our clubs on their viperish necks." But the old commander, no coward, would have preferred the remedy of peace, for were not some of his best friends, even a great nephew, there in that brambled wilderness?

"Take heart, great commander," said Pfumojena, "I swear by my father who lies buried by the ant-hill, no man, or group of outlawed men, while I live and behold the light of day, shall be allowed to lay violent hands upon the men of the sacred nation of the Vanyai. We were born to rule; we must prepare to lay down our lives to preserve the total dominion our ancestors gave us!"

The great commander for a while remained silent as if putting his thoughts together for a new way of suggesting, one last time, a more peaceful way. "Changamire, my Chief," he said, slowly and thoughtfully, "we are dealing not only with a handful of rebellious outlaws but with a silenced mass who know not how to, or feel they dare not, express their dislike of our present conditions. I have longed to disclose this thought to your Highness for a long time, but feared the wrath of my Lord."

At this, Pfumojena's face expressed outrage. Looking at his general squarely, he said, "We have done so much for the people—yes—so much. Everything has been done in the interests of the peoples' wealth—and their security. Even our ancestors know how dedicated we are to the common good. To sweep clean away all the wicked people in this nation for the safety, security and happiness of our people, by any means at hand," he added grimly, "has been our one wish—our one goal." He gripped his fearsome white spear until his black knuckles grew grey-pale on the waxy shaft.

But the Commander stood resolute, looking him in the eye, and Pfumojena remembered his fierce old father telling him, heaving his wounded chest on the battle-field, "Be careful, my son, about disregarding your advisors—they are seasoned men—they speak for the good of the nation!" So mambo said more softly, "The truth must stand, Sari-ramba. The true path is ours!" and this more fiercely, "We are here to govern the people with honour. The honour and dignity of the nation must oppose any odds, any dissent."

"I will stand and fall with you, Changamire. I am

your servant—and a servant must divulge the truth to his lord and master, as he sees it, or he is another kind of traitor," Sariramba assured his chief. "But not everybody agrees with us, Changamire. When the truth is said, we'll have to stand alone, for we've made enemies far and near," and he shivered, thinking of his daring.

"Then the solution," retorted Pfumojena, throwing his own caution out, "is to execute, hold in serfdom, or exile all who engage in, or have the semblance of engaging in, any treasonable thoughts or acts against the Vanyai. Our force will make our good rule better!" And he half-shouted.

"This, Changamire," replied Sariramba, very humbly, "is seemingly our greatest problem. Mixing good eggs and rotten eggs together spoils the mixture instead of improving it. It is like cooking the bitter gall with sweet meat. The gall cannot but turn the good meat bitter, my Lord. Men flee our land because they fear our decrees. Will violence bring them back to our hearts and hearths?"

"We cannot give up our laws for the sake of dirty traitors who seek the jungle for refuge because they refused to admit our rights. We cannot change or compromise for the sake of a disgruntled few who want to destroy the strong state we have been building among the Vanyai for immemorable generations."

In this angry mood Pfumojena expressed his resentment. "These weaklings," he muttered, "have not earned their right to tell us what to do."

"Changamire," observed Sariramba, emboldened one last time to object, "it is because of our unchanging nature that we must suffer. Remember the Varozvi of old who, lords of vast lands, conquered peoples, allowed all to live in peace and plenty. They reigned long and quietly and only lost their empire in the course of many generations, not from rebellion. Customs and traditions which are resistant to change destroy peace in the end. Things go askew more and more if there are no adjustments. And the Vanyai must realize the need for accommodation, for change, where called for."

Pfumojena was listening now glumly, not saying a word. His sullen expression revealed a stubborn man whose character and experiences allowed him to ponder, but whose relentless will and pride would brook no true limit to his ferocious desires. Nothing could change him. Not even death itself.

The silence grew long. The weary general knew he had to yield. "Oh, Wise Mambo, the last men we deployed to Mudzimundiringe forest a few days ago are due to return today," he alerted his Changamire. "About thirty of our most valiant warriors went out to hunt out these outlaws again, their report will soon be in our ears."

"Very well, great commander. Very well. I expect word from you on this matter and the state of our nation."

No sooner had they concluded their talk than a group of Vanyai men arrived at the far end of the village with two captured outlaws, their hands roped behind them, and almost naked. They suffered as best they could the thrashing they were receiving from the over-zealous guards, flailing away at them with cow-hide whips.

A sub-commander panted up to Sariramba; they whispered, and the two trotted off to the place of the prisoners where interrogations were held. The general was eager to see the outlaws and to question the Vanyai men as to their fight and experiences. If the prisoners would not talk he would order their execution. The capture of such men of the forests of Mudzimundiringe was a sign the bandits were not out of reach forever. The mambo was angry and the regiment must soon move out to crush the run-aways once and for all.

A valiant man, the old commander still hated torture—yet the prisoners must tell who led them—and where they hid. . . .

Chapter VI

The Adventures of Feso

As Feso left the *imbahuru*, the chief's house, he was excited and proud in the thought of taking on such an unusual adventure for the mambo. He had never been to the land of the Vanyai before. He had only heard about it, and now he was faced with the actual fact of entering and spying out his objective in a hostile and unknown region. Knowing that the journey would be long and full of hardships he asked his wife Musekwa to get ready his victuals to last him as long as his journey would take him. "Yes," he told her, "enough for three days." And he didn't speak the rest of his thoughts: "After that I'll either be back with the princess or dead in the enemy's lands, an assagai in my throat."

Accordingly, his wife prepared him boiled beans and peanut butter, raw and cooked sweet potatoes, biltong, good jerked beef it was, cooked black-eyed peas, mealie-meal, and she hunted up an earthen pot for cooking. Other food, wrapped in pumpkin leaves, was packed in an old calabash, red with smoke and soot. These foods were stuffed into a woven bag called *nhava*. She also got ready a sheep-skin bag for carrying water. All these his wife prepared in the evening prior to Feso's morning departure.

You would have heard Musekwa ordering: "Maravanyika, my son, get me that pot that I may cook your father's sweet potatoes! Get me down that basket with nuts and help me crack them for his roast-nut lunch. There, Rudo, my daughter, pass me that bag that I may pack it with cooked maize for your father!"

Very early, even before the cocks crew in the starry illumination of the new morning, while the village was still embraced by the serenity and tranquility of the peaceful predawn, and the moon still high up in the sky, Feso's mind, set to wake early, snapped the man up on this worn reed-mat. Shivering in the cool darkness he prepared himself for his journey while his now active Musekwa helped him gather up all his provisions. He seized his four spears and his axe from the weapons wall, and strode out of his house after a quiet and quick farewell to his wife. He walked by the gate keeper's hut unseen and left his dearly beloved village to face the dangers of some unknown country. His wife, in the doorway, peering into the misty gloom, prayed for his return. Behind her the dog growled and the first chickens began to cluck and stir.

Feso, after walking a little distance, turned and, looking back, could see dimly in the hazy moonlight the quiet and sleeping village, his tumultuous thoughts running in his mind, wondering if he'd ever return to his family and to his young mambo again. But, shrugging his shoulders under the cord of his *nhava*, he manfully dismissed the womanish worries and walked briskly toward the rim of sun now redding the hills far to the east. This day his path was through friendly country, and he was almost happy, facing the exciting and fearful adventure that now awaited him. Tonight he would rest awhile and then strike for Mudzimundiringe forest where he hoped to make contact with the outlaws holed up there. Someone there would know how to slip him inside the Vanyai territories—someone hating their mambo would lead him to the captive priestess. He walked with long steps through the familiar grazing pastures and maize fields and crossed the streams that he knew so well and by name and by noon he had passed through the Gombekombe mountain ranges and hill passes that in his youth were his hunting grounds. Here the familiar honey bird if carefully followed might lead the hunter through the shadowy forest to the buzzing swarm and the precious white combs of sweetness.

And soon he was passing through unknown and less familiar tracts, farther and farther from his natal village. Now with less familiar trees and weird stony outcroppings, his mind, despite his resolution, was full of fondness for his village, common sounds and sights, and its people, old and young, flooded for a moment his eyes. Why this strange task? his treacherous inner-voice asked—why not turn back—to say the way was barred—that Vanyai prowled all the passes and no guides could say how to cut inside hated Pfumojena's land.

But the mambo's charge imperative forced him to continue, and he half-grinned, shaking his soldier's head, no, no; so ruthlessly he crashed his way through the grass and toppled trees of a storm-lashed hill—warm though his Zezuru heart was for Zezuru things, he must seek out the Vanyai. For, was he not a Muzezuru of the land of Nyan'ombe? Was not theirs a life of calm happiness, free from the shackles of body and spirit; was not their life full of respect and decorum among the men and women of his land; was there not an abundance of food and a warmth of life unparalled anywhere? These and other things, the core of the life of the Mazezuru, Feso's mind and fondness now took strength from. This kind of life—possibly unique among all their neighbours, friend and foe alike, keeps the Mazezuru close to home and, unless provoked, unwarlike, happy in their fields, proud of their well nourished children and animals.

Feso, after a rest, his first since setting out, braced up against an orange-lichened granite boulder to ease his sore back muscles. He had now moved beyond the region of the hills of Chouchi, Nharira and Gunguhwe in whose valley flowed the sparkling waters of the Chirayire river. He had reached as far as Gombekombe town (adjoining the modern villages of Jeranyama, Matsvororo and Madombwe). His obsession with thoughts of home had slowly begun to leave him as he seriously faced the mysteries of entering the alien regions which he was now about to invade. All day, as he walked and then dog-trotted to the north, the sun had climbed up in the horizon, but now the shadows were long and his nhava-sack was dark in the purple pool of the giant rock he leaned against.

Oh, he must be careful. He must skulk and hide, not be seen nor heard, for one false step and he knew he'd be pinioned from behind, or caught in a net on a strange trail, or brained without a blink of warning by a Vanyai club. The strange forests of Mazoe were eerily garbed in deep blue loveliness and the twilight bird-songs rang strangely in his ears in the quietness of the uninhabited wilderness. He recognized the sun's dipping behind earth's edge by the darker purpled gloom—and almost with an effort of will he brought to mind the month of an old September, long ago lived as a boy. He had last seen these woods garmented in a frosty rustle of reds, oranges and yellows of loveliness. The hills and glades of Mazoe then had spoken only of crisp youth and hope.

Now, after such a hurried trip, the heat of the long spring day tugged his back, added to the weariness of his calves. The pain even of his straining heart told him to hunt

51

out a safe lair for the night. He longed, too, for a drink of water, for his water pot now contained only a few tepid, brackish drops. Fortunately, nature had supplied the region with many bubbling and swift-flowing streams of clear, sparkling water and after just a moment's hesitation, he turned to his right and in no time was standing at a pool of crystal water emanating from a spring silver in the last touch of light at the foot of an unwooded hill. Here grew flags, water-lilies, reeds and, through the shallow, glassy water he could see a few large, slow moving fish swimming in and out of the rock cavities under the clear surface. Moths and dragonflies fluttered all around him and above the water in a gentle breeze. Notwithstanding his weariness, Feso didn't have much difficulty making a fire from his flint. Drawing water from the spring, he quickly prepared his simple meal, and fed himself.

Revived, he began to look around. There was happily no sign of human life anywhere. As he prowled about he came upon footprints of bucks, eland, and the kudu that come to drink at the fountain. Then at the far end of the pool where the forest came down, he saw the footprints of a large cat—could they be a lion's? Seizing more firmly his spear he warily pushed into the woods—having discovered the smashed path of a small herd of elephants. He was surprised, for he had not believed such beasts were in this area. A few night birds came hovering above him, flying away scared by the stranger. Feso was, for a while, alarmed, for normally one didn't pass the night, alone, in the forest and who knew what sort of ferocious animals might be stalking him that very moment? A host of other scary creatures, crawling, lurking, flying, he imagined all around him.

As he returned to his original place he took notice that night had fallen. There was no time to waste. He murmured to himself, thinking he should seek out a high tree and tie himself into its bushiest part for a safe night's rest. Certainly it was not safe to sleep on the ground. No sooner had these thoughts crossed his mind than he was suddenly met by two men whom he recognized, at once, as robbers or renegades.

Their very appearance betrayed them, for they were half naked, wearing only a front apron and with the mops of their hair as large as an ant-hill. In their hands they carried spears, fighting sticks, and hunting knobkerries. One of these outlaws had straddled across his shoulder a bleeding rabbit.

Seeing these human spectres, Feso reeled back and would have liked to have shown a clean pair of heels. But, was he not a man of war himself? A warrior of no mean importance? a scout and chief's messenger who had resigned himself to whatever danger he had to face without flinching? Feso stood tall then, adjusting his face muscles to show sternness as the outlaws, themselves surprised, approached him. The diviner's bones had been cast and the fate of the mission decided. So, the Chirayire River was crossed!

"Who are you, stranger?" the heavier one called out.

"Feso is my name," he replied unhesitatingly.

"What are you doing here at this time of day?"

"I'm a bee-hunter seeking the honey-bird and its sweet target," he said.

"Where do you come from? Speak up, stranger!" And both men took a step closer.

"From the land of Nyan'ombe."

"Ha! ha!" Marasirapi the outlaw laughed scornfully at Feso, and slowly relaxing, or appearing to, he sneered, "Look, Mutowembwa, let's fill our eyes with a specimen of the low castes from Nyan'ombe, at a man who has dared to cross the Nyan'ombe-Pfumojena line."

"Ah, yes," the companion grinned, staring impudently at Feso, "these are they who eat the entrails of an animal together with its skin and call that meat. Ha! Ha!" he laughed. "They also eat locusts and caterpillars and call it a dainty dish. Ha! Ha!" laughed Mutowembwa.

"Ha! Ha! Ha!" together they ridiculed him. They joked, but they also watched him warily.

At this Feso was cut to the quick. His fiery temper rose high like the mid-summer's noon sun. With a snort he turned his back and started off in the direction he was headed before running into these jeering night birds.

"Hey, where are you going, smart one?" they hurled at him and then forced him to halt by pricking his shoulders with their fighting sticks.

Wheeling, Feso angrily answered, his eyes seeking theirs, "to hunt honey—and I have come far; I need to find a resting place."

"More likely a traitor! An enemy! A spy! a collaborator with our arch enemy," they both muttered, standing on guard a few feet away. Feso knew he would be killed if he made any false move—and he could hardly hope to attack both at the same time. But he had to wait for some opening—either of friendliness or—whatever?

"You lie, stranger! You don't come from Nyan'ombe! The Vahota of Nyan'ombe don't have the guts to cross into the territory of the land of their masters. You are one of these damned and confounded spies of Pfumojena on an errand to find out what we are doing here—a damned tool of that cruel mambo who's killing us all."

"I am no spy, listen to my speech. Does any Pfumojena hireling speak like a Muhota?" Feso retorted.

"Who's your father?" Mutowembwa growled.

"Madyavanhu!"

"Yea!" yelled Mutowembwa, "the collaborator with Pfumojena who lives just a stone's throw from the royal residence of that wicked, despotic ruler."

"No!" Feso remonstrated, "That is preposterous! Would I tell you that if I knew you were outlaws from Pfumojena's power? No, I am from Nyan'ombe's country and am not a liar (though I am a spy!)" he admitted to himself, but for a better master than theirs. "Give me justice," Feso argued. "My father was Madyavanhu of . . ."

"Justice! Just listen to this hypocrite," interrupted Marasirapi. "What justice resides in Pfumojena's brain and his cronies like you? We've been driven into this jungle by the taxes of a despotic ruler, so-called stranger! We intend to make you an example of the kind of revenge we'll have on your wicked ruler, if we ever get our hand on him."

"No, no!" shouted Feso as the men backed off and then raised their spears into stabbing position. His heart was pounding like a two hundred-weight hammer, and he made one last effort to avoid the violent battle that seemed inevitable. "I don't talk like him, or like you do," he pointed out. "Just listen to me," and he had an inspiration, "look at my cooking pot—and the design of my net sack. Are they of Vanyai making? None of these things are in your people's hands." And Feso knew he must somehow get these men to trust him, aid him in his mission.

But his words went unheard and they charged. Feso deftly leapt aside and scrambled into the bush and then tum-

54

bled and twisted into the thicket as fast as he could.

"Catch him! Catch him! Let's get him alive and sport with his hide later," shouted Mutowembwa. So saying they plunged after him, and soon wrestled him to the ground, buffeting and kicking him, and ripping off his sack. His calabashes now lay broken on the ground and they dragged him several hundreds of feet to a hidden place nearby under a large tree. Here they were met by a gang of other outlaws who had remained camped there. Altogether there were about ten men. No sooner had these outlaws seen him than they started to dance around and howling insults at him. Endless questions were showered at him.

"Who are you, stranger? What do you want here, you red-eyed woodpecker? A sneak-eye of that scheming prince? Do you know who we are? How did you get here? Do you know where we can get others like you?" They all congratulated Mutowembwa and Marasirapi for capturing one of their enemies.

While the outlaws ate their carnival-noisy meat dinner, they tied Feso's hands and feet and passed a stick under his knees and elbows so that he lay there helpless. Mutowembwa looked over at the man some yards away on the rocky ground and gave a scornful smile, as he took pride in capturing such an enemy.

"You've made a grievous mistake, stranger, by passing through this way at this time of the day," snarled Mutowembwa the leader of the outlaws, seated on a fallen tree trunk, a chunk of half-cooked flesh in his hand. Your ancestral spirits have not been much of a protection against you, have they, by allowing you to pass through this way of Mudzimundiringe? We, too, had our homes and families that we loved dearly, but through oppression and persecution we left them all and fled here for refuge. That's why our anger kindles within us when we see our enemy's spy pass this way." Turning to one of his subordinates, he ordered:

"Loosen that damned man, and pull him before me!"

Feso was untied and dragged and shoved to a spot a few steps in front of the leader. Feso quietly stood before Mutowembwa.

"It is customary that you talk to your superior more respectfully—and more naturally—so sit down. I can't bear your towering over me even though you'll be answering questions with a quivering, shaky voice like a frightened rabbit," Mutowembwa growled. "This is a life-and-death-matter as you shall soon see."

"Sir, and all you honourable men before me, I swear that I am not one of Pfumojena's men, but," and his voice grew urgent, "a stranger in this land—a visitor—a traveller— and not a spy or confederate," Feso swore with all the courage he could muster. "I shall be grateful to you, Sir, if you'll let me go," he pleaded. "I do not refuse to die," he asserted, "or to take punishment over what I know I have done. But certainly, since you, too, abandoned your homes and your country for the sake of your freedom, I too, would love to ask for the justice you say was denied in your own homeland," continued Feso. "So give me my freedom!"

"Homeland? Justice? Freedom!" sneered Mutowembwa. "There is no such thing in this world. And, besides, your pleadings mean nothing, stranger. We have no mercy, no compassion, and, certainly, no experience of justice to share with anyone. Our ruler brutally treated us to his justice and you'll taste it today. You have seen your last. We will take your skin, make it into a drum; your head shall hang along the pathway as a warning sign to the passersby. Oh, gods, how I hate Pfumojena and all his gluttons and thieves!"

At this Feso, despite himself, was shaken. He was close to trembling from head to foot, he held his muscles tight, strengthened by his conviction he was innocent—not guilty of anything for which he should die. He remained brave and true to his training, his ancestors—and to his mission.

While Mutowembwa was still fuming with the emotional outburst of his anger, one of the men remarked:

"Changamire, when this man came here he held two sticks. Now we have a tradition whereby, in a doubtful situation like this, we can try to settle the innocence of a man by letting him prove it in a duel against our best man. You might order this stranger to fight it out in a duel with one of us and end the case this way. If he wins he saves his life, but if he loses he dies the death. Either way, we need the sport—we haven't had a rouser for a long time—not since our last ambush." Mutowembwa who was much less convinced of Feso's guilt than his speech had indicated, pained as he'd been with his sense of wrongs, was not difficult to convince. "I didn't ask your opinion, little barking-dog," he said, "nevertheless, if that's what you all want, I'll consent," and he boomed it out, "Marasirapi will fight the duel with Feso, using the fighting sticks."

At this Feso was overjoyed. He prayed his ancestral spirits to give him victory. He had fought many a battle before and was a hard, crafty battler. His new courage rose in him like the flood waters of a spring stream.

In the silvery brightness of the just risen moon, the two men took their fighting stances—alert—strained—in the center of a clear spot with green grass. Visibility was excellent and Feso felt himself, despite his long journey, in great shape and in high spirits. The two men held their short sticks tightly in hand—one in the left hand for shielding, the other in the right for attack. Feso felt a rare strength filling his bones and sinews; the ancesters were helping him. He was ready for any trick of his opponent.

Squarely, they faced each other and, for a harsh moment, stared at each other. Then, with one heave, Marasirapi rushed forward, attacking fiercely with left and right thrusts. Feso defended himself with remarkable dexterity of hand, thrusting aside all intended blows. Click-clack the hard sticks clattered—sounding like devils' teeth in the forest. Marasirapi grinned and made a few wild shouts in an effort to demoralize the stranger. Feso kept his cool head and, unsmiling, glared back. Both men were breathing heavily after the last exchange of blows and counters. Feso, after several feints, attacking methodically, always aiming at the most vulnerable spot for striking, bore in again and again. He lifted his stick then and, for a split eye-blink, and aiming well, struck his foe on the left side beneath the ribs. Marasirapi groaned, staggered, but as he, too, was a strong man, he stood his ground, and even returned to the counterattack. The men watching started to roar with laughter and excitement. This was a good match. The captive was putting up a fine fight . . .

"Ha! ha!" they laughed, "Come on, Marasirapi! Strike a fatal blow! Prove your manhood! Strike! Strike! And finish him up!" they cried out. But all admitted in their hearts a grudging respect for the other man.

Rising from his near defeat, Marasirapi aimed high and well, breaking through his opponent's defenses, and struck Feso on the right shoulder, sending him reeling and wincing with pain. But the sting was not intolerable, for Feso had partially warded it off and the blow had landed in less than full force. He rushed back at the outlaw.

In the new yell and excitement, Feso suddenly landed a volley of blows on his foe, poum, whack, breaking apart the enemy's sticks, hitting Marasirapi several blows on the head, shoulder, here, there, all at once. With such blows he bashed the grizzled and bearded old outlaw to the ground. Falling flat on his back, the bandit's champion lay there groaning, bleeding. Removing him to a nearby bubbling brook, the others attended to him, pouring cold water on him, soaking him from top to bottom, to resuscitate him. Only a groan and hissing through his broken teeth announced he was still breathing.

Feso was delighted with his victory, and he stood, almost fainting, his bloody sticks hanging from his aching arms.

"Very well, stranger," said Mutowembwa, "You've fought a good fight and proven your innocence. You deserve the freedom you have earned. You are a free man. Go your way! But, if we ever hear that you disclosed our rendezvous to Pfumojena, you'll never again pass safely this way," he warned. "We will hang you like a dog. You've had a chance we never got from our vulture-king."

Feso just nodded his head without saying a word. (No hope for the bandits' help now!) He gathered whatever was left of his belongings and rubbing his bruised shoulder quickly hurried away, disappearing into the deep shadows of the forest. He sped as swiftly away as he could though every muscle now was crying for rest. He must get as far away as he could from these new enemies. Soon he realized the forests thickets were beginning to give way to open glades, and knowing he could go no further—nor dare sleep in the open, he searched out a shaggy tree to climb. Building himself a makeshift nest high in its branches, he crept up there, tied himself to the trunk and fell immediately into a dreamless sleep. When his eyes opened, his whole body was sore, every muscle screaming from his awkward position and bruises, the sun was up and the birds were twittering all around in the trees. Quickly he slid down the tree, and after a splash and quick drink in a green pool he had spotted from his perch, he started on his way. After a long, weary journey, dog-trotting, resting, and then, slower and slower, walking, Feso saw a large village some distance away as he crested a hill. Somehow, he knew, or guessed, that was Pfumojena's royal residence and its surrounding houses. At long last he was where he could begin the actual mission of hunting out the princess. His heart beat with joy and gladness as he entered the alien village.

Chapter VII

Pfumojena and His People

It was at high noon when Feso arrived at the royal residence of Chief Pfumojena. He was amazed, if not astonished, at the sight of so many crowds that were now in the third day of the observance of the Celebrations of the Magnificant Princess and in the confusion he was not looked at—or even noticed. As he strolled about he saw the crowds seated within and without the councillors' houses, in makeshift huts and sheds, beneath the shadows of trees, and in every conceivable place wherever room was found.

This celebration coincided with the End-of-Year Ritual which it was customary for the Vanyai to observe annually. The people came ostensibly to observe the lovely girl, the nation's priestess, but also to enjoy and even to participate in the ritual dances honouring her. There were, of course, those whose sole attraction was food and drink who also had found their way to the royal village and who carried away home whatever they could salvage from the chief's table of abundance.

Feso wearily pushed his way through the throngs toward the palace and found himself a place among a group of men who, sitting quietly, were even in a contemplative mood. He had quickly sensed a feeling of uneasy tension among the crowds, and there had been little of the joking and shouting so common on feast days back home.

As he silently slipped into an empty place he had a premonition of something terrible happening, or about to happen. As he settled down as inconspicuously as he could, his heart pounded within him, for here he was, in the very heart of the enemy and now he must learn where the girl was, the country-wide famed daughter of Pfumojena. No sooner had he caught his breath but his eyes fell on the lovely princess; he was even close enough to catch the sparkle of loveliness and beauty in her eyes. So, at last, as fate allowed it, his eyes fell on her whose beauty had brought him to the land of the Vanyai—the proud and strong in arms.

The princess was soft-skinned, aloof, thoughtful,

seated just a few arms' lengths away, on her royal stool. On her head was a coronet of beadwork with plaited grass tassels hanging down. She was wearing a choker neck-band of beadwork made from cowries and other river shells, interwoven with wild, dried, seeds. Her heavy necklaces, of a special bright alloy of tin and copper, shone warmly with a golden colour while her earrings were made of pure gold nuggets gathered from river beds. Her arms, as well as her legs, were just loaded with brass and copper bangles. Around her waist she wore a finely embroidered leather covering. Straddling over and above this were thick rosaries of beads that loaded her waistline above the leather covering. Her bare bust showed a youthful pair of brown breasts projecting out round and erect with the belts of beads crossing in the front and held in the back by the rosary-like belt around her waist.

All these rose and fell, shining in the curious and furtive, speculative eyes of Feso, sitting there in the company of men who would tear him apart in an instant were they to discover this "guest" and guess his reason for being there. Feso, old fighter, masculine mind, carefully studied the rare woman and in a flicker concurred with all the reports: he now fully accepted the fact that this poised, almost disdainful, Chipochedenga was the most beautiful girl in the world, a princess truly in all ways.

"Here is a girl, vibrant with youthful bloom, fit to be my chief's wife," he soliloquized in his inner heart.

"Such loveliness is, indeed," he thought, "an attribute of a goddess—a charm bestowed by the grace and favour of the ancestral spirits and, magnified, exalted, and extolled by man's earthly mind to a point where she can be found worthy of worship." But he frowned at the latter idea, for Feso rejected any mortal being considered sacred. There indeed was madness—or slavish servility.

"Yes, she is beautiful," he reasoned with himself, "but she is no goddess. For, indeed, what attributes of body and spirit does she possess more than any other woman? Beauty, yes," and he stole another look at the proud woman so close before him, "beauty even is in a man's mind, and we all grow older—even a girl like that one will have wrinkles one day. I admit she is attractive and beautiful," he said a fourth or fifth time. "But that is all—and all that a man needs," he concluded, chuckling. "Oh happy king our king will be, with such a wondrous bride!"

It was while he was, thus, lost in his thoughts that he saw the chief's retinue with members of his body guard emerge from the *imbahuru* as the women's ululations filled the air with their shrill voices, while the men clapped in unison. The proud in arms and austere warriors of the Vanyai flanked him and came sauntering with their spears glittering in the sun and their shields half concealing their bearers, and crying out: "Changamire, Nzou, Samanyanga!" At the head of the rustic procession was a medicine man holding an ox-tail and spraying everyone before him with a concoction of herbs immersed in an earthen pot. A second long ox-tail trailed behind him like a natural tail from his back, and jouncing over everyone's head was the sorceror's plumed head gear, proud with ostrich feathers. Here was the nation's chief medicine man—Mhindudzapasi—the Diviner and Priest.

As the procession marched in, the drummers began to beat their drums and the men and women nearby began to dance excitedly before the princess. Apparently this activity announced that the princess was about to retire. Rising, she joined the royal retinue and disappeared into the *imbahuru* to take her rest. The crowds had seen her long enough.

In the interim period, Feso, who sat there quietly observing all the proceedings, was greatly astonished as he noticed a great silence pervading the crowds—a silence as of death, as of some power that grips the mind and paralyzes the body from action. Then a deep voice hit Feso's ears.

"It is being rumoured that there are some among you who are planning and plotting to bewitch our great and beloved Pfumojena because of their desire to have Chipochedenga. These sorcerers, witches and wizards must be dealt with here and now," Nyamambishi sternly announced—for so was this councillor's name who represented the chief.

A chill ran down Feso's spine. He could hardly believe such a cruel thing could be done on those he believed to be in the very heart of the people—and on a feast day.

"I have here before me Mhindudzapasi—the nation's diviner—whose occult powers are beyond all expression and whose many successes in hunting out culprits has made him our chief's oracle. He represents the chief's absolute power. He has been appointed by our most supreme council to use his esoteric wisdom to find out who the culprits are. This action is being taken in order to purge this nation of all those undesirable people who are out to destroy Pfumojena. The findings of Mhindudzapasi will be honoured and the verdict he proposes will, without discussion, be accepted by our supreme council. Death, banishment and servitude will be the three forms of punishment that will be meted out to those found guilty," concluded Nyamambishi.

Feso heard these stern and unusual threats of punishment with much astonishment, and he remembered the bitter, ragged outlaws of the forest. The hunger pains, too, which had increasingly been reminding him of the need for food, vanished immediately. If the sage was so prescient, he, Feso, was a dead man. He trembled, not knowing how to escape from the crowd.

Mhindudzapasi quickly moved in. He was a lanky, ghostly, and ghastly looking man. His head gear sat stately upon his head with the ostrich feathers glittering in the sunlight. His waist was covered with a many patched skin covering sewn together and adorned with many animal tails dangling all around him. Laying down his age-old bags, he took out his medicines of roots, oils, seeds, and herbs of all kinds, and a set of six bones which he used for divination. Strange horns, too, hung from his weird dress and made him a spectral figure that filled the minds of the people with awesome wonder and terrible fear. Then, after a pause, he whirled.

"You, and you, and you!" he said pointing to the alleged culprits, "are the witches and wizards. Stand over there!" Moving to another part of the crowd, he came and proclaimed his awful ordeal to those whom his eyes fell upon—his finger pointing. Strident, his voice accused again and again:

"You and you, and you! Step aside. Today the spirits have revealed your wickedness and you must either die or serve the chief throughout your life time, or be banished from the face of the earth." Mhindudzapasi screamed their fates. While he moved among the heaving, terror-stricken people, Feso noticed that the witch wore a pendulant made of sea shells that dangled and tingled as they rubbed against each other. Also the bangles in his arms and legs jingled and tingled as he darted from one part of the crowd to another.

Feso thought the old male hag did very well, lean and sinewy that he was, with hardly a tooth left in his mouth. Then Mhindudzapasi quickly changed his direction and headed to where Feso was seated. Looking straight ahead, his eyes fell on Feso who sat quietly among others in his presumed innocence.

"You and you, and you! stand aside. And you, too, stand with them!" he said pointing right at Feso who, knowing himself a spy, yet had no evil intent against the person or power of the mambo (except for his daughter!). How could the diviner single him out for anything?

Feso sat there stunned. His heart heaved within him and he deeply felt all his sore spots, his hunger, his leg weariness. Fear and shock, this unknown and unexpected punishment, left him unable even to try to break away.

"All of you are the enemies of the chief," the wizened witch screamed, dancing, rattling, pointing through the shivering crowds. Feso wondered how this crazy man could have suspected him since he had only just arrived. His medicine indeed must be fearsome.

But there was nothing he could do. All his protests could avail him nothing. He was in their clutch, right or wrong, innocent or guilty, for life or death, and all around him the groans and tears of those singled out in honor of the holocaust were pitiful. Men and women weeping their lungs out either for themselves or for their friends, made one imagine the scene after a disastrous battle in which innocent people had been slaughtered or driven into the enemy's camps as slaves. Their tears were such as to fill a creek and their groans were as of a thousand people together. In the diviner's hand now appeared a cow's horn, filled with water and a fresh concoction of herbs. With this he sprinkled the people again but actually spat out the same on those he deemed enemies of the chief. Finally, when all his predictions and accusations were done, he took out three sets of bones used for ascertaining or predicting the fate of each accused person. He held the white bones in his hands and started to throw them on the ground, saying:

"Nhokwara kwami dzine chirume!
Nhokwara kwami dzine ngwena!

Matokwadzimu ane ngwena!
Nhokwara chirume!
Nhokwara mbiri!
Rutokwadzimu!
Rune ngwena!
Kwami!

Tell me, my bones, who the culprits and witches are!" Hence, by observing the position these bones held on the ground, he interpreted whether the innocence or guilt of the people concerned was established. He went past the lines of old men and women, middle-aged, and even young people, too, throwing his bones and casting this terrible disaster on them. Then was heard Nyamambishi's terrible voice, in which some were banished from the land, or set aside to bear the burden of servitude at the chief's village—amongst whom was Feso—while those not in this lesser category heard the most horrible order.

"Take them out of the village precincts and kill the witches. Leave their corpses to the ravages of hyenas, and jackals." And so would die many people that day amid groans, wailings and bitter weeping. Women cried out, one saying "O, my son! Who shall look after me now that you are gone? Now I'm left alone!" and another "Oh, Mushonga, my husband, you're leaving me lonely and desolate in this world! Where shall I go now? Where find protection?" So these moans and complaints continued into the night. But Pfumojena, angry at the clamor, and perhaps even shamed a little by his daughter's ever-strong protests, sent a proclamation prohibiting any further weeping, wailing, or crying aloud in or near his village. Thus, the execution was carried out a good distance away from the royal kraal while the diviner sprinkled charmed water around the village to scare off the evil ones and the *ngozi* (angered spirits) of those who had been freshly executed. Feso had felt the brush of death even before he'd been in Pfumojena's village one hour.

But there went out a doleful, prayerful plaintive cry of one old man whose relatives once again had been implicated in this disaster, for most now had been executed, or driven into lawless exile. Chanting, crying, the brave but dispirited elder prayed:

"O Nehanda Nyakasikana!
How long shall we, the Vanyai, groan and suffer?
Holy tutelary spirit!
How long shall we, the Vanyai, suffer oppression?
We are weary of drinking our tears.
How long shall we have forbearance?
Even trees have a rest
When their leaves are shed;
Then, when spring time comes,
New leaves and blossoms sprout to adorn them
To attract wild beasts and bees by their scent.
As for us, when will peace and plenty come our way?
The young ones our women bear, given us
By you—Great Spirit—who should be the inheritors
Of our hard-earned substance, all have an uneasy time
In their own land; and grope for a period of calm
And happiness. Everywhere they stand as on hot ashes.
Their feet with blisters are covered through hot oppression
Of the forces of Pfumojena. How far will the tyrants go?
In every house and every village
Our people are being pulled out and punished;
In every place and every court
Where they are accused, they are treated like flies,
Killed without reason—without an honest trial.
Today all the wealth of the land has been taken.
The top-dogs, the kindred of Pfumojena, share the spoils.
Today they are eating the fat of the land,
And we are reduced to eating the pus of our wounds.
Today they are as fat as pigs,
And we are lean as diseased dogs.
Today they live in wilfull freedom,
And we are gagged, strangled with bindings.
Where is our freedom, Nehanda?
Won't you come down to help us?
Our old men are treated like children
In the land you gave them, Merciful Creator!
They no longer have human dignity,
They possess nothing.
A great calamity has befallen them.
Holy Father, Merciful Mountain!
Won't you hear our cry?

What foul crime have we committed
That you should abandon us like this?
Nehanda Nyakasikana, how long shall it be
That we, the Vanyai, must suffer?
Holy Tutelary Lion Spirit! How long shall it be
That we, the Vanyai, must suffer oppression
By this cursed Pfumojena who is devouring our land?"

Chapter VIII

Feso at Pfumojena's Village

Grateful that he had been spared his life by some twist of good and bad fortune, Feso, quietly served a full year at Pfumojena's royal village, for in that way he would be able to plan out some way to lure the princess away. His appointed tasks were to look after the chief's numerous heads of cattle which had been confiscated from supposedly "guilty" persons. Feso joined many other men whose duty it was to tend these animals, to milk them, morning and evening, and to make sure they were led to good pastures and rounded back home every evening. (Several other herds were posted elsewhere in Pfumojena's domain and there tended by appointed vassals.) Every evening, in addition to rounding up the herds, Feso and his fellow serfs, gathered and brought in well cut and bound cords of wood for the men's fire place.

The age-old tradition among the Vanyai was upheld in which food for the men was brought to the men's place—called dare—every noon and evening from each established household. Strict division in eating was observed. The older men and younger men and boys ate separately and strict codes of etiquette were enforced. Thus, for example, boys may not leave the dare, nor wash their hands, before or after eating, until the older folks had done so. Domestic utensils were always carried away by the boys back to their respective households. The younger men must kindle and make the fire at the dare and, they must always sit down, clap their hands, obsequiously, when speaking to, or when spoken to, by their seniors. The women had their meals apart in their respective houses and seldom appeared at the dare, except when bringing the food and drink for the men. The reason given for the separation of men from the boys was that the latter ate carelessly, like chickens, and did not observe the proper decorum of clean eating. Besides, it was a mark of respect to eat apart from men who were in the age bracket of one's father.

The second of Feso's duties was to participate as an active member of a hunting party during hunting expeditions.

Occasionally, during the summer months, when the grass was dry, the men would go out, surround a chosen area of the bush land, burn it, and kill the animals as they try to escape the fire. In spring time when the trees and the bushes were green, the men went out hunting with hunting nets—called *mambure*. The mambure would be set up at a convenient spot with armed men hiding beside them. A second party would go out and half surround the area in a crescent shaped formation. In this way they would try to drive the game into the mambure.

Feso's third duty was sometimes to help in the clearing of virgin land for crop growing. Once this was done, he was to labour in the cultivation, sowing, hoeing, and tending the crops and finally, aiding in their harvest and storage. This was hard work and Feso found himself doing what he would normally have been doing in his own land—except now he was a bondsman. The Vanyai grew their fingermillet, African corn, maize, sweet potatoes, black-eyed peas, ground nuts, okra, pumpkins, cucumbers, and squashes, on raised mounds of earth. Feso found himself toiling in the heat of the blazing sun day after day. Because of his great physical stamina, diligence, and obvious frank character, Feso distinguished himself as a good, reliable, honest, and hard-working man. In the course of his stay, Pfumojena—being satisfied himself with his general character and deportment, actually promoted him to be the head of all serfs in his royal village. Feso was, thus, remarkably able to come in and go out as he pleased. He would, indeed, have worked his way out of serfdom had he stayed longer than he did and might have become a free man once again. But, nevertheless, the actual period of time of such freedom was indeterminate and often some lived in this state for all their lives and never actually became free men. His only problem was to speak as carefully as he could so as not to speak Chinyai with his own accent too differently.

One lovely, sunny afternoon, while Feso was busy in his work in the field and wiping away drops of sweat from his face, he was suddenly dazed by the unexpected appearance of none other than Chipo herself and Rumba her maid-servant. Heading for a cool spot, they had slipped silently under the cool shade of a nearby *muhacha* tree. As

Feso turned to rest a moment, lo and behold, there was Chipo in all her glory. The unexpected had happened, and he was astounded beyond measure to see her in that place. He could not fathom any earthly reason for her being there. But, nevertheless, he was delighted to be honoured by so gracious a woman like Chipo, and he would seize the opportunity for whatever it was worth.

"Why do you continue to work in the great heat of the sun?" were the words from her gracious lips. "Why don't you take your rest until the heat has abated somewhat?"

"Well, your royal highness," Feso was emboldened to reply, "your presence does place me in a rather difficult position," but he was very cautious, not quite knowing what to do in a risky situation like this. "It would be most unseemly of me to idle around, and besides, my master—your father—would consider me mean, indolent, and negligent of duty if I acted otherwise. My position defines my course of action and robs me of such freedom as you cherish, your royal highness."

"Why, what are you saying? Freedom is a word that I haven't known from birth. I wish I were you spending such glorious days in the open air and enjoying freedom of work and outdoor living," Chipo bitterly retorted.

"I cannot believe it," Feso said incredulously, "that one who is surrounded by all the wealth and pleasures of the land could express so much desire for a peasant's life."

Chipo looked up, smiling a little, and said softly, "We are human, too, and though we seem privileged we are often not—and as for me. . . " but she stopped.

"But you *are* different," Feso affirmed.

"No, *we* are not," she retorted.

"This is how we've come to regard you! We are beaten if we do not bow our heads to you—and secretly envy you."

"But you are wrong, that's only a myth—a pitiful myth," she insisted.

"How?" Feso looked up at her as she now stood up showing a little smile radiating from her face. "You are there, a princess, and I am here, a serf. One complaint from you about me and I would be a dead man."

"We still share human attributes of touch, taste, smell, sight, and hearing, and all other things that make human life complete and enjoyable," she explained. "It is wrong that we are all so separated."

"Well," grunted Feso, "if your royal highness is so much like the rest of us, then why do the Vanyai look down on common men, and especially on the Vahota, as if we were God's most loathesome creatures?"

"It's human pride that degrades the human mind. The blood that courses in you, in me, in kings, and even in the least of us, is as red and pure as yours and mine. The pain you feel and the pleasure you enjoy, and the death you suffer is common to all men. There is no difference. Though my position seems immutable, I would wish it were different—different in social position, though otherwise I'm happy to be me."

Feso was astounded. He took out his tobacco and started to smoke his pipe. A smile pervaded his lips as he pondered over the bridging of the incredulous gap that had previously existed between them. Could it be true? Did she really mean it, or was it merely a trap? How may I go one step forward—to seize this golden opportunity, he thought.

"I thought you were a goddess, high and lifted up, untouchable, and unapproachable."

"There's nothing like that," Chipo smiled, dismissing the carefully nurtured myth her father had invented.

"Me—just me. Human, a simple human being. Indeed, if I had something to take me away from this predicament," she continued, "I would gladly welcome it. It's been a long time since I've been in my invisible fetters and only *my late mother knew* how I felt about it all," she concluded, using an expression peculiar to her own people.

Delighted with her honesty and humility, Feso decided now he must broach his long cherished goal. But he still hesitated, not eager to go against his fear of the mambo, ingrained in him over the past year.

"But you are like a treasured biltong hanging above a fire place where neither fly nor cockroach can reach you," he allowed himself to say.

"I'm not a biltong. Besides, fire does not burn on the hearth all the time and, hence, in the quiet moments of the day flies and cockroaches do find their way to the biltong if only they desire to do so," Chipo philosophised obligingly.

All the while Rumba listened to the argument with

her head down, without saying a word. Custom prohibited her participating in such a conversation, and her duty was merely to take care of the mistress's needs.

Encouraged by such reasoning, Feso decided not to waste any more time, but to say what he had to say, right then. It was a very tender moment and one that he had waited for, so long.

"I hardly know what to say, now." stalled Feso, nervous, overwhelmed by the chance he saw to be too good to be true.

"Aren't you a man?" she taunted him.

"I am not a prisoner of war, princess. I came to the land of the Vanyai for a special reason. To see you," he started.

"Me? Why?"

"I came in order to win your love for my worthy and beloved Chief, Nyan'ombe. He is a noble man—young, strong, vigorous and, in every way fit for a charming woman like you. I am his messenger, his ambassador."

"Flattery! He has never seen me. How can a man love a woman he has never seen?" A woman's quick answer startled him. Otherwise she seemed not surprised at the amazing confession of Feso's.

"Those who have seen have been his eyes, his ears, and have represented in every way his own feelings and desires in life. I, myself, testify to that fact."

"You mean, you already love me for your master?"

"Precisely so. I mean I love you for my brave king. I assure you that you'll find him worthy of your love. It is for him I risked my life; it is for you I'm here, and I can only hope that my risk and devoted duty will not have fallen on rocky ground. I would have the pleasure of greeting you and clapping my hands to the Mother of the Imbaharu of Nyangombe." In making these gestures he clapped his hands with one knee down and the other genuflexed as he would actually have done before his lord and mistress in a real situation.

Chipo was impressed and felt highly honoured.

"What's on your mind, then?" she inquired earnestly.

"I know that your quarters are in the innermost parts of the imbahuru where you and Rumba, and her little sister—Hamundide—sleep. No one can approach your place without going first through the imbahuru and arousing suspicion and risking death. And you could not easily slip out at night either, without someone casting an eye." Chipo listened in a rather pensive mood as one who is deliberating a weighty and serious matter. She remained silent.

Feso thought for a while. Suddenly, he was seized with a weird idea.

"Tonight—and I mean tonight," he emphasized, "in the dead of night when everybody is asleep, I'll enter the imbahuru, my face and hands and body all dabbed in red and white clays. I'll look like a ghost with a head gear adorned with ostrich feathers, and a flaming spear in my hand. Everyone in the imbahuru, including your father, will be so frightened when I stalk in to take you and Rumba by the hand to dart away in the excitement, away from the imbahuru. If anything happens, slip away as soon as you can to meet me here, under this muhacha tree. Then we'll be on our way to Nyan'ombe's. And I'll have time to prepare food for the journey."

"How can this plot succeed?" she inquired doubtfully.

Feso replied with a voice of deep sincerity,

"You are at the centre of the success or failure of this plot. You are my salvation, or my destruction. And you said, yourself, you hated the prison your life has become. A handsome king is awaiting you."

And as she stood looking at him, hard and long, trying to doubly convince herself of his trustworthiness, Feso added, "Although the fear of ancestral spirits and of night ghosts is steeped in our people, still, I'll have to depend on you and on your sincerity. This night we must be brave."

"Don't fear. I'll be on your side," she assured him. But then, in a gush of womanly fear she added, "But what if I don't like your king?"

"Then I'll bring you back again—and everyone will believe you've been with the spirits," Feso answered strongly.

With a strained, tearful look, the young princess and her handmaid quickly left the scene and hurried back home, leaving Feso to resume his lonesome and arduous task and to ponder over the consequences of the dangerous scheme that he must now carry out, all alone, in the middle of thousands of enemies. When he arrived home in the evening he went to the dare where the fire was burning and the men engaged in the usual topics of conversation, the weather, the hunt past, the hunt future, the strange ways of women. . . Only Feso had something different on his mind.

Chapter IX

The Ghost of Feso

The Vanyai, who were an integral part of the Vahota—though the former boasted of a direct lineage from the great Vatapa of King Monomotapa—shared the same traditions and customs as did the Vahota of Nyan'ombe. The men's dare was a common tradition. It separated the men from the women and this was perfectly in harmony with the ancient practice and tradition as this gave each sex its own desired privacy and independent growth and development. Sex was regarded as a sacred attribute of the creator mediating his will through the intercession of the ancestral spirits. Thus, when the men sat at the dare and partook of their food there and engaged in manly talks and conversation, and the women repaired to their homes, took care of the children, and prepared food and drinks for their men, all this was regarded as the normal thing to do. The younger men learned life's experiences from the older folks at the dare and there they developed masculine attitudes, while the girls became women in their mothers' and grandmothers' houses.

The women took great pains in preparing food and desired to excel in the dishes they produced for their men. As each household brought its food to the dare, great care had to be taken in the cleanliness of the utensils, the quality of the food—i. e. its taste and palatability and the manner in which it was cooked and prepared. If nothing was returned after the men had eaten their food, it was a sign of excellent cuisine, while the reverse was, likewise, a sign of poor cooking. The main dish of the Vanyai—called *sadza*—was prepared from either cereals or maize meal, African corn meal, fingermillet meal, or rice meal. The thick porridge was served with either stewed meats—including beef, chicken, venison, fish, or any other available flesh—or served with vegetables of any kind, or milk, roasted seeds, or eaten as it was if nothing else was available. The Vanyai liked it, and cherished it greatly, and nothing could take the place of sadza as the main dish in the serving.

When the men had finished their evening meal, they

sat down in a relaxed mood, and this evening talked about the great heroic deeds of their lives. A drink or two made from the fermented seeds of the fingermillet often completed the dinner as the men prepared to go to sleep in their respective houses. Often, when the occasion permitted, some older folk would tell fables and interesting stories to the younger people for their entertainment or edification. The stories of the lion and the baboons, or the tortoise and the hare, were a rich store of treasured legacy among the Vanyai and these were more often than not laced with moral teachings for the young. They were aimed at imparting wisdom and understanding and a preparation for life's troubles.

Feso sat in the dare and listened to what was going on, and often participated in the story telling. He was witty, and spoke rather fast with a distinctly, and yet pleasantly, different accent—to the fascination of the young hearers. Notwithstanding the show of happy mood that Feso put on, his mind was as perplexed and as troubled as a turbulent stream. He pondered and churned the matter of his escape with Chipo and the idea haunted him like a ghost haunts an enchanted dwelling. However, in no way did he doubt the integrity and sincerity of Chipo's intentions and he forced himself to believe that all would be well that night. For good or ill, for better or worse, the die had been cast and the Chirayire River would have to be crossed. There was no turning back.

In time the dare was a deserted place. The men had abandoned it, and, likewise, Feso stepped over to his hut to sleep. For hours his heart pounded in his chest and robbed him of his sleep. But he was also afraid to sleep and to fail in his mission, for this would be his only chance. The royal village that was lately vibrant with life now lay quiet and still. The early hours of morning have such an overwhelming power that even the strongest of us soon find ourselves succumbing to their irresistible drug of sleep. Even the gate keepers were dozing off in sleep to the unheeded wild hoots of the enchanted owls. Feso, judging the time by the moon, rose up, girded himself, and then began to smear himself with the potter's red and white oxide clay, plastering it on his face, hands, and entire body. He lost his natural appearance and in moments became a ghastly spectre of some bad dream.

It was the "ghost" of Feso. He then adorned his head with feathers, and made his spear red hot in a fire lit for the purpose and blown by the goatskin bellows of the blacksmith.

Slipping by the sleeping guards, Feso entered the imbahuru where the excited pair Chipo and Rumba were housed; quickly he stood before the slumbering Pfumojena and shouted: "Pfumojena! Pfumojena! Arise! Mambo, great ruler of the people, arise! See the mighty one sent here to tell you the ancestor's desire the visit of your most charming and beautiful daughter, she whom the gods have so graciously blessed you with. Her voyage to the great and noble ones of the underworld is called for and she must leave forthwith."

Pfumojena arose on one elbow and, lo and behold, a ghost—an apparition from the ancestral spirits—stood before him. Seeing this terrible figure all daubed in red and white, wielding a fiery, deadly spear in its hand, the chief trembled from head to foot and believed what he saw to be a spirit in truth. He tried to speak, but words wouldn't flow from his mouth, nor even form in his terrified mind.

"Obey!" the voice urged, "and you shall live, Pfumojena, and do not resist the changes required of you in your life and that of the people!"

"Who are you, my father?" the Mambo finally stuttered, still half asleep.

"That you shall know later. Obey now before a greater calamity befalls you, Pfumojena! I have called your daughter. Do not hinder her visit to the other world. . ." and here Feso held the red hot spear point under the chief's nose.

The door of Chipo's room flung open and, there, in obedience to her own will, if not to the ancestors, Chipo stood calmly, composedly—a perfect symbol of royal beauty and dignity—waiting for her distant, unseen lover's ambassador to take her away. Standing next to her was her faithful maidservant—Rumba. Without a word, or even a glance at the quaking mambo, they followed Feso out to freedom, unimpeded, and unafraid, Pfumojena enshrouded in fear, still lay twisted on one arm, as if in a trance.

"Stay in your room!" the last peremptory order had come from the ghost's voice, "and there remain silent till the break of day! Or you shall not see your daughter again."

What could any being do but obey. The ghost's voice barked, "Good-bye! till we meet again in blood and fire."

Pfumojena curled back onto his mat, unable to make utterances, or to understand the meaning of it all. There he anxiously awaited the break of day in order to find out from the diviner's occult powers what this eerie, inexplicable visitation from the *vadzimu*, the nation's ancestral spirits portended.

Chapter X

Feso's Flight with Chipo

Leaving the *imbahuru* where he had sown seeds of confusion and terror, Feso quickly returned to his hut, washed his face clean of the red oxide, and put on his normal attire. No need now for disguise. Without losing any more time, he led the women through the main gates of the village past the sleeping gate keepers.

As they went past the familiar haunts of the village, Feso was very pleased and proud of himself for having hatched a plot so successful. The princess—the most beautiful and most loved woman in the whole land—was now by his side. What a wonderful thought this was! For a moment he forgot everything and laid aside his hate of Pfumojena and the bitter memories of humiliation and suffering that he had silently endured for a whole year. He thanked his midzimu for having so strengthened him and blessed him with so precious a gift as he now had in his possession. All this for the sake of his beloved Chief—Nyan'ombe.

There was still much of the night left and they must hurry. Too soon might Feso's hut be found empty—too soon might the not unintelligent mambo realize the trick played on him.

The small party, now well on its way to Nyan'ombe's country, would dog-trot for a period, and then rest, then walk when there was a hill, rest, then run. They took the same way back that Feso had followed previously, for it was direct and though it led through the dangerous pass of Mudzimundiringe Forest where he had fought his successful duel with Marasirapi. It was just over a year now and whether the outlaws still occupied the same haunts, or had moved to some other sites, was the question that Feso pondered laboriously and painfully in his mind to resolve the issue. Whether the latter supposition was now true or not he would still take the same route. The only other way home would mean they must climb savage hills and find a track through unknown mountains, and even more dangerous because of wild beasts. No, they must risk the outlaws.

As dawn broke they reached the first stretch of trees along fast flowing streams, and occasionally they had to cross open grassy plains. All of this was a novelty to the young women who never before had dared venture away from their quasi-imprisonment. The rolling hills they now climbed were bright with flowers and green bushes, and the bubbling, flowing waters, clear as crystal, fascinated the young women beyond description. Not being used to walking long distances, however, their steps became shorter and shorter. The pace was too fast so Feso had to slow down and even halt for long periods, despite his own impatience, in order to avoid undue weariness and exhaustion on their part.

From time to time the girls would sleep. When they finally came to the place of his former captivity, having been in the deepest part of the forest for some time, Feso kept his silence. No sense was there in scaring Chipo and Rumba with the thought of dangerous outlaws who might still be lurking here. His heart throbbed in his chest, as they very slowly followed the dim path and he quietly and earnestly prayed his ancestors to watch and protect them from harm and danger. But suddenly they had pushed out into a new plain, the trees behind them. The Nyangombe-Pfumojena borderline had been crossed and, once again, Feso was in his native land.

For another period, after a long nap, he encouraged the girls once again to keep on, despite the aching legs and tears from branches and thorns. At last they sat down near the quiet and gentle flowing waters of a stream and ate the food Feso had packed for them. Resting, sighing, they could look down into the open glades, for from their little hill they could see for miles around. Suddenly, the wide, open-eyed Chipo fearfully cried out,

"Look Rumba! Look what's coming our way! An animal something like a cow!"

"Not a cow!" corrected Feso, "but a buffalo, Chipo."

The women huddled behind Feso in fear of the animal racing past them.

In a moment a different animal swept out of a hidden crack in the hills and sped by, startled to find strange shapes in its grazing grounds. Finally a whole herd of the beasts galloped down the valley below them.

"What are these called?" asked Rumba. "I don't

know their names."

"These are called antelopes. They live in herds and are so swift footed that even the fastest hound finds it very difficult to outrace them."

The fear that had gripped them left them slowly as they regained their confidence under the protection of their experienced guide. These were "*guta*" girls, sheltered, and the ways of wild beasts were mysterious.

"The dried meat we just ate was that of an antelope," he explained, and they nodded their heads with a half embarrassed smile on their faces. "These gentle animals won't hurt us," he reassured them. "But be prepared to see many more as we proceed, for they are very common in my country—which will soon be your country."

Chipo was thrilled and, having regained her usual poise, mentioned the stories of wild animals her mother told her. All this to show she was not a complete village ninny about wild life.

"Has anyone ever told you of koodoos, bucks, rhinoceroses, the red deer, the long eared grey hares?" asked Feso.

"Yes, my father used to relate stories of all kinds of animals, but he didn't give me any idea of their size, or colours, nor of their swift-footedness. Only the hulk of the elephant was clear, for it was as a small grain storage barn."

"Yes, there are all sizes and colors of animals. Some, like the elephant, are of a mighty build, capable of uprooting small trees and breaking down large ones," Feso replied, and, standing up, pointed to an elephant trail traversing the plain in front of them. "Some beasts, especially the one horned rhinoceros, are almost as powerful and even more fierce. It takes many men to subdue one of those brutes with spears and axes. The tawny lion, of course, is the king. Several tribes of cats are spotted, or mottled, and they easily hide in the brush before springing on men or beast. All the animals try concealing themselves from one another. In the case of the buck, his brown and white colors blend with the brown grass and the white streaks of light in the open forests, thus making it difficult for his enemies to spot him. Even the noble lion, afraid of no creature, shares the same need to hide and he is as brown as the grass in which he lurks and hunts.

"Some, of course, like the koodoo, in addition to

their camouflage, are keen of hearing, and are very swift-footed. They can rapidly clear away from big leopards or lions." These and many other details fascinated the women and, giving them something to think about, heartened them into travelling on the still long path without homesickness or worry about the future in a strange land.

And after another long march, ended on another grassy hill, Feso related anecdotes of his hunting experience to them, Then, looking away in the distance, he pointed out a herd grazing in a secluded plain in the valley below.

"Those animals you see in the valley are buffaloes," he started. "They, too, are common in this country."

"They look like cattle," observed Chipo.

"Yes, indeed, they look so, but they are the wild brothers of our docile beasts," agreed Feso.

"Are they fierce? Would they attack us?" inquired Rumba.

"Not unless we attack them," Feso assured them. "A buffalo can be a fierce animal; but even a domestic cow can be dangerous if irritated. But the wild buffalo has great strength and with its horns can easily, with one swipe, gore a person to death." With a twinkle on his face, he added, "No, we won't try to get too close to those bulls and cows, if we can help it." He then began a story.

"Once when our men went out on a hunting expedition—led by one of our best men, Gwanzura—we were fortunate enough to kill many antelopes. We dressed the meat in the bush, smoked it, and bundled it together in the hides for easy carrying. We had been away from home several days when, suddenly, crossing a half-wooded area, we ran into a herd of buffaloes. Our fierce hounds attacked a buffalo bull which plunged into a dark thicket. We followed closely behind, armed with spears and axes, ready for the assault. Our brave dogs fought fiercely. Alas! All the dogs who dared to come too close were brutally trampled down. In a short time we had lost seven dogs. Some of the hunters said, 'Enough, let us retreat and leave it alone.' But some, like Gwanzura, insisted that we attack the bull. It would be shameful to back off before just one beast.

"So, we all followed behind Gwanzura as he led the assault. Then in one swift lunge the buffalo broke at us, bellowing fiercely, and we scattered in all directions. Some climbed trees, others scaled boulders. But Gwanzura stood his ground as the infuriated animal swung his way. He hurled his spear and it landed deep in the bull's chest, as his faithful dog at his side barked and snapped at the bull's very nose. Undeterred, the fierce brute charged sticking its right horn into Gwanzura's side, killing him instantly.

"Though we timid ones immediately came down to try to rescue him, it was of no avail. His spirit was gone, and gone the triumphant bull."

"Oh, my! Poor Gwanzura!" cried Chipo. "Why didn't he, too, run away?"

"Because he was a brave man—a fine warrior—and a man who would never flinch from facing any danger. He fought like a man, and died like a man," concluded Feso.

Again, after another march, this time less hurried, for even Feso was footsore now, they came to a cool shade of a big rock overlooking a stream. There they sat down to eat their evening meal and to rest.

The Princess and Rumba exhibited high spirits after their simple repast of sadza thick mealie-meal porridge, and roasted biltong and stamped groundnuts. Their weariness seemed half gone and this new life—far from restrictions and confinement—seemed to have revived in them a new zest, a new spirit. They were now looking forward to the prospect of a different and happy life. Chipo was vibrant, and Feso was ready with a clever tale. He cleared his voice like one ready to deliver an oration before an audience.

"In a far off village—called Mbiriyedenga," he said grandly, "there lived an ambitious young man called Muhwati and a beautiful young woman, called Rudo. Their love affair became the talk of the village and the envy of the people. It was love—plain love—such as exists between two simple people. Something had happened and the two suddenly blossomed into one tender plant." Feso then paused.

Chipo gave a radiant smile, showing her dimples and her winsome beauty. "Go on," she urged him, "we're listening."

"Now Muhwati came of poor parents who could not afford the traditional dowry—a love token—to give to the parents of his beloved. He, therefore, decided he must leave his betrothed and go to a far off country to labor for the dowry—it being understood that she would wait for him till he returned home.

"What a faithful girl!" exclaimed Rumba.

"Not unlike me," rejoined Chipo.

"Why?" asked Feso.

"Following the trail of a star I've never even seen!"

They all laughed.

"I hadn't thought," said Feso, "that you two could be taken in just by a story." And looking at Chipo, he said seriously, "The star you are following is a real and true star."

"Very well; go on, sir," she ordered with a smile.

"Muhwati journeyed many a day, risking hunger, thirst, and the many hazards of his long journey. At last he arrived at King Nyatsanga's royal village where he lived and labored for five, long years. For his well-earned reward, the king generously gave him goats and cattle and even a wife but Muhwati refused, as diplomatically as he could, the offer of a wife, saying he had a betrothed woman waiting at home. Saying goodbye, he drove his four-footed wealth before him, hurrying home as fast as he could.

"While he was yet afar, he met a man who immediately recognized him and informed him of the mishap that had occurred while Muhwati was away. 'Oh poor man; What a pity! Your betrothed girl got tired of waiting. She already has a one-week-old child.' he said.

"Muhwati was dumbfounded and would have shed tears but for his manly courage. He thought of his arduous tasks and the many years he had labored for her and his dreams of a good and happy life with Rudo. Now all gone—gone with the wind!"

"Maiwe!" Chipo cried, "What a despicable and shameful thing! What an unfaithful woman!"

"I would have drowned her in a river pool," shouted Rumba, ferociously.

"I would have whipped and flogged her," continued the princess.

"I would have stripped her and lashed her lazy skin with a cow hide strap," reiterated Rumba angrily, adding pictorial details.

"Then what followed?" asked Rumba, rising in her

anger, and looking Feso in the face.

"It was a painful decision for Muhwati to make. Should he turn back to reclaim the woman he had just refused—or go on to his village? Well, he did go on, though he no longer hurried, and his heart beat slowly, his mouth dry, his eyes too wet. After some days at home, Muhwati met Rudo at the village well. He approached gently and forced himself to speak.

" 'Well, what happened?' he inquired softly.

" 'I was enticed,' she replied in shame, face down.

" 'Nonsense! You didn't love me.'

" 'Not so. You men are tongue twisters,' she attacked.

" 'My husband said you wouldn't return to me, and I believed. Years I waited. I was attacked on all sides by my parents as well until I gave in.'

"An anguished look filled Muhwati's face, but Muhwati slowly said, almost cruelly, 'How could you hurt me so? You told me you would wait, no matter how long.'

" 'I'm sorry. Forgive me!' she implored with tears rolling down her cheeks.

" 'You are still dear to me,' he assured her, seeing her pain.

" 'And, you to me, too.' she sobbed.

" 'Do you understand what this means, Rudo?' he asked as he came closer to her.

" 'No!'

" 'It means giving up everything—everything! And starting anew with me. We must flee.'

" 'Yes,' she conceded.

" 'Will you come with me?' he insisted.

" 'Where?' And her startled eyes showed her sudden hope.

" 'Anywhere,' he replied in desperation.

" 'Yes, with you, Muhwati. Yes.'

"Thus, it became true, once again that men are tongue twisters, deceiving and being deceived in return. A weak moment leads to even worse moments. Muhwati knew then, without a doubt, that she still had love for him big enough to move mountains. The two then hatched a plot whereby that very night the woman would go out in the dead

85

of the night and pretend some one was attacking her. When her husband rushed out to save her he would be met by a murderer awaiting him in the dark. And thus it happened, for Maravanyika—Rudo's husband—responded to his wife's cry that dark night; he was brutally stabbed to death, his neck cut with one stroke of a sharp panga, and the two left the village, flying away from their gory deed. Maravanyika had lied to Rudo and died for his haste to claim another man's bride. But now the lovers were outlaws."

"Maiwe! What a tragic story." moaned Chipo.

"Couldn't Rudo have divorced her husband?" Rumba asked with a painful look on her face.

"Divorce was unthinkable, not even possible in those days. Once married—always married," Feso explained.

"And what happened to the baby?"

"Your Highness, this is what followed." Feso lit his pipe and began to smoke as if to stimulate his mind to recall all the further details of his bloody story.

"Fleeing their village, the two lovers and the baby, too, travelled to a far away land, in order to escape punishment. Escape they did, but it was not long when they came to a river in flood. They were now in a remote and uninhabited part of the country. Everywhere wild beasts prowled, owls hooted, snakes slithered away, and rock lizards shrieked their mournful and doleful sound at night.

"The lovers reached a spot much like this one and turning around, Muhwati faced Rudo, and said, 'I know of a truth that you love me. But there is still one barrier between us.' Rudo was startled. She was unable to account for the stern face before her.

"Turning to him entreatingly, her side-long glances more loving than ever, she said, 'What is it, dear Muhwati?'

" 'The baby! I mean the baby!' he said, pointing to it. 'You know it is not my baby, not my blood, not any part of me.'

" 'What's wrong with it,' she asked, sickened in her soul, almost comprehending. . .

" 'This baby is a danger to me—a real danger—I mean when he's grown up.'

" 'In what way?'

" 'He will seek after my life. He will destroy me when all is revealed about the death of his father.'

" 'What do you think I should do with him, then?'

" 'Cast him away!' he replied dryly.

" 'Where?'

" 'Into the flood,' he suggested.

" 'No! No! No! You can't do that with an innocent baby!' the mother remonstrated. 'No one will ever tell him he is not your very own son. We will go so far from our village no one will know our story.'

" 'Then you are none of me,' he said, with a hardened heart. 'I will not accept him as my son.'

"Then, slowly, and painfully, the mother's emotions began to rise. She could not restrain herself as tears rolled down her cheeks. She looked all around her—thick forests—with all those prowling beasts—no sign of human life anywhere near. Then, closing her eyes, she threw her baby into the surging flood. It gave one cry and disappeared in the dark rushing waters. Muhwati stared out over the turbulent stream, then turned round to face the woman again, 'I left you in trust, believing you would be true and faithful to me. But instead, upon my return, I found you had married another man. Then I asked you to join me in my plot to get rid of your husband, and you agreed. Here, you have just now flung your baby into the surging flood. You are a foolish woman, inhuman, and untrustworthy. I cannot but believe that you could do the same to me if you felt you had to. You are much too gullible and much too simple and much too savage for me.'

"So saying, Muhwati entered the flood and was, likewise, quickly drowned. Rudo shrieked, fell howling on the ground. Mad, she wandered in the forests for days, her clothes torn from her body by brambles, her feet bleeding. Howls coming from her bloody lips. Finally, she fell a prey to the wild beasts of the jungles." Turning to the women, Feso said abruptly "What do you think of such a love affair?" There was no answer.

Both Chipo and Rumba were crying, their hands covering their eyes in grief. Feso regretted having told them such a tragic story, and he apologetically mumbled, "Such strange things do happen in life and all in the name of love."

The girls were weary. Emptied of their own fears by the wild tale, they huddled together. Feso quickly built a makeshift shelter of boughs and grasses and there they spent the night. Only a sob from first one girl and then another during the long night spoke of their tragic dreams. Braced against a tree, the dozing Feso watched over them, sad with his long absence from home.

Chapter XI

Chipo's Royal Welcome

There was no doubt that when the princess arrived at the imbahuru of Nyan'ombe she received a joyful and uproarious royal welcome, for Feso had almost been given up as lost—even dead. At once, Feso's arrival marked the triumphant return of a hero and the beginning of a new royal family.

Chipo became the talk of the country, the center of attraction, and soon the pride of the nation. Her youthful charm and vigour captivated her beholders as she moved and smiled with all the elegance of a young princess. The announcement of the forthcoming royal marriage of Nyan'ombe to Chipo had spread like wild fire throughout the land. Chipo's presence as the new mother of the nation seemed to have uplifted the spirit of the people and word spread around praising the shrewdness, cunning and intrepidness of Feso in bringing to the nation such a good looking woman. She seemed beyond the reach of human ill and the image of her future motherhood enhanced her graces so much that her presence even raised the hopes of the Vahota nation under their young paramount chief that they could overcome their enemies.

Nyan'ombe now no longer acted like a young man, but like a mature king, father of his people. No one addressed him any longer as Ishe—the Chief, but as Mambo—the King. What once was mere ceremony was now said in all seriousness.

It was no wonder this was so because the mother image is paramount in the philosophy of life of the Vahota, for woman as mother precludes and even overshadows the idea of woman as lover. In joy or pain, in good health or illness, in prosperity or poverty, in life and death—yes, in practically everything, *amai*—the mother—is at the centre of every cry. She rules at the heart of her children and, in her advanced age, she is honoured even more. She is the future of the nation, the basket of prosperity. Little wonder, then, that the whole nation was moved by the appearance of the 'new

mother' of the nation—and such a fine girl as she was—and so
mysterious alien in her nurture—so wonderful her appearance
in the midst of the Vahota.

On the occasion of that great day when Nyan'ombe
was to take Chipo to be his wife, a large crowd gathered at
the Mambo's royal village to celebrate the marriage festival.
People from all the villages around gathered in the thousands.
You could see people in houses, in huts, in shelters, and in
every available space. Big, strong men came strutting,
strolling here and there pompously, proud of their mambo
and his new bride.

Then Nyan'ombe ordered to be slaughtered one
hundred and sixty head of cattle to provide meat for those
celebrating the royal marriage. Numberless sheep and goats,
too, and chickens in the thousands were baked on spits and
served to the crowds. Everywhere you looked you saw some
fires burning, the great black cauldrons bubbling, simmering
with their hot meats. The traditional sadza was as ever served
with the tender flesh. Oh, and don't forget the people's
beer—doro—in two kinds, the intoxicating one for warriors,
the sweet one for women and children. Doro, doro, it was
everywhere. All goblets spilled with its foam. So the people
ate and quaffed the drinks to their hearts' content. Their
bellies puffed, their teeth bit, everyone laughing, crying. . .

As they neared the critical moment when all should
see the royal bride and hear the public orations, Jeranyama—a
junior Army Commander, received orders from Senior Army
Commander—Mapondera—to gather the people together at
the appointed place in order to welcome officially the young
princess and her handmaid—Rumba.

Strutting among the crowds with an air of military
pride and superiority, and dressed in his full warrior
accoutrements, Mapondera sought out Jeranyama to give him
orders.

"Jeranyama!" he called, "let the people gather
around, have them face the pavilion."

"I will, Changamire," he responded.

"See that there is space enough for the royal
procession and leave free the open forum facing the
pavilion."

"It will be done, Changamire."

"That is where the warrior parade will take place

under my command," Mapondera ordered.

All this, the young shepherd Chokumarara heard. He grinned as he stood near to the Warrior Commanders.

"Have you seen the princess?" he asked Manzira, his friend.

"No, I have not."

"She is beautiful—I mean beautiful! When Nyan'ombe's aunt saw her, she quaffed a whole gourd of water in praise of her," Chokumarara explained.

"Ha! Ha; that's funny," Manzira laughed.

"Fascinating is the word. Not funny," Chokumarara corrected him. "Oh, such a woman!"

"But she is a Munyai girl," Manzira added, teasingly. Why should we want a foreigner?"

"Don't be ridiculous! She is a person—winning our old enemy's daughter is a fine thing. We have spited old mambo the cruel one—and we shall soon have brave babies in the royal kraal, and that is what matters," Chokumarara proclaimed.

"Well, I agree, but what about her handmaiden?" Manzira joshed. "I hear the princess came along with one. Have you seen her, too?"

"You mean Rumba?" inquired Chokumarara.

"Yes, I mean her, if that is her name."

"She, too, is a fine looking woman," he added.

"Whose wife is she going to be?"

"No idea," replied Chokumarara, "that remains to be seen." At this point the two boys were interrupted by the peremptory orders of Jeranyama.

"Everybody to my right and left, move now, leave way for the royal procession," he shouted directing the crowds with his hands.

"Attention now, as soon as you see them coming I want all of the men to start clapping your hands, and the women to ululate. Welcome our new mother. Show her we love her!"

Led by the elders of the nation, the mambo came majestically down the column of people. He was dressed in his robe of a lion's skin, and regally girt above his shoulders was a leopard's skin. His kingly crown sat royally on his head with its glittering ostrich feathers, quivering in the slight breeze. In all his majestic splendour, Nyan'ombe proudly moved along amid the clapping of hands and the women's shrill ululations. Behind him, and led by Feso and the mambo's mother and his aunt, came the charming princess. Her elegance and gracious smiles enchanted the crowds and she received a tumultuous reception as was never accorded any woman before. Beside her was Rumba, her faithful handmaid, also looking as attractive as can be.

When the people were finally quiet, Mapondera stood up and cried out:

"Behold, the mother of the nation!" A new roar leapt from the crowds.

"Behold, her faithful handmaid!" Another thunder of applause followed.

"This is an occasion I should like to share with you in welcoming to this royal village, to this country, yea, to this nation, Chipochedenga—the new mother of our nation. May her ancestral spirits attend her, and may she be happy and fruitful among us," Mapondera concluded. The crowds went wild, with the men clapping their hands, and beating drums, and the women dancing and screaming, expressive of their joy and gladness.

Then bringing the mambo to join his bride, Mapondera boomed out:

"Your Royal Highness, Changamire Nyan'ombe, behold your wife!" And turning to Chipo, he, likewise addressed her, thus, "Royal Mother, behold your husband!" Again, the crowds applauded and danced in an act of approval. Then, Vanyarambi—the mambo's mother, and his aunt, the royal ambuya or tete, danced before the bride and bridegroom to the amusement of all the people. Nyan'ombe, overwhelmed with emotion, ceremonially hugged his wife to his breast, and then giving her over to his mother in the old, honoured way, slowly, raising his hand, saying in the sudden silence,

"I am grateful to you, my people, for your approval, for your words of encouragement, and for the wonderful welcome you have given my wife. We will ever seek to live up to your expectations and serve you as our ancestral spirits give us health, strength and wisdom." Turning around, and seeing his great commander sitting next to his wife, he then addressed the crowds, saying,

"Now I want to address myself to my loyal and

faithful friend—Feso. Here is the man who deserves all the credit and praise for his loyalty, intrepidness, and unlimited courage. I am deeply indebted to him for my wife." At this point, the people gave him a roaring ovation with their applause.

"Feso the Great! Feso, the Great!" They shouted.

"He is, indeed, Feso, the Great!" Nyan'ombe acceded.

"But today, I have the pleasure of making him greater still. As of this moment Feso will be the First Army General and second only to me. In him I invest all the powers of a warrior commander of which no doubt you will all agree he more than deserves." The people once again applauded and went wild with excitement.

Turning to Rumba and lifting her up by her hand, he said,

"Another surprise I'll give you, Feso," he said, addressing himself to him, "behold your new wife; she has royal blood in her veins. And woman, behold your husband!"

At this juncture the crowds went wild again with a joyous surprise. The two young herders who were in the crowd could not be restrained from wild excitement, too, as they nodded their heads and clapped their hands in an animated conversation about a matter they had discussed before.

"I knew Feso would have that girl," boasted Chokumarara.

"He deserves her for all his courage," Manzira replied. "Now he has two wives and we'll have occasion to visit her as the younger wife and see how well a Munyai woman cooks," concluded Manzira.

"And to listen to her pleasant, foreign accent, too," added Chokumara.

"Ha! Ha! Ha!" they both laughed together for joy.

The warrior parade and dance which followed under the direction of Army Commander, Mapondera, was even more impressive than the preceding ceremonies. The men, dressed in their traditional garbs with their plumed headpieces, bright spears in their right hands, their small ox-hide shields in their left, presented a spectacular sight. The older warriors were armed with battle axes and swords ensheathed in scabbards which they wore on the left side, the warriors danced and put up a violent sham battle in the open forum, dancing to the rhythmic sounds of drums, chanting a war song. One man was so carried away that he accidentally cut himself on his own blade, while another swooned from the intense heat of the sun and, perhaps, a bit too much of the potent doro beer. Then, from all the dust and sweat and noise, the royal party retired to the imbahuru for food, and drink, and rest.

Now, after a brief pause, as the evening shades closed in, the royal drummers heated the drum heads gathered on little fires to tauten the skins, preparing for an all-night celebration. Likewise, the younger people also made ready for their *jeketera* dance.

So it was that when the people had eaten and had had their share of the beer, they stood up to dance and to enjoy themselves. In the crowd was a man called Chanyuruka, a remarkable dancer. Indeed, no one in the nation was as distinguished a dancer as he was. He was tall, standing well over six feet, lanky, and of remarkable strength and agility. He wore a loin covering of a fawn skin, a bead-belt ringed round with tails of the white-tailed mongoose and a longer tail of a baboon trailing behind him. On his head he wore a cap of bead work decorated with brightly shining feathers. On his upper and lower arms he wore bangles of brass and of grass, around his ankles he had rattles which jingled at his rhythmic movements. All these added to his weird appearance and made him look more like a magician than the nation's most original dancer whose wild yet clever work delighted all the people.

Tonight, Chanyuruka was particularly brilliant. Sometimes he would make strange leaps and unbelievable whirls and twists, then he would stand upright on his head, now he is walking on his hands with legs up; finally, like a monkey, scaling small huts and barns and jumping over them—to the amazement of the spectators. He even would lie on his back, allowing women to place their wooden pestle and mortar on his chest to pound their fingermillet. In between he would shake all over as if in a hallucinatory trance, or in a seizure. He received numerous gifts of appreciation from his admirers, and young women wept for Chanyuruka, some of them barely restrained from creeping close to him to hug him, suffering from Chanyuruka-mania.

While this dancing was going on in the open, inside the huts the older folks were, likewise, suffering their own form of craziness. Enchanted by the rhythmic beat of their drums, and the tingling rattles in their hands and around their legs, they danced themselves away all night long, amid the wild cries and ululations of the women. The bangles jingled and clattered producing an enchanting and alluring whir of sound. There were those who danced the lion dance, some the baboon dance, some the ancestral-spirit-dance, and they continued dancing until they fell down to the floor from sheer exhaustion.

Even more frenzied, some others seized live chickens, ripped open their throats, and drank their blood—mimicking the wild cats of the grasslands. Those who were so seized by the mashave spirits fell into trances and terrifying visions. And so it went on the whole night long. Those who had over-eaten and were surfeited, or those who had taken more than their share of intoxicating drinks and were drunk, or those who were merely tired, all were seen to lie down sooner or later in one place or another till the break of day. Most hardly stirred till the late afternoon.

Finally as the evening once again began to close in upon them, the crowds began to disperse from the royal village. Some were seen carrying with them the remnants of pots of beer and the leftovers of meats from the festival. Such behavior could not escape the keen-eyed young herders who stood at their cattle enclosure. Seeing the women carrying away the pots, Chokumarara pretended outrage, "Hey, women! Don't carry away the pots! They belong to us. We're still hungry."

"You've had your fill, you should be ashamed of yourselves bringing things here and then sneaking them out of our village," taunted Manzira.

But the two boys got no response from the women who silently were more keen to get away than to be involved in the banter. Their men went by singing, still tipsy and gay, they, too, carrying with them whatever they could salvage from the leftovers of the festival.

"Don't worry, Manzira," Chokumarara soothed him. "Let them salvage whatever they can. We might as well sweep food out of the village. There won't be anything more left altogether."

"What do you mean by that?" asked Manzira.

"Because last night I overheard General Feso ordering Commander Mapondera to send off four hundred head of cattle for the dowry, or love token for the two girls, to Pfumojena. After all, though the women came here on their own, they must still be paid for."

"Then, indeed, there won't be any cattle left for us to look after," observed Manzira.

"That is so, at least for a while. But remember, Nyan'ombe has had grazing elsewhere many other cattle throughout our land, and most will be taken from those places to make up the number. Here we'll lose some but in a year or so we'll have just as many as ever."

And so ended the memorable marriage feast of Nyan'ombe and his lovely princess, Chipochedenga—the Gift-of-Heaven.

Chapter XII

The Troubled Land of Pfumojena

Recall the night Feso eloped with the princess and Rumba.

The next day, a frightful atmosphere pervaded the royal village. People spoke in whispers about the miraculous disappearance of Chipo and her handmaid. The whisper soon grew into a gossip, and the gossip into a scandal of the royal house. Some expressed shame, others pity, and still others secret approval of a situation they had always thought unnecessarily oppressive of the poor girl. They felt she had worked out her own emancipation and, consequently, could not be blamed for it. In no time, the entire kingdom of Pfumojena was involved in the scandal so that everywhere in the surrounding country you saw two or three engaged in talk about the mysterious disappearance of the princess.

Then, when the slave Feso was found to be gone, everyone guessed he had escaped with the girls with the intention, perhaps, of making Chipo his wife and, possibly giving away Rumba in marriage to another man. Such a possibility made the outrage even more sensational.

That first morning when the still stupified Pfumojena collected his scattered wits, he called out "Hamundide! Hamundide!" shouting for the girl who shared the room with the girls.

"Come here. Quick!" Hamundide came in panting and shaken.

"Tell me, my child! Where are Chipo and Rumba?"

"I don't know, Uncle!"

"You should know, child! You should know!"

"I don't know, Uncle!" The young woman started to cry.

"I saw them leave last night and thought they did so with your consent," she said. "They walked right by you—and you only looked at the ghost with the burning spear."

"Tell me! Where did they go? Tell me!" he sternly ordered.

97

At this point the girl could not answer. She broke into sobs and wild outcries.

Leaving the imbahuru, Pfumojena strode outside.

"Sariramba! Sariramba!" he screamed out.

"Samanyanga! I am listening, Changamire!" So saying the man called came running to Pfumojena. Standing before him, he said, "What can I do for you, Samanyanga? Your servant is listening."

"Tell me, General—and I want to know right away. Where is my daughter, and where is Rumba?"

Sariramba replied, "That is a question I cannot answer, Samanyanga. Tell me what has happened?"

The mambo spoke, as best he could, still mystified about the previous night's vision.

"Well," finally responded the general, "it is conceivable that since Feso—your trusted servant and convict—is also missing, that he in some fashion is involved in this matter. Possibly they are all together."

"What does this mean? Can we not send a search party after them?" Pfumojena groaned, feeling more and more duped.

"Not a chance, Samanyanga! Not a chance!" his commander grimly replied with a pessimistic look. "They have been gone most of the night. By now they should be in the Mudzimundiringe Forest—if, in fact, Feso has fled with them to his homeland."

"Are you certain you can guess where this Feso could have gone?"

"No, Samanyanga! I have no sure knowledge," he replied. Then Pfumojena's anger was kindled against his general.

"You should have made it your business to know where these convicts serving here come from. I shall punish all of you who failed to prevent the mysterious disappearance of my daughter."

Sariramba fearing further to provoke his already irate chief, said, "Samanyanga, human weakness is everyone's lot and I apologize for this negligence."

"This is no time for apologies! I do not wish to hear such apologies. They belong to the weak and the ignorant who know no better," Pfumojena rebuked him. "Go, now, and inquire from his fellow serfs. They should know where this lewd slave came from. Also find out why the gatekeepers failed to stop him—and why they saw nothing of my daughter!"

"Samanyanga! Your servant hears you!"

"And report to me before the sun has dried the grass. The death drums will mark your carelessness unless you learn what has happened this night!" he added in a peremptory voice.

As the troubled Pfumojena returned to the imbahuru, Sariramba hurried to the dare where the men were gathered. He ordered the gatekeepers and the serfs to be brought to the dare.

"You! and you! and you!" he shouted at several of these men serving at the royal village, as well as at the gatekeepers, "Answer me! You know what has happened in this village, don't you? Tell me what village Feso comes from. Who among you were his friends?" When the men hesitated, he ordered them beaten. They had all heard the scandalous news by now, but knowing Feso or not it seemed a terrible thing now to admit anything.

"What? No answer?" The commander screamed, himself wild with fear. "All of you will be stabbed to death, by noon and your bellies sliced open by *pangas* unless the truth comes out of your mouth," he threatened. "Speak!" The other nobles of the dare glared at the guards and serfs.

Fearing for their lives and the immense torture they shivered, but all but one had nothing to say. That one, deciding to save his comrades if not himself, spoke out at last, stammering.

"I knew Feso, very well," he said. "He was—he was, a great friend, yes, a friend, of mine." The serf, a large boned man, stumbled on. "Feso spoke softly, in a dignified way, his tongue was a strange tongue, a foreign accent."

"What accent?" one councillor shrieked.

"A southern accent," he said.

"That doesn't mean much," said Sariramba.

"An accent of the Vahota people."

"Of Chief Nyan'ombe?" Sariramba shouted. "I know he was a Muhota."

"Yes, Changamire," said the man. "Indeed, you are right. He spoke with that accent though he endeavored to conceal it many times. And he was from the mambo's royal village. But he never said anything else about his life."

"He was a clever spy," said Commander Mhingepinge, standing next to Sariramba, as their worst fears were realized.

"No wonder he was so patient—so good a servant," said another with a ferocious sneer.

"We will soon find out how smart Feso's master was to send him here," Sariramba retorted. "Put these men under guard. We may have more questions." So saying he straightaway went back to report to Pfumojena.

The mambo listened to this new information, his eyes popping from his head.

"Very well, General. I, too, have come to believe this spy was of Nyan'ombe's army. But we shall now fasten our teeth on this Nyan'ombe! He is only a youth. Our armies are mightier by far than his—a hundred times! Great commander, I swear by my mother buried on that anthill that there shall not be a soul, not a blade of grass, left in Nyan'ombe's kingdom to tell the story of how they tricked the royal princess right out of my own palace. Beat the war drums!"

"It shall be done, Samanyanga," answers Sariramba, turning to go.

But the mambo had not finished yet. "We cannot allow these Vahota barbarians to touch and abuse our women folk. It is an outrage that the conquered curs of the Vahota should make such fools of us—and of me." And the chief ground his teeth. "Mobilize all of our forces against Nyan'ombe. Call out our fastest runners and send them with orders to your regiments. Prepare to march to Nyan'ombe's land within three days. Then attack across the mountains. I will join you at the frontier with my own home legions in ten days."

Pfumojena thus sternly ordered his Army General to prepare for war with the Vahota. The Supreme Council—Dare Guru—of the Vanyai, unanimously approved the war resolution against any king found guilty of this elopement. To whatever land the princess had flown, blood and death would follow fast.

But the very next week, while the elders were seated at the dare pondering over the future, a man called Marangwanda suddenly arrived at the royal village bearing an important message.

"Samanyanga, and all the councillors present here," he started, "while travelling not far from the outlaw's forest, I saw a mysterious thing on the plain."

"What did you see, Marangwanda?" they inquired.

"I saw a large herd of cattle being driven by twenty men—horned cattle, polls, bullocks, cows, heifers, cattle of all sizes and colours filling a whole countryside—such magnificent animals!" he recounted, "and coming this way!"

The old men looked at one another—only their eyes talking to each other, but "What's this all mean?" interrupted Sariramba, anxious to set out, now that their spears and clubs were ready, their food prepared for the invasion.

"I talked with the men. They said they were driving the beasts to Mambo Pfumojena as a dowry for his daughter and Rumba. They go only a short distance each day by reason of their numbers."

The men looked at each other with a look of amazement, as if to say: "That explains the mystery of the disappearance of the girls. We were right. Feso was at the bottom of the whole outrage."

Pfumojena spoke the words himself, but then he declared, "We don't accept a gift for our extorted daughter. The Vahota must still pay for their crimes. No insulting bribes will be accepted. Only war can teach these primitive people not to tamper with the Vanyai women," he snorted. "We shall slaughter those beasts for meat to feed our invading warriors. I have enough of my own cattle; I don't need anything from the barbarians."

Again the war drums menaced the ear-drums of the inhabitants of the royal kraal.

The next day, Vanyai warriors of the palace guard and Sariramba's troops took the path to Nyan'ombe's kingdom, to ravage the land of the treacherous Feso and his foolish mambo. Pfumojena himself, doubly incensed, and his Army General Sariramba now marched together. Elder Councillor-General Zambara would bring up the main peasant army as soon as he could. Dust rose beneath the thousand heels. Looking down a pass the next day the Vanyai could see the large herd of cattle. Disregarding the startled, placating cries of the Vahota herdsmen, the Vanyai attacked them and scattered the herd of cattle, killing many, and driving away the remnants into the neighboring hills. The surviving Vahota fled before the fierce warriors and after skirting the great force of the enemy brought back news of the invasion. Thus, war was declared between the Vanyai and their neighbors, the Vahota. All for a stolen princess.

Manzira and Chokumarara were with these cattle and escaped in the dust of the stampeding beasts.

Chapter XIII

The Troubled Land of Nyan'ombe

No sooner had some of the escapees of the brutal attack arrived at Nyan'ombe's royal village with the disturbing news of the impending invasion than Nyan'ombe immediately proclaimed a state of siege in his country.

"Changamire, Mazvimbakupa," said the agitated Feso, "We are caught by our enemies unprepared."

Nyan'ombe merely stared on the ground as they sat at the men's dare. His peaceful mission had been shattered. Now the nation must fight for his bride he was thinking.

"We cannot sit here merely pondering over the matter, we must be putting our thoughts into action. Immediately!" warned Mapondera, irked at the mambo's silence.

"The Vanyai contingent coming against us is small but they are all well trained, well seasoned, and war-loving warriors," Mapondera added. "Let us mobilize our warriors and defend our country the best we can. After them no doubt will come their main forces."

"What did the messenger say who returned from our well-intentioned mission?" Nyan'ombe inquired, looking at Feso.

"The messenger told of horrid attacks on them and the cattle. The cattle bellowed and scampered all over the place under attack from the fierce and brutal assault of the warriors. A pitiful sight to see," he said. "If they can attack wild brutes like that, how much more will they attack men who are their real enemies?"

The council listened and a feverish tension seized the men.

Looking Feso full in the eye, Nyan'ombe said, "Tell us, General! You've lived with the Vanyai. Tell us, what sort of men are their leaders? Will their men fight as well as their fathers? I know you've told me this when you first returned but I want everyone to hear you again."

Then Feso carefully recounted his experiences, finishing, "Mazvimbakupa, the Vanyai are a very proud people who look down on us as primitive, backward, and

103

uncivilized, and as being totally unequal to them in arms."

"Why are they so proud?"

"They trace their geneology from the great King Matope Nyanhehwe Monomotapa who they claim led a powerful and highly civilized kingdom which once held sway throughout this entire area. They also claim that it was their ancestors who built the many stone ruins and forts in this land, including the Great Zimbabwe in the ancient land of Guruuswa a long, long way from here," explained Feso.

"But we are also descendants of Monomotapa, we all know," objected Nyan'ombe. "My late father, Gombekombe, often talked about the great empire of Zimbabwe," the mambo reminisced.

"Yes, Mazvimbakupa, but the Vanyai say we are a minor line, and they further laugh at our regiments, throwing scorn at us as being unequal to their military strength."

"In your opinion, are they very powerful?"

"Yes, Changamire, they are very powerful. And we now need to act like men to fight the best we can, as has urged Commander Mapondera."

Mapondera who had been listening quietly to all this and other discussions now rose up again and, raising his voice, said vehemently, directing his remarks toward Feso, "I do not dispute your account, General. But it would be cowardly of us to assign so much military strength to these Vanyai. It is not so much who they are or think they are that counts, Changamire, but the personal qualities of the men and the training they've had, plus their morale. Feso shouldn't forget how we, at one time, routed the Vanyai under Vumbamusakasa, and how we scattered the regiment of Gondomutsa, and also how we made the warriors of Zhangedwa beat a retreat near the village of Harare. Were we not the same Vahota that we are today?

"I believe that a nation seems strong and invincible sometimes, but I do not believe that a nation or people are strong and invincible all the time. The Vanyai today must re-earn the reputation won by their ancestors. It is my conviction that we should order our regiments to fight them in the hills and in mountain passes, where we can surprise them. But if we must we shall fight them in the plains, in the forests, in our villages and hamlets even, and in every conceivable place we can find them. They will feel and know our strength," and he firmly concluded. "And we fight for a loved king and a happy people. We, too, have our great victories."

"I do not doubt," said Feso, "the truth of our past glory. But as was said, what was is not now. But we must realize that ever since the old days the great Commander Mapondera spoke about, the Vanyai have since grown even mightier in arms. While we only have at most twenty regiments of well trained men, they have fifty. We only have about thirty thousand men scattered in three hundred villages; they have well over thrice that number of well trained men spread all the way down to the Zambezi river in Dande. And, besides, all they ever train and prepare for is war and all we know and live for is brewing beer, tending to our cattle, and getting wives." At this sardonic humor, all the men grimly laughed.

"I do not contradict Mapondera's words of courage. Most certainly, let us prepare for the invasion and behave like men. For, indeed, deep pools do turn into shallow fords, sometimes. But, we must gird ourselves for a long, hard war. And early defeats must not discourage us—nor prevent our continuing the struggle."

The thoughtful Nyan'ombe now rose from his stool.

"Very well, my people. Our ancestors are waiting to see how we acquit ourselves. They will help us if we deserve it." And pointing to Feso and Mapondera, he said sternly,

"Great commanders, see to it that our warriors are equipped and in readiness to meet our enemies. Send out scouts to the borders. Send our most ready warriors to bar the way at the frontier. Then the rest of our men will march with me to meet the enemy full force." So saying, he dismissed them all, to prepare his own weapons.

The village lived the next days in strange quietness. The women worked on provisions and the smiths were busy with the repair of weapons.

Within a few days, Nyan'ombe's country was invaded by the fierce warriors of Pfumojena and the Vahota frontier forces driven back from one skirmish to the next. Under the command of the General, Sariramba, and numerous other experienced commanders like Mhingepinge, the Vanyai swept the lands clean before them. Armed with short handled big-bladed assegais and small shields, the Vanyai moved

105

swiftly and deadly. They did not throw their spears but stabbed at close range, holding on to them. It took courage to use the short assegai, but once the Vanyai line could stab it wiped out the opposing line and broke resistance. On the other hand, the Vahota, like most Africans, were armed with long-shafted spears and large shields. In the battle they threw their spears at their enemies and often lost too many of them, rendering themselves vulnerable to counter-attack by their foes.

One early morning, in that region which lies between the Nyota hills and the hills of Gombekombe, in that lovely land watered by the perennial waters of the Ruya, Chipfururwi and Chirayire, the blood-thirsty warriors of the Vanyai and the Vahota met. Springing down from an ambush the Vahota had the initial advantage, but for much of the day the battle raged. Spears and battle-axes glittered in the sun and commanders rallied their men to battle reforming the broken lines. Nyan'ombe's warriors fought like lions under the command of their leaders and though their casualties numbered in the hundreds, the brave men still kept fighting.

Then Mapondera, the son of Vahai, slaughtered many Vanyai with his single spear. At one time the combined regiments of his men met Zambara's men and engaged in the fight against the Vanyai for a long time, each side striving to overcome the other. When the battle became very fierce, it is reported that Mapondera was seen in the fever and dust of battle, lifting himself up from the ground and flying like some magical beast, then invisible, he was able to get closer to his enemies, to slaughter them unseen.

For his part, Feso was faced with the fiercest regiment of all under General Sariramba. Though the Vanyai were cut down by the fierce pangas of the Vahota, they kept coming up in ever-increasing numbers, for Pfumojena had sent back for more legions once he knew the strength of the Vahota. Tired by the weight of the fresh warriors, Feso's forces fell back.

Pulling back into the rugged hills through which the Chirayire river flows, Feso met Mapondera—his troops also regaining their breath after the heavy combat.

"We've been cut up very badly," said Feso, "I think the best thing we can do is to withdraw to our most southern and mountainous areas to regroup. We will call up our older men and the strongest of the newly circumcized class."

"What, General? Did you counsel retreat? What virtue is there in retreat?" questioned the fiery Mapondera disapprovingly. "What good will it do us, General?"

"Save our men! That's all! Save our men!" Feso answered somewhat breathlessly. "We cannot attack again today—but I think the enemy are well-bloodied too, and not eager for another bout. We should withdraw in darkness, leaving only our spies here to watch the Vanyai's movements."

At that moment, Nyan'ombe arrived at the scene with a handful of men, most of them slashed and bleeding.

"Our men have been very badly mauled," he said in despair. The entire royal regiment is gone. It was a good fight but we were too few."

"And we have no further troops to replenish them," confirmed Feso. "We must fall back and call up older and younger men—even if it leaves our villages defenseless for the while.

Then looking at his chief, he said to Nyan'ombe, "Changamire, Mazvimbakupa, I have received a special message to deliver to you from our worthy mother—your wife—at home"

Nyan'ombe, still distraught by the sad turn of events, cocked his head, "Say on, General," he ordered.

"Our worthy mother desires your presence, for a weighty matter presses upon her mind."

"What matter," the mambo retorted angrily, "could be more pressing than the one before us?"

"I have only the message delivered by our emissary, Mazvimbakupa."

Before any further discussion could be engaged between them, they heard the jubilant shouts of the enemy, and looking across the Chirayire, they could see a whole army of warriors surging towards them and soon, they recognized they were additional contingents of the Vanyai, some surprisingly with armed women in their ranks, being led by none other than Pfumojena himself.

"Our scouts report many more are on the way, Samanyanga," said Feso. "There is very little useful resistance we can offer now, Changamire."

So, painfully and grudgingly, Feso and Mapondera

ordered the remnants of their warrior legions to retreat. Pfumojena, wielding his deadly white spear, burned to meet Nyan'ombe face to face—though they never did meet. But for now he was exultant to see his enemies retreat to the hills. That night the Vanyai pursued the Vahota, fighting rear-guard actions, all the way, to the royal village in the foothills of the Mazoe river. Plundering and laying waste the fields Pfumojena's men moved ever more deeply into the land of the Vahota as the Vanyai continued their now large-scale invasion. Thousands of women and old people fled into the neighboring hills of Nyamuhumbe, Mbeve, Gwiranenzara, and Manungwi, the children subdued, wondering.

When he reached his royal village, with his enemies on his heels, Nyan'ombe met his wife and mother crying and unable to run for safety.

"Chipo, my wife, and my mother, all is lost for the moment. All is lost! It will not do to carry you with us, for the army must live like beasts in the wilds until we can strike again for our freedom. So I must say good-bye!" But as the king strained Chipo to his breast, she whispered something in his ear as tears rolled down her cheeks. "Yes," whispered Nyan'ombe, "I shall remember your words—my wife. But now I must say good-bye! I shall indeed remember your words and come back for you no matter where you are." Then Nyan'ombe disappeared and all his commanders and men were not seen for many days.

The very next morning, the Vanyai warriors, led by Pfumojena himself, entered the village, seized Chipo, Feso's two wives, and Vanyarambi, Nyan'ombe's mother, and killed everyone else they could find, mostly old cripples and the blind. Setting this and the other captured villages on fire, they left burning embers and ashes all over the once proud kingdom. The jubilant Vanyai, having successfully overrun the country of the Vahota, and having retrieved the object of their conflict with the Vahota, returned home, singing songs of triumph, one of which was:

> *Behold, Pfumojena's regiment comes!*
> *(Hondo ya Pfumojena, inouya—*
>
> *See, the bull will soon be here!*
> *Hezvo, mukono uchauya pano.*

What a year!
Gore iwe!

Ha, hiya!
Ha, hiya!

What a successful hunter (warrior)!
Hombarume!).

Raise ululations to Samanyanga!
(Ridzirai mhururu Samanyanga—

The elephant that trampled the Vahota!
Nzou yakatsokodzera Vahota.

What a year!
Gore iwe!

Ha, hiya!
Ha, hiya!

What a successful hunter!
Hombarume!).

Chapter XIV

The Crushing Defeat of Pfumojena

No one who saw the defeat of Nyan'ombe and his warriors could have ever thought that he would rise up again to face the formidable aggressors of Pfumojena. The villages lay waste and in cold ashes and the distraught Vahota remained scattered in hills and plains for many a month. Many of their cattle had either been driven away, or slaughtered on the spot by their enemies. Much of their food in barns had been burned down or carried away. The whole country smelt of blood, desolation, and death. It was not going to be easy to restore battle-courage to the distraught warriors who had been so badly beaten and scattered. Indeed, the Vanyai now appeared to be so powerful as to be regarded as invincible by the Vahota. It would take time to build up the morale of the people and, once, again, lead them to mount a fresh attack on their enemies. It would take great minds with vision to convince the people that there were no invincible nations that had never known defeat at some time or other and that the liberation of a nation demanded the concerted effort of everyone.

The remarkable work of building up the morale of the people and rehabilitating their regiments was a task that could only be accomplished by Feso and Mapondera—the two most distinguished leaders among the Vahota. Slowly, but surely, they gathered their men together and started the formidable task of rebuilding the villages and resettling their people in the land. Mambo Nyan'ombe and his army commanders built a new royal village in the foothills of the Nyota hills so that he now occupied a more central and more protected position in his kingdom than before. The Vahota had learned a bitter lesson from their defeat and they were now ready to meet their enemies with new tactics, or those at least they had learned from their victors, making some modifications of a surprise value.

"Feso! Feso!" Nyan'ombe called out as he stepped out of his imbahuru.

"Changamire! Here I am!" the commander answered,

coming towards his mambo.

"Tomorrow is a great day and we must instruct our warrior commanders in the new tactics we learned from the Vanyai, and the stalking spear, too," Nyan'ombe said.

"There is another new approach we shall introduce into the regiment," Feso added, "which is also strongly supported by Mapondera, Changamire."

Just then Mapondera came up and joined them as they sat at the dare—or men's place.

"What is your new scheme, General?" inquired Nyan'ombe.

"It is that we should include women warriors in our fighting ranks" was Feso's response.

"A commendable idea," said Mapondera, smiling, "and I support it wholeheartedly."

But Nyan'ombe stood there, stunned and unable to accept the idea of women joining the ranks. For him women were to attend fighting men's needs, and to bear children—not to carry arms, or to fight.

"That's not what we learned from the Vanyai, my Lord," said Mapondera. "You will recall last year that when Pfumojena arrived with his contingent there were women disguised as men in their ranks. And they fought just as fiercely as the men. We, who have even fewer men now than before the invasion, should enlist our most courageous females."

"I have never given much thought to it," replied Nyan'ombe. "It still seems barbaric."

"Nobody did, Changamire," said Feso. "It is only recently that Mapondera and I discussed it and we now see how useful an idea it is. After all, some women are as aggressive and as courageous as men are and, as such, could fulfill special positions in the warrior ranks."

"What position could they fill, great commander?"

"Changamire," said Mapondera, "they could draw water and cook for the men, comfort the wounded, and actually attend to them. Besides, they could also encourage our men by their presence, entertain them, and help to raise their morale. The more militant among them could actually take up arms and mix with the men and fight."

"Why would we have to do this to subject our women folk to a dangerous war? Do we not have enough men to train and actually meet our foes on the battle field?" Nyan'ombe fiercely attacked the commanders. But there was also sadness in his voice, for he was thinking of his own lost queen, and Feso's wives, carried off by Pfumojena.

"We have more women among us," Feso observed, "than men, so I have already commented. And strangely enough, I have observed lately that many of our despondent men have been receiving beatings from their wives at home, which proves women's militancy." At this remark, his listeners roared into laughter.

"Why should we not, therefore, make use of such resources as we have in women to help us beat our enemies?" The Vanyai are doing it, and I think we should do it, too."

"It sounds a useful idea," slowly conceded Nyan'ombe. "But when will you put the idea into practice?"

"Changamire," replied Mapondera. "For months we've secretly been training women warriors together with the men and the idea seems to work well." Feso was glad to confess their covert actions.

"One thing, great commander, you should enforce the strictest moral code between our men and women," emphasized Nyan'ombe, still greatly disturbed.

"Indeed, Mazvimbakupa," interjected Feso, "our warriors are subject to court-marshalling if they fail to observe correct moral conduct while in training or in combat. This, as your Highness knows, is part of our national and traditional code of conduct."

"How do you actually put this into practice?" asked Nyan'ombe.

Mapondera replied, "We keep them apart in different camp regiments and only allow them to meet in simulated combat, and at officially organized drinking, dancing, or social parties." He finished by arguing, "Women are not expected actually to engage in close range fighting—except when it is absolutely imperative. Their presence is merely intended to swell the numbers and to give the enemy the visual impression of being overwhelmed. But, however, with prolonged exposure to fighting, women do become just as aggressive as the men."

Nyan'ombe nodded, apparently satisfied that the idea was good and could be implemented in practice—and in war.

"Another thing we have learned from the Vanyai,"

Feso now added, "was the use of the short-shafted assegai for close range fighting in place of the long-shafted spear. Our soldiers now fight easily and confidently with their new weapons. This I know you have personally thought much about."

Then, Feso, looking at Nyan'ombe with a curious look, inquired, "Changamire, I am curious to know what it was that Chipo whispered into your ear? You've never divulged or shared that secret with us. Would it be an act of impropriety to ask your Highness about this?"

Nyan'ombe smiled, "I'm glad you asked that," he said. "On the night of our retreat, my wife whispered a very important message to me."

Feso and Mapondera waited very intently. Continuing, the mambo said, "She told me that three hundred days from that day her father would be holding a feast festival for her. That is an annual celebration. On that day, she suggested, we must make an invasion of Pfumojena's royal village and land. For then the people would be eating, revelling, drinking, and getting drunk, and they would be least prepared for the invasion."

"Ah, then we will catch them—and avenge our losses," grunted Mapondera, grinding his back teeth.

"That is the Festival of the Princess Day," reminisced Feso. "I remember that day—a great day it is. We still have some months ahead of us. But we must prepare for it every moment. It should be our only concern."

"Chipo is a wonderful woman—a wonderful mother of our nation!" observed Mapondera, "and we must have her at the head of the nation."

"She is my wife, and some day, we will bring her back home," Nyan'ombe avowed his intention, "and with her, our other lost and captured ones."

And so—each day, their plans ratified by the king, the great commanders trained their men—and women! Feso and Mapondera could be seen instructing and giving orders to the national leaders in the new tactics they were to observe in training their warriors. The tactics arrived at in their previous private meeting were to be implemented. The leaders, thus prepared, returned home better strengthened and more determined to meet their foes than ever before. In each outlying village the new tactics and weapons were worked with. More and more women were accepted in the companies and regiments, so bitter was the memory of defeat, so sharp the wish for revenge.

Far away, Chipo, who had been taken back to her home kraal, was now restored to her former position by her father. She had been "cleansed and purified" according to tradition and custom, in a ritual which included, among many other things, sprinkling her body with specially prepared herbal conconctions, and forcing her to inhale smoke from burning leaves and roots—all this to banish the Vahota demon-spirits. Resuming her daily walks with her old friend, paying visits, guarded though they were, to Nyan'ombe's mother, the days slowly passed. She was in exile even though at home, and her wild father strained to win her faith and love—but with little success. And no one dared speak the name "Feso" aloud.

The sun rose and set, and the copy-cat moon did the same. One after the other they paced through the sky or hid behind storm clouds. The day of the Festival of the Princess had now arrived. The celebrations this year were not only held in honour of the Princess, but also to celebrate the great victory over the Vahota the year before. There was an air of arrogance and pomp as the warriors danced and exhibited their military strength in an ostentatious parade. The whole village became a great, giant celebrant as men, women, and children were engulfed in a vast mood of joyous celebration. Food and drink were in abundance. The people ate and quaffed to their heart's content. All day long the din and noise of the celebrants rang far and wide with hilarious people dancing and singing out to the melodious rhythm of their drums. No doubt, Pfumojena had restored his kingdom to its former glory with the once lost princess now restored to her royal place. Forgotten were the outlaws, the run-aways, the enslaved.

And, as usual, during the festivals, there were those who were possessed by the various *mashave* spirits: the lion, the baboon, the *mazenda* and the *magadairwa* slave spirits. Quickly the seized souls fell into trance and began to speak in tongues, and to mimick the beasts and spirits riding their backs.

Some of the less religious simply slept all over the royal village from sheer weariness or from surfeiting. Oh, it was a great day! (But, alas, this great day was soon to turn into a day of tragedy as great as the celebrations had been one of happiness and pride).

The proud Vanyai who had fortified themselves all around and had thought they were truly invulnerable to any attack by the Vahota, now stood face to face with their foes. For, towards the early hours of the morning when all the Vanyai regiments that had come for the celebrations were asleep, they were suddenly taken unawares by the Vahota and attacked. The foreigners came thick as a swarm of locusts and as determined as a fierce flock of rhinoceroses, to destroy and conquer the Vanyai. They had hidden in the forest and guided by the outlaws unseen had approached the exhausted capital.

The clatter of war soon became a din, and the din a pandemonium as the warriors entered the royal village, screaming, spearing, laying it waste. The Vahota swarmed in fiercely, killing a great many of the resistors. The Vanyai—completely stupified—were unable to stem the tide of the invading forces. Though they tried to close ranks, to fight the old way, they met the same tactics and better. Battle as they would, their resistance could not match the planned and savage revenge of the Vahota.

Entering the imbahuru, and those of his councillors, a special detachment captured Pfumojena himself and his commanders, themselves only half awake, and sought out Chipo who stood there in tears, pleading for her father's life. Feso and Mapondera led their captives away to the place where Nyan'ombe was waiting. For the first time Nyan'ombe and Pfumojena met—not in battle but one king's total defeat.

"Changamire, Mazvimbakupa!" cried out Mapondera, "we bring forth to you your enemy, Pfumojena."

"Not so!" responded Nyan'ombe, "Not so, great commander—but my truculent father-in-law."

They all stood amazed. Likewise, Feso came forth leading Chipo by the hand and crying out, "Tembo Mazvimbakupa! Behold your wife!"

"Indeed, welcome my dear wife! But more importantly—our nation's retriever and new mother of the nation!" So saying, he took her in his arms and embraced her gently and lovingly, while she, overcome with emotion, responded tearfully.

"Today is a great day," shouted Mapondera jubilantly. "We've subdued our once formidable and invincible enemies."

"Not so, great commander! Not so!" shouted back Nyan'ombe. "But rather we've retrieved our friendship with the Vanyai in a rather unusual way. We've broken the barrier of pride and prejudice. We've bridged the differences that have divided us for so long. Now the Vanyai will know we are as good as they are—or better still—that we intend to be their friends and, to show them we are as noble and civilized as they are."

The commanders and others stood there amazed and astonished, for they had awaited Nyan'ombe's command to execute their enemies.

"From now and henceforth," Nyan'ombe decreed, "if the King here accepts, we shall endeavor to build peace between us and Vanyai—peace for all, with honor and respect for all—and for all time. And all serfs will be freed, for we are all men—and there should be only respect for the older and wiser, and compassion for the weak and old."

"Mazvimbakupa! Your wisdom is wonderful!" they shouted, amazed at the magnanimity of his thoughts. Even the captured Vanyai joined in.

"Since we all share one common heritage from Monomotapa—our great, great, grand ancestor—for that's what he was—" Nyan'ombe emphasized, "we shall now treat one another as cousins. Better, since the rift between us has been broken down by reason of our common bond of marriage, we shall, henceforth, call one another brothers and sisters."

By this time the bellicose mood of all parties had changed into a jocular and relaxed mood.

Turning to Pfumojena who stood there, stripped of his royal power, but still full of his manly pride, Nyan'ombe asked,

"And what sayest thou, noble king?"

"Nothing, Changamire! Nothing! Or, rather this—that what you are saying is the truth—and the truth must abide while all else falls apart."

Happy his enemy, his father-in-law, wanted to end the blood-letting, Nyan'ombe shouted, "Now, let us praise the woman whose subtle, innate powers have enabled us to be brought together, ending our foolish strife and hostilities. The freedom of the woman has become the freedom of the man."

"Changamire! Mazvimbakupa!" they all applauded. "We cannot fathom your knowledge and wisdom."

"For a woman works in a mysterious way to change, yea, to transform a man's heart. The true power of a man comes from a good woman whose presence and purity makes the man worthy of his tasks—and equal to them. But once the woman is absent, all the weight falls on the man, and he remains helpless. He cannot wield his power or influence the future anymore."

"Changamire! You are great!" the commanders praised him. "Go on, Sire! Go on! Give us more of your wisdom!" they urged him.

"Therefore, remember, noble commanders, what I said, at first. Changing a woman changes a nation. And changing nations changes mankind. Today, as clear as ever, the woman has bridged the gap between us and the proud Vanyai."

Stretching himself up as if to revive his strength, Nyan'ombe continued, "Since the land of the Vanyai has now come under my control, from now, hence forth, there shall be no more Muhota or Munyai. Instead, we shall all be called Vatapa because we all share a common heritage as descendants of our great and noble ancestor—Matope Nyanhehwe Monomotapa."

"Long live Nyan'ombe!" they shouted.

"Long live the Vatapa! What a noble idea from our wise father!" All around, the troops echoed such praises.

In this mood, they led the humbled Pfumojena and his captured commanders away. But not to death, but to respected retirement.

And so, Pfumojena, having been forced to bury his white spear, and having been stripped of all his power, lost his kingdom forever, now to live in quiet exile in a border village. His people, once peace was restored, and the noble terms of surrender announced, rallied to their princess and the generous Nyan'ombe. War was banished between them.

In the meantime, only where there was resistance, did the Vahota continue to overrun the land of the Vanyai, burning, looting, and laying waste the villages, and driving away hundreds of cattle as booty.

The triumphant and jubilant Vahota returned home then with their captives before them, singing triumphantly and in jubilation:

Oh, Munjeri! Won't you listen?
　　Nhai, Munjeri wee! Chimboterera!
We've left them (the Vanyai) perched in the mountains—
　　Tasiya tavakwidza mumakomo—
Just what we'd said!
　　Ndozvatakareva!
Oh, Chiweshe! Won't you listen?
　　Nhai, Chiweshe iwe! Chimboterera!
We've left them perched in the mountains—
　　Tasiya tavakwidza mumakomo—
Just what we'd said!
　　Ndozvatakareva!
Oh, Pfumojena! Won't you listen?
　　Nhai, Pfumojena! Chimboterera!
We've perched you up in the mountains—
　　Tasiya takukwidza mumakomo
Just what you deserved!
　　Ndozvawakada!
Oh, Vahota! Won't you listen?
　　Nhai, Vahota imi! Chimbotererai!
We've left them perched in the mountains—
　　Tasiya tavakwidza mumakomo—
Just what they deserved!
　　Ndozvavakada!
Oh, Negomo! Won't you listen?
　　Nhai, Negomo iwe! Chimboterera!
We've left them perched in the mountains—
　　Tasiya tavakwidza mumakomo—
Just what you had said!
　　Ndozvawakareva!
Oh, Pfumojena! Won't you listen?
　　Nhai, Pfumojena wee! Domboterera!
We've left you perched in the mountains—
　　Tasiya takukwidza mumakomo—
Just what you deserved!
　　Ndozvawakada!

118

Thus sang Nyan'ombe and his warriors as they triumphantly returned to their own villages. They were met by women ululating, singing and dancing to meet their men—and some women warriors, too—in the procession.

The Vahota—now collectively called the Vatapa—built a new, even more prosperous and free society in peace, unimpeded by the threats and intrusions once imposed by the belligerent Vanyai. And many marriages brought the "cousins" together.

And so, Nyan'ombe and Chipo, his wife, and all the people of the new Vatapa nation, lived happily together ever after, eating well, sleeping well, welcoming each new day with quiet joy and sure hope for the future.

Chokumarara and Manzira grew to manhood, having survived battle, and youth, to become great cattle breeders in the lush meadows of Mazoe.

Poetry of Zimbabwe

(Dual texts: Zezuru and English)

Back View of Soapstone Bird
Found in Ruins of Zimbabwe

3CP ⓒ **By THREE CONTINENTS PRESS**

Table of Contents

Preface

Traditional Zimbabwen (Shona) poetry served a different function and purpose from that to which verse has been put in this book. Here, we attempt to express complex thought processes, perhaps never before attempted in our oral poetry. In this respect, modern Zimbabwen verse differs structurally and in its form and content, as well as in subject matter.

Much of Zimbabwen traditional poetry is in the form of canticles, with a verse and a chorus specifically serving to arouse feeling and emotion. The songs are about the joys and sorrows of man and neither abstract nor philosophic. They are, thus, anthropocentric. Often the verse is an instantaneous creation of the lead-singer in his fantasy and this required an innovative and quick-thinking mind to maintain the coherence of the emotion and feeling so aroused in the participants, as well as to engage the imagination and attention of those concerned.

Traditional poetry can arbitrarily be divided into perhaps six classes. Class 1 includes general work songs which comprise communal grain-threshing, harvesting, grinding (by women) on mill-stone, or pounding grain in wooden mortar (also by women). Class 2 deals with general social gatherings and dance party songs for both the old and the young accompanied by rhythmic drumming. Class 3 deals with the ancestral, or *mashave*, dancing spirit songs (some religious) of which there are several kinds. These are sung to the accompaniment of *mbira* music (the so-called African hand-piano) and, perhaps, form some of the best and most beautiful social dances of them all. Perhaps here we can also include the *Chiremba* or *N'anga* songs sung in praise and honour of the healing medicine man, herbalist, or doctor, e.g.

Watore n'anga, Watore n'anga
Waona Chiremba iwe nhasi pano

He who has invited a doctor, etc.,
has desired a doctor's healing art

Class 4 includes war songs, or patriotic chants. Wars and unrest, as well as times of peace and tranquillity did not fail to have a share each in the evolution of poetry peculiar to its own era. Thus, when faced with the distresses of war the people chanted:

> *Yowerere!*
> *Baya wabaya,*
> *Yowerere!*
> *Mkono unobaya dzose*

> *Cry out!*
> *Kill whomsoever you may.*
> *Cry out!*
> *A bull [a warrior] kills every enemy in his way*

The well-known Mbire song invokes nostalgic feelings of patriotism, e.g.

> *Kuenda Mbire, Kuenda Mbire*
> *Vakomana imi, etc.*

> *Let's go to Mbire, Let's go to Mbire,*
> *Oh, Boy!*

Class 5 includes children's or didactic poetry. This is, no doubt, the most common of traditional poetry, and is perhaps, the most widely known and appreciated. The cheery, litany-like and onomatopoeic nursery songs such as the one following exemplify children's traditional poetry:

> *Yanga iri njiva,*
> *Guu!*
> *Nekana munyhasi*
> *Guu! etc.*

> *It was a dove,*
> *Guu!*
> *With its little one below,*
> *Guu!*

Class 6 is praise poetry, perhaps better known as laudatory praise incantations. Such incantations exalted the individual for his heroic deeds, eulogising his heroism in terms appropriate to his clan totem and his ethnic group.

Traditional poetry has no set pattern of meter and rhyming scheme and, certainly, observes no rigid set rules of form and structure, except for chorus repeats in certain incantations. Much of it is instructive, moralistic, religious, philosophic, with little sentimental love poetry as found in English prosody.

"Mother love" is uniquely at the centre of much of unwritten African (Zimbabwen) poetry and this seems to have formed the basis of all traditional love poetry. In pain, wonderment, excitement, and in the pangs of death, one cries *"Mai Wee,"* [Oh, My Mother . . .]. It is, indeed, the fountain of all amorous sentiment.

Although Zimbabwen poetry is a communal contribution of anonymous composers—there having been nothing committed to writing until recently—yet each poem, or incantation, brings out individual potentials in performance and sharpens the mind of the reciter who is obliged, as an intellectual exercise, to remember the verses, or to create new ones while the singing or performance lasts.

Times of wars and suffering, and times of peace and prosperity, had each a share in the generation of poetry peculiar to its own time. However, in recent decades we, the contemporary poets, because of having studied British and American writers, have become pioneers in our own new native literary art, and at first we did not give thought to the traditional poetry of our forebears. The colonialists, especially the Christian missionaries, put a devilish stigma on everything that was indigenous to our culture. This brain-washing was indeed thorough until our recent realisation of how deeply we needed to know and preserve our original culture, and how often distorting the European influence had been. Hence, the poems in this book (many having been written during those years of "tutelage") have not attempted verse in any of the traditional forms. Rather, they have followed by and large the pattern of English poetry, many with regular meter and specific rhymes and dealing with topics never before treated in traditional Zimbabwen poetry. Despite the obvious European influences, the new kind of Zimbabwen poetry should not be looked upon as a bad thing or an aberrant form deviating from the tradition. Rather it should be looked upon as a healthy development since, just as a living thing grows by absorbing new things, so must any literature which, by increasing its vocabulary, forms, and subjects and ideas, gains new powers and expressiveness. Accordingly, I hope that the reader finds much in this new verse.

The next thing I should like to comment on is the problem we faced in translating the poems into English. This was enjoyable yet hard work. Sometimes African ideas do not lend themselves too easily to translation in a European tongue and often the philosophic or cultural outlook of the African is difficult to capture. Of course all poetry loses something in translation. Each people has its own way of life and there can be no hard and fast rule by which to measure the qualities of one literature from the point of view or standard of an alien literature or culture. So, we did our best to realize in English the qualities of the Zimbabwen poems, and we allowed ourselves a considerable latitude in rendering the original thought.

Of possibly greater significance, historically, and I hope, esthetically, both Zezuru and English texts are here presented, something unique so far in the literature of Zimbabwe and providing my countrymen with the opportunity of reading this work in both the original and the English. Zimbabwen dialects are widely spoken in southern Africa, being the major speech of Rhodesia, but they are also used by many in Zambia, Mozambique, Botswana, and even as far away as Vhendaland in the Transvaal. And, of course, the poetry in English permits many other Africans and non-Africans to come to this work.

Now let me discuss briefly a few of the poems. In "Kumhandara Yangu" (To My Full Grown Girl) we see:

> *Norujeko rwunobaka rwuri mumaziso ako,*
> *Kwete, usandivheneke,*
> > *handidi zvokutosvorwa*

> *With that sparkle that beams from your eyes*
> *I'm hit, please lower your lids in looking,*
> > *I can't bear the blaze*

This kind of exaggeration was not only foreign to the culture of my people, but requires the expressions that are unique and appropriate to this new theme. I believe this aspect of our problem was satisfactorily accomplished, proving that the Zimbabwen language was not only flexible enough to accommodate such thought processes, but also that it had the vocabulary with which to express quite original experiences.

In "Mudikani Wangu" (My Loved One) we find the following lines:

> *Mudikani wangu, unenge chipfeko*
> *Chino mwema mutsva,*
> *Unenge sorumbo; unenge kudziya*
> *Komoto pachando*

> *My loved one, you're like a new garment*
> *Upon my body, with its smell of newness;*
> *You are like a fresh song that delights;*
> *The warm red tongue of the winter's fire.*

The meter is duodecameter (12 syllabic beats), regular, but there is no rhyming scheme. Again the topic is reflective of foreign influences.

The use of repetitive or alliterative pattern is more fully exploited in our modern Zimbabwen poetry. This concordial agreement (of prefixes) with verbs, nouns, and other parts of speech, is common in East African languages. The alliteration thus gives a pleasant, musical, euphonic sound to the words following each other, as in the poem "Nguva Yokufudza" (Herding Time):

> *Zvakwaichinge chirimo chichinge chasvika, . . .*
> *Hozi dzizere dzichinge dzisingazopera*

> *Remember, when spring had just come, the wind soft, . . .*
> *Our barns still packed as if we could never eat them up*

Another excerpt illustrative of alliteration is in "Dambiro roHwangu Hwana Uduku" (The Playground of My Youth):

Nemi makomo eGunguhwe! Harahwa dzemhanza dzakare,
Pasi pamakatukunyudza, pasi pevu pasichigare

And you, Gunguhwe Hills! Bald-headed omens,
Eroded, hard granitic, residual humps, eons-old—

Of course the ancient Zimbabwens perhaps had no specific knowledge of earth science and, hence, could not reckon the age of hills and mountains in terms of geologic eras. Therefore, such concepts could not have crossed their minds and they could not be expected to express this idea so explicitly.

My collaborator has observed the nostalgia running like a silver lining in many of my poems, with mixed themes of depression (death), elation, frustration, hope, aggressive resistance, etc. Indeed, no one is more sensitive to the vicissitudes of a passing culture and its traditions than a poet who speaks in his peculiar "prophetic" way. Some of my lamentations reflect memories of my young days when, for example, I recall in a poem the now vanished life of the villagers at Dengu, now in utter ruins. This nostalgic poem therefore ends in the following lines:

O, musha uya waDengu waive megomo mujinga!
Hakuchina nemheremhere—kana neinochema nhengu,
Asi zvino rangove dongo—dongo romusha'yo waDengu.

Oh, oh, lost men and beasts and huts—foothill village!
No more joy quivers in your many hearts—
                    not a breath of life:
All abandoned, shattered hutments, rotted,
                    wind-turned Dengu
                    at the bottom of the hill.

The poems in this book have tried to embrace a wide variety of topics. For example, an appreciation of nature per se is not known to have been a preoccupation of traditional poets. No grown up in his rightful senses smelt a flower and eulogised about its sweet fragrance. Nor did any man get into an ecstasy as a result of observing a beautiful sunset. These were taken for granted. But modern Zimbabwen poetry has broken tradition as in the poem "Kuchirimo Chisingafe" (To Spring that Never Dies), for here we introduce Spring in a dramatic way:

> *Chirimo: hecho, piriviri,*
> *Norunako rwemandiriri!*
>
> *She is the Spring, bountiful,*
> *And beauty unsurpassed!*

Luke Chidavaenzi's "Bvukutirwa" (The Turtle-dove) is an example of an attempt "to dovetail" the old and the new together. This may lead to more verse of this kind by our other modern poets.

> *Muswero wose rinongoimba,*
> *Pamasikati napamauro!*
> *"Guku kutizwa nehama!*
> *Guku ndosara ndoga!"*
>
> *Sun up or sun down it sings,*
> *Bright day or shadowed evening:*
> *Coo! to be deserted by one's kin!*
> *Coo! I'm left so alone!*

Mutswairo's poem "Bembera kuShiri yoRushishe" (An Ode to A Bird of the Sand) is another example of the blending of the old and new together. The refrain is:

> *Ndiko, ndiko, wodandaura—dandaura!*
>
> *(Ndiko, ndiko—wildly chattering!)*

borrowed from an ancient folk-tale relating to a bird wildly chattering and yet decoding some secret information to a perplexed group of listeners.

Herbert Chitepo's: "Soko Risina Musoro" (The Tale without a Head), exemplifies the only epic poem so far written in Zimbabwen. It deals with a highly complex philosophical thought and is, in essence, an observation, if not a lamentation, the elaboration of a passing culture and the manifold problems lying ahead and how much we have suffered a loss of control of our destiny. In his concluding remarks, King Mutasa speaks:

> *Ndini ndakamira pano*
> *Ndichiringisa shure nemberi.*
> *Kwatakabva irima,*
> *Kwatinoenda irima.*
> *Uyai nomwenje, imi vakuru,*
> *Mutitungamidze muneri rima.*

> *I stand here*
> *Looking behind and before.*
> *Whence we have come is darkness,*
> *Whither we go is darkness.*
> *Bring a light, you elders,*
> *And guide us in this darkness.*

Chitepo's epic is a vivid description of the passing age, and I believe a great contribution to Zimbabwen literature carrying as it does a message to our people that the rulers and leaders working without the blessing of their spiritual ancestors are doomed to failure. Perhaps there were early Zimbabwen epics now lost, but Chitepo's long poem is, so far as I know, the only published one in this form.

Dintweng Kousu's prose-poem "Ndevo yeN'ombe Luvizho" (The High Place of Cattle) is an excellent example of traditional philosophical thought in prose-poetry. This work has been included here mainly because of the interesting light it sheds on what I have termed the "Old Zimbabwen language" spoken by the Rozvi Kings of Mambo Changamire. The remnant of it is still spoken as Lilima, Kalanga, and Shangwe dialects in the south west districts of Rhodesia and, indeed, elsewhere also, as in parts of Botswana, and Vhenda-land of the Transvaal in South Africa. Kousu is, perhaps, the first to write such an account in his native dialect and his poem offers the reader the full flavor of traditional herding or pastoral poetry. He has, indeed, recaptured the spirit and life of outdoor living in traditional life and the high place cattle held in society.

So far we have made a cursory study of the development or evolution of Zimbabwen thought in poetry. The present trend seems to be toward westernization of our literary art. There is still a wide and, almost, untapped, field of study and research in this respect. Our traditional poetry suffered a paucity of imagery, though it was rich in idioms, similes, and aphorisms. Everything referred to man (anthropocentric) and little attention was focused on nature per se. The language itself was rich in descriptive words but the poet preferred general statements.

Many of our budding Zimbabwen poets, who have attempted to write modern poetry, are struggling consciously, or unconsciously, to express new ideas in forms outside tradition. Their efforts are encouraging and do point to a bright future although no doubt some poets will choose to work in a more traditional vein. Writers such as Joseph C. Kumbirai, C. S. Ngwerume, M. A. Hamutyinei, E. M. Muzeze, the late Wilson E. Chivaura and others (and I here include myself), have all written modern poetry, hopefully with a reasonable degree of success, each in our own way. The themes have varied from commonplace topics to quite complex ones, moving away from the ancient anthropocentricism that seemed to have dominated the old poets. This present effort, as noted, will obviously lead to modernization rather than a return to traditional poetry. Whatever the case, the people will dictate the trend and we can only hope that popular acceptance as well as critical acclaim is not far from realization.

Finally, let me say that the thought of attempting something new and seeing one's work in print can only be a rewarding experience.

In closing I wish to recast in optimistic vein the last two lines of the first stanza of my poem "The Picture of Nehanda and Kagubi":

> *Rabuda hero zuva renyika yedu,*
> *Nebasa redu guru zvino rasvika*

which is:

> *The sunrise of our country is come,*
> *And our great task is now begun.*

S. M. M.
Washington, D.C.
January 1974

133

SOME ZIMBABWEN (ZEZURU) PHONETICS ENCOUNTERED IN THIS BOOK

Vowels are open (as in Italian).

Consonants—mostly as in English, except the following:

b — used with h,e.g. bhande (belt),is bilabial explosive,

   — used alone,e.g. baba (father),is bilabial implosive

c — always used with h,e.g. chechi (church),as in <u>ch</u>urch

d — used with an h, e.g. dhadha (duck as in <u>d</u>uck), is dental alveolar explosive

   — used alone, e.g. dada (be insolent, conceited), is an implosive,

   — used with z,e.g. dzimba (houses), or with v, e.g. dzviti (sp. of grasshopper),is denti-alveolar affricative

h — is glottal fricative,e.g. Haha (Haha hill), as in <u>h</u>arm

m — is bilabial nasal,e.g. a<u>ma</u>i (mother),as in <u>m</u>other

   — in combination with v, e.g. mvura (water), is denti-labial fricative

   — with w,e.g. mwana (child),is velar-nasal

n — with ('), e.g. nyan'ombe (cattle owner) — originally nyagombe, is a velar sound as in ha<u>ng</u>

p — used with f, e.g. pfumojena (white spear), is dentilabial affricative

   — used with w,e.g. pwere (youth), is velar bilabial

r — used with explosive w, e.g. rwangu (mine), is a rolled dental alveolar

s — with v, e.g. svika (arrive), is a whistling fricative

t — with y, e.g. kutya (to be afraid), is an alveolar flapped lateral as in Chi-cago

v — alone, e.g. vana (children), is a soft bilabial fricative

— with h, e.g. vhara (close), is a labial fricative, as in the English Vatican

z — with v, e.g. zvino (now), is alveolar labial fricative

— with w, e.g. izwi (word), is both fricative and semi-vowel

Some Comments on Translating Zezuru Poetry

What do you call someone who puts into his own language, the best he can, the ideas, images, feelings and qualities of work in a second language of which he knows not one word? Even with a rough draft translation one must still strain toward coherence, toward accuracy of feeling, and reach for strength, if not beauty, in alien words which do not dishonor the original.

The author of most of the poems in this collection, fortunately, is a wise, well-travelled man, an university graduate several times, and skilled in the English language. Yet, the drafts he offered me to begin our labors on were sometimes stiff, puzzling, not musical, and even stylistically quaint, often reflecting conservative British curricula of a generation ago taught by men most probably untouched by 20th century poetic developments. To such, the thinking and experiments of Yeats and Pound, Eliot and Auden, were as nought. So, the effort must be made to make clearer, crisper, harder, more visual where possible, the rather vaguely late 18th century or early romantic rhetoric of a worn-out English poetic voice. The Zezuru originals my Zimbabwen friends assure me are beautiful, supple, and fresh. So something like qualities had we to seek in our contemporary English versions without slipping into merely modern jargon or tempi.

"Solomon," you say, "let's hear this poem again, in Zezuru, read the stanza once more"– and as he speaks the lines with excitement or sadness—you look at his rough draft and check words or phrases that seem the nucleus for patterns or images which might come just a little closer to the sounds and surges of the original. Again and again he reads his poems, line by line in the original, so the flow, the color, the rub and bang of the consonants, gets into you. Finally you begin to work out the new English lines—pithier, more muscular, more intimate or whatever, sometimes with pauses, or repeats, that try to catch something of his caught-in-the-throat reading, a touch of the mood or tone of the Zezuru—if not its actual music.

Then you both stop, get up and move around the study, maybe make a new cup of tea or pour out a new cold coke, and then you read your new version. "Yes, yes, no, yes, no, well yes, here, let's stop a minute", so Solomon agrees, or doesn't, to what you've caught his thought as being. Once in a while, to break an amiable but hopeless cultural deadlock, he stops to explain a game, or tell how a certain vegetable is cooked, or how a girl in Zimbabwe sits on the lap of her lover with her back to him (a bizarre picture to most Westerners I imagine) while the brave lad sits on the hard ground, and so on, and then, when you finally understand, you can find a better word or a more zesty expression to capture the Zezuru—something that is graphic, yet honest, too, and good English to boot.

Occasionally, though not often, an hour can pass while one line or a short stanza is fought over this way. Usually a poem of 30-40 lines would take three, possibly four hours—just to get a strong poetic vessel blocked up well on the English ways of oak. Then, tired, both of us, he goes home and I, if I have time and energy left, go through the whole poem again, trying to get the run and dip and brightness into one organic whole. When Solomon comes back the next Friday, you start off with a newly-typed poem, in English, the product of this final, private effort. He consults the original and, with luck, you can hear: "Well, that's fine. Except for line three there where . . ." And so we polish this poem up, including the recalcitrant line three, and send it down to sea to float on its own now, and we turn to start afresh on the next one.

So the weeks went by, and now, some year and a quarter after we began (and we worked on the novel *Feso* the same way though less intensively) we have some twenty of Solomon's poems fixed in the amber of our English along with a few others by Kousu and Chidavaenzi.

One could write a long essay on what I learned, or didn't learn, about Zimbabwen culture and poetry during this long process, but it may boil down to this: Zezuru poetry is very ruminative, didactic, and in Solomon's poetry at least, nostalgic. Even anger and bitterness is softly, almost sadly expressed. The development of ideas is often lyrical—internalized—then put into a poetic context rather than into dramatic scenes of theatrical intensity. Finally, love, a new theme in most of the African continent, is gentle, never erotic, hardly even, in Western terms, agitated. Everywhere in this new poetry from Zimbabwe are the beasts domestic and savage, the mountains and flowers and fast-moving streams, and the people in all their variety and in happy and tragic moments. In all the verse there is an unworldly (meaning an un-Western) present-ness, a calm, a dreamy joining of the poet's inner moods with the deeply evoked qualities of the lovely valley of the Mazoe. Poet and poem, land and landsman—all merge.

The work here presented then, is a joint effort, of translation and re-evocation. Far from perfect no doubt, but Solomon tells me the English verse does not do unjustice to the original—at least in sense and purpose—and once in a while, we both feel, the new English versions are quite possibly poetry on their own merits. Zezuru readers who know English will be happy to judge the first—and the rest of you be the jury on the question of whether or not we have verse here that is manly, sweet, and, hopefully, memorable.

This work accomplished, perhaps the world interested in such matters will note the lot of Zimbabwe and agree:

> *How brilliant is the land of Nyota!*
> *As the first rains kiss the blossoms from the trees:*
> *Low flowers, too, of the plain, look white as ash,*

and we all, with Solomon and his brother poets from Zimbabwe, can stride in the petaled home seas, beyond the Gweshe, and near the Sawi River.

D.E.H.

POEMS FROM MAZOE

Shiri Dzangu

Dzose shiri dzomumvura ndedzangu:
Madhadha anonwa mvura ndeangu,
Kanyururahove, kose ndekangu,
Gukurwizi romumvura nderangu.

Shiri dzinobhururuka ndedzangu:
Njiva nenhengure, idzi ndedzangu,
Nzvihwo, nenjivam'tondo ndedzangu,
Hoto nekondo netsoro ndedzangu.

Neshiri dzinotizira ndedzangu:
Matendera nemaguhwi ndeangu,
Hwata namunditi, idzi ndedzangu,
Ngarukuni nemhou, ndidzo dzangu.

Dzinodududza muruwa ndedzangu:
Hwerekwere namarenge ndedzangu,
Horwe nendova nehwari ndedzangu,
Huta nehuku nehanga ndedzangu.

Dzose dzinoimba shiri ndedzangu:
Huvirikuviri nenjikenjike,
Mhupupu netsutsunhwa, shiri dzangu,
Muswewadepa nakuwe ndedzangu.

Shiri-idya-shiri, hadzisi dzangu:
Chikondomasvinu, hachisi changu,
Chipungu negondo hadzisi dzangu,
Rukodzi nengavi hadzisi dzangu.

Shiri dzousiku, hadzisi dzangu:
Dahwamaringa, harisi rangu,
Chipotono, chigunda, handi dzangu,
Namazizi evaroyi, kwete! haasi angu!

Siku nesikati—ngavi nenjiva,
Pane imwe shiri—zvibvuwo zvedi,
Inoimba runyararo mumabwe—
Ruvimbo rwomusarapasi rweZimbabwe.

My Birds

All birds that swim are mine:
The ducks that drink neck-arched are mine,
The kingfisher—he is mine,
The pondfowl is also mine.

All birds that fly are mine:
The dove, the drongo-shrine are mine,
The black bird and the turtle-dove are mine,
The hornbill, the hammerhead, and the honey-bird are mine.

And all birds that run are mine:
The ground hornbills, the korhaans are mine,
The secretary-birds—these are mine,
Turkeys and ostriches are also mine.

Birds that crouch in running are mine:
The bush partridges, the giant-breasted bustards are mine,
Francolins, spurfowls and partridges are mine,
The quail, the fowl and the guinea-hen are mine.

All birds that sing are mine:
The starling and the waxbill,
The hoopoo, and the skylark are mine,
The widow-bird, and the Go'way bird are mine.

Birds that eat birds are not mine:
The lizard buzzard is not mine,
The eagle, and the falcon are not mine,
The hawk, and the kite are not mine.

Nocturnal birds are not mine:
The pennant-winged nightjar is not mine,
And the owlet, and the house-owl are not mine,
All the large owl species, no, these witches are not mine!

Day or night, wet or dry, hawk or dove,
There is one better; indeed, the finest,
Silent singer in carven stone—the symbol of peace,
Remnant, hope, love—the unruined bird of Zimbabwe.[1]

---

1. This bird is carved on the excavated soapstones of the ruins of Zimbabwe
    and now is memorialized on modern Rhodesian coins, and is the national
    symbol.

Makoma Enyota

Anoyevedza sei makomo eNyota
Akashongedza nyika yaMambo Chiweshe!
Zvinondifadza sei kana ndichirota
Ndiri mhiri yaSawi pedyo nokwaGweshe!

Ndinoyemura sei makomo eNyota,
Kutiva mumimvuri yawo richabuda!
Napakunge rodoka usiku ndorota
Ndiri mhiri yaRuya, nzvimbo dzandinoda!

Kuyevedzawo here kwenyika yeNyota!
Munhuruka wosvika miti yotungira,
Maruva omubani achena sedota,
Nepfumvudza yemiti nyika yopfumbira!

Ndinogodisa sei kuva kwaChiweshe,
Ndichinzwa nziyo itsva dzeshiri mugan'a,
Nenziyo dzavagere mumisha tekeshe,
Vachigere chinyakare, vasinai hanyn'a!

Iyi nyika yeNyota pedyo kuna Sawi:
Inyika yomupunga, chibahwe nezviyo.
Inyika ine hova dzinosarukira;
Vanhu vagere imo vazere nenziyo.

Kunyange ndova kure nenyika yeNyota,
Ndichiri nyika dzino dzinenge masowi,
Zvinondifadza sei kana ndichirota
Ndiri mhiri kwaGweshe, pedyo kuna Sawi!

The Nyota Hills

How assertive are the Nyota Hills,[1]
Bold, they clothe the horizon in the land of Chiweshe![2]
How glad I am when I dream myself back
Beyond the Sawi River near Gweshe![3]

In exile I long for the Nyota Hills.
Lonely, I want to bathe naked-souled in their shadows at dawn!
How I dream when I dream myself back at sunset
Beyond the Ruya River,[4] to places I long for!

How brilliant is the land of Nyota!
As the first rains kiss blossoms from the trees:
Low flowers, too, of the plain, look white as ash,
My mind strides in the petaled home seas!

How I die, then, to be in Chiweshe land,
Listening to the young birds chirp in the bee-hummed plains!
Hearing the work songs, the cradle-croons of the calm villages,
Sounds of a carefree life, safe from alien pillages!

That land of Nyota near Sawi[4] —
A land of rice, maize and finger-millet—
A land of ever-rushing streams—
There, the people have joy; there, my dreams!

Though I may be far from the hills of Nyota
As I fight the foreign cliffs and deserts,
I delight in my dreams, for dreaming,
Beyond the Gweshe I am, and near the Sawi[4] River!

---

1. *Nyota Hills,* in Chiweshe Tribal Trust Land, Mazoe District.
2. *Chiweshe,* Chief, and Tribal Trust Land.
3. *Gweshe,* village in Mazoe.
4. *Ruya* and *Sawi,* rivers in Mazoe.

Kuchirimo Chisingafe

Nokunge Chirimo chasvika,
Napanguva yomutsva mwaka,
Pasisina mhepo nechando,
Panguva'yi zvinopepeta,
Nenyika'yi zvinofefeta,
Nokuvhuvhuta nokupuva,
Dzivaguru—Tenzi wemwando,
Munisi wemvura nerwando—
Wozvinyn'udza Chirorodziva.

Yose nyika yotsvukirira,
Namakomo osvipirira,
Oshonga somutsi wemvura;
Misasa yotsvuka pfumvudza,
Nemipfuti inopfumbidza
Nomugomba nomumipata:

   Chirimo: hecho, piriviri,
   Norunako rwemandiriri!

Sejira remarasirapi—
Saanobva Dande maponde
Dzavapfumi anowaridzwa
Mudzimba dzisina hanambwa—
Nyika yenge guru rehanga
Kana yazvuura kutanga—
Sohweshato unyerenyete
Hune ganda referefete,
Richinge gungwa ramavara
Rinovhunga mhuka musara:

   Ndozvinenge mudiwa wangu
   Anodiwa nechido changu:
   Chirimo, ndiro zita rake,
   'Norunako rwemandiriri.

Zvino dzomerera neshiri—
Dzinododoma mbiri mbiri,
Namanhenga dzoshonga matsva,
Dzichipapama mumitohwe
Dzoimba: Ndiyo! Ndiyo! Tsohwe!
Notuhuro twunofadzisa.
Kana eshiri mazinyn'ana
Anoyevedza madzvanzvana,
Notudodoma omirisa
Achiimba achizeeswa
Mumapazi anoveyeswa
Notudutu twaNyamavhuvhu
Twunokumba zvose namavhu.

To Spring that Never Dies

When Spring has come,
When the new year ushers in,
And the wind and the cold are gone,
Whose blasts and gales blew fiercely,
Winnowing the great plains of the land,
Then tamed, blowing gently,
Dzivaguru[1] —the Master of the winds,
And the Rainmaker—
Drowns them all in the pool *Chirorodziva*.[2]

The earth turns bright
As the hillsides blaze and bloom
And put on a cloth of rainbow glory;
The *Misasa*[3] trees turn scarlet with blossoms
Alongside the *mipfuti*[4] trees;
Deeper hued, hugging their valleys—

Full Spring: hillsides amazed with brightness
Overpowering—unsurpassed!

Like a cross-patched quilt—
Like the mats made in *Dande*[5]
For sitting in the rich men's houses,
In the *dzimbahuru*[6] of those who shun uncleanness,
The land, like a guinea fowl,
Like the enchanting colours of a python
When he has freshly shed his skin,
With his shimmering, shifting spots.
That cover his enchanting skin—
Like the play of colour on the ocean's spray,
He hypnotizes his wild prey!
This is what my loved one—who has enamoured
My heart—this is what she does.

She is the Spring, bountiful,
And beauty unsurpassed!

Now, as the nestlings put on first feathers,
They flutter in pairs to and fro;
Clothed with new pinions,
They flap their wings in the *mitohwe*[7] trees
Singing: *Ndiyo! Ndiyo! Tsohwe!*
With pleasant little voices.
First the fledglings are
Appealing and soft, then,
Stretched, they tense
To trill out as they rock
In the swaying boughs—
As the breezes of August
Sweep all dust away.

Nezvihuru zvetupfumvuti:
Tutsvuku, tutema mumiti,
Muchavhuvhu twunopembera
Twuchingaima tworembera
Pamatavi twenge tuvete
(Twuchidedera setumhete
Twunorengarenga panzeve),
Twune nziyo dzisingareve,
Twunongopenya setuzuva:

 Ndozviri pamudiwa wangu
 Anodiwa nemwoyo wangu.
 Ane uso sohwe pfumvudza
 Yemisasa inokungudza
 Nezvihuru zvawo mavara
 Omuruwa rwomuruvara
 Rwemakomo omuMazoe.

Naizvozvo, iwe Chirimo
Zvauri somudiwa wangu,
Uchagara murudo rwangu;
Tichadana norudo rutsva
Panguva'yi yomwaka mutsva,
Haungafe kunyange wofa.

 Sokuuya kwegore idzva,
 Newewo, pakare womuka:
 Narinhi, uchazosaruka.

146

Like a thousand blossoms—
Brown and dark in the trees
    Proclaiming jubilation in the breeze,
Bedizened with dew drops,
    Their glitter spangling the branches, quiet—as in sleep!
(So like trembling ear-rings
    Hanging on the tender ear-lobes)
They are silent songs of light—
Sparkling tiny suns—
All this my loved one wears;
    She has enamoured my heart—
    Her face, fresh as the leaf-bud
    Of the misasa trees which coloured
    With a thousand tints
    The unspoiled slopes
        Of the hills of Mazoe.

    Thus, since, oh Spring!
You are like my loved one,
You'll remain my love.
You and I shall love each other afresh
At the breaking in of the new year.
    You'll never die, though you may die away.
As the new year breaks in,
        With a rush you'll green again,
            Forever, you shall exist!

---

1. *Dzivaguru,* a once celebrated rainmaker among the Tavara people of Tete District in Mozambique.
2. *Chirorodziva,* a mysterious subterranean pool and caves near the town of Sinoia.
3. *Misasa* (sing. *musasa*), tree species—*brachystegis spiciformis.*
4. *Mipfuti* (sing. *mupfuti*), tree species—*brachystegia bohemii.*
5. *Dande,* a region in the northern part of Rhodesia.
6. *Dzimbahuru,* houses of nobles, or notable persons.
7. *Mitohwe* (sing. *mutohwe*), a quarter tree bearing edible fruits—*thespesia garkeana.*

Mufananidzo waNehanda naKagubi

Nhai, Nehanda Nyakasikana!
Watsinzireiko, Mufakose,
Nouso hwako hwokotamira,
Kana maziso anotandara,
Ojenga mvura oringe pasi,
Nepfungwa dzako dzopinde rima
Dzongopesana sebuvebuve?
Hauchisina kunyemwerera,
Radoka zuva renyika yako,
Nebasa rako guru rapera.

Kana Mazoe yaive yako,
Uchiitonga patsoka dzako,
Nhasi, naiyo, yokupe gotsi:
Hezvi umire panze pejeri,
Hausisina navateveri.
Unoshamisa, samharekadzi,
Pamadzimai omuZimbabwe:
Wave kufira nyika yokwedu,
Neropa rako idiramhamba—
Rusununguko rwomuZimbabwe.

Wakagopara mhakayi huru
Yakakupinza tsambwa'yi huru?
Hauna here vaikurwira,
Kuzenge, hezvi, umire woga?
Vaikupesva, vamire'piko,
Nhai, Nehanda Nyakasikana?
Kana Kagubi newe amire,
Kunyangoshaya kana mumvuri,
Asi amire segamba guru
Rine dambudzo, pasina kutya.

Tarisa, nyika yaikutunha
Ichikumisa pamberi payo,
Ichikubata samambokadzi,
Pari kwanhasi, yomira kure;
Vaikupesva vokudzvamuka.
Rino repasi harina kwaro:
Nhasi rokupa ngundu yamambo,
Rechimangwana rigokuponda,
Mabasa ako okanganwikwa,
Wenge usina kumbove mambo.

The Picture of Nehanda and Kagubi

Why, now, *Nehanda Nyakasikana*,[1]
Do you close your eyes, *Mufakose*,
With your face gently lowered,
And your eyes staring long,
And looking down—heavy with tears;
Your mind muddled,
And, as a torn cobweb, perplexed?
Your smile is now gone,
The sunset of your country is come,
And your great task is done.

Even Mazoe, once your domain,
(You—the ruler, all under your feet),
Today, they, too, turn their backs on you.
There you stand outside the prison!
You have no more followers.
Still, you are wonderful, our heroine!
Alone, of all the women of *Zimbabwe*[2]
You are about to enter the door of death for our land,
To spill your heart's blood—a living sacrifice
For the freedom of Zimbabwe!

What great outrage did you commit
To bring you to this sad state?
Why was there no one fighting at your side?
Now, silent, you seem to stand, even more alone!
Where are those who placed you in the forefront?
Indeed, I ask, Nehanda Nyakasikana.
Even *Kagubi*[3] who stands there beside you,
His glory, too, no longer bright;
Yet, he stands still a great hero.
The picture speaks of pain
But we "see" the fearless heart.

See! the country which called you forth,
Exalting you, following you,
Glorifying you, Nehanda, as its queen,
Today it stands aloof.
Those who petitioned you have turned away.
Alas! This world is good for nothing!
Today the people offer a royal crown,
Tomorrow they rise in arms against you;
All your deeds are quite forgotten,
And you depart—noble one—as if you never were.

---

1. *Nehanda Nyakasikana,* a celebrated woman spirit-medium associated with the rebellions of Rhodesia of 1896-97, and hanged in Salisbury.
2. *Zimbabwe,* African name for Rhodesia.
3. *Kagubi,* a celebrated man spirit-medium associated with the rebellions of 1896-97, who suffered the same fate as Nehanda.

H. S. Clapp

Musangano Kubare

Pasi pawo mumvuri wedombo guru,
Ave mangwana, pakave ndinde huru,
Pakaungana vanhu chitsama chezvihuru.
Murunyararo yakanga igere misha,
Yakasvikirwa nemheremhere yomweya mutsva,
Pakuvheneka kwezuva mujinga meBare
Rakatarisana nerokwaMakope Dare.

Pachikomo ndakamira'po ndikagoyeva
Sowemasvesve muzinga une zhinji nzira,
Besanwa nebvakapfaka mumisasa yepasi,
Nohwendaenda hwavaizhamba muzasi;
Naiko kwavo kutaura kunge kuimba,
Kuchizadza gomba ravaivemo mariri,
Kuchinge sokunge yomubvumbi mvura;
Kana sokunge kweinoririma muhore,
Zvimwe sokunge kweinowira pabopomo;
  Nengoma dzichiridziwa siku nesikati—
  Vose vachida kuonana nokutaurirana
  Kukunda kumurumbidza Musiki wedenga.

Pamasikati vakaungana ndokufora:
Madzimai achikunyirira nguwo chena,
Nemireza iri utsvuku, ushora, upfumbu,
Riri ravakadzi pavarume gumbukumbu:
Havo, vari bvakapfaka voyambuka kakova,
  Vose vane chido chokuona Kamandadi
  Kukunda "kuona" Murume weGararia.

Nyika yakanga yasuwa yakabva yafara,
Namakomo akafarawo namaungira,
Nekakova kachiyerera zvinyoronyoro,
Namashizha akapepera norufarowo,
Neni pachikomo ndikave nomweya mutsva
Naiko kwavo kuimba kuchizadza denga.

  Gungano'ri ravanhu ndakarinamatira
Chavatorwa chitendero, rakagam'chira,
Chine simba mumwoyo yavanhu kusandura:
Chikuru kuri kutevera, kwete, kuziva,
Kana chematsvene magwaro kunzwisisisa.
Hezvo, ndiri paBare ndakafunga nerudzi
Rwuri pasi pomumvuri wegomo reBare,
Rwave nomweya mutsva pedyo neRuvhudzi,
Munyika'yi yemakomo yaMambo Makope.

Conference at Ba-re

In the shadow of a great rock—
That morning, there gathered a large crowd,
Way up in the thousands.
The villages which up to the time had been peaceful,
Were overwhelmed by the din of the new movement
In that light, beneath the Ba-re foothill,[1]
Overlooking Chief Makope's citadel.

Atop the hill, I stood and looked down;
The crowds were like an army of ants following intricate paths,
Criss-crossing in the valley below,
And pushing along and shouting before makeshift shelters;
And the tumult rose up like a giant's song
Filling the crowd-filled valley;
Resounding like the lashing rain,
Or like the echoing thunders of rain-clouds,
Or like the pounding, thrumming of a waterfall;
And the drums beat night and day—
The people seeming more anxious to talk and visit each other
Than to worship the Creator of Heaven.

At noonday they assembled for a match;
The women, dressed neatly in white;
The flags fluttering—the red, yellow and blue—
Everywhere, more women than men:
Marching, now the army surged across a stream—
All more eager to see the Commandant
Than "to see" the Man of Galilee.

The folk who once were unhappy, now are glad;
For even the hills echoed with their joy;
And the stream, gently flowed,
While the leaves rustled as if in a gleeful mood.
And, I, high on the hill-top, felt lifted by a new spirit
As their sky-filling anthems rose up.

I prayed for this gathering,
For them who had accepted an alien religion
With its power to transform people's hearts:
For many, to follow was more important than to understand,
Or the truth of the Gospel to comprehend—
All this I thought while the people crowded
Beneath the deepening shadow of Ba-re rock—
The Ruvhudzi hill overlooking the zealous people
In the mountainous region of Chief Makope.

Hazvinei kuridza ngoma, kana kutamba;
Harusi ruwando, kani, rwaiwo makore,
Kana hwomuromo kutaura uchenjeri,
Kana kusvikirwa nomweya unopotera,
Kana kunyudzwa mumvura yorwizi Monera,
Zvingaratidze yoruponiso nzira nyn'ore—
    Asi mhando yorutendo rwake muteveri,
    Pam'soro ngoni dzaShe kunavo vatendi.

Murume weGararia mwoyo anotsvaka
Kwauri unotendisika kuti apinde
Muhana inozvipfavisa, chinyararire.

It matters not beating of drums, or dancing!
Not even the number of years of service—
Not even the eloquence of a preacher—
Or being taken in a spiritual trance—
Or even being immersed in the waters of *Monera*[2] —
Can accord an easy way of salvation:
Only the quality of your faith counts,
And the grace of the Lord to the believer.
   The Man of Galilee seeks
   A faithful and humble heart,
   Quietly, to enter.

---

1. *Ba-re,* a residual outcropping in Chief Makope's Tribal Trust land in Mazoe District. The Salvation Army often holds annual religious congress meetings here.
2. *Monera,* a river near *Ba-re.*

Guva Raasingaziikanwi

Pano parere muviri usingaziikanwi,
    Unotonhodzwa nomumvuri wedombo guru.
Nenguva dzine madutu,iye mudikanwi,
    Dzinomusiya arere hope dzake huru.
Pano pavete mapfupa aimbove munhu
    Waifemawo nokuimba nziyo dzenjari;
Waigunzvwa nokushatirwa nohwedu unhu,
    Nenziyo dziya dziya dzokusoka ukari.

Pakaiswa gate pamusoro paro guva
    Isu rokutiratidza pakurota kwake;
Asi chegore chiratidzo kana chenguva,
    Hapanaba, chingazivise isu nezvake.
Izvi zviratidzo zveyokusaziva nguva,
    Rima'ro rokusaziva repaguva rako;
Heyi hari yakakwidibwa iri paguva,
    Namatombo akarongwa akaringe bako.

Pasi pasi paro ibwe rotofefenuka,
    Iye wake musoro ndipo pawakanyn'ura;
Mhundwa nedendam'mera zvongobibinuka:
    Zviratidzo zvayo nguva ndefu yapfuura.
Pahari'yi yakadai tingaverengei,
    Pasinai norunyorwa rwavakasvinura?
Paguva'ri rakadai tingagozivei,
    Kunongove kusumwirwa kwaasopindura?

Tarisa, pawakarinzwa musoro'yu wake,
    Navanhu chitunha chake ndokuunganirwa;
Nerima rakwidiba radoka zuva rake,
    Ndokumusiya asumwirwa afukatirwa.
Chokwadi, chokwadi ramunoona ivu'ri,
    Rakadya vamwe vasina kuipiwa nguva
Yokuvhurura somukukurume romubani
    Rinorurutsa mwema wakanaka weruva.

Zvichida gomo'ri rakarara banzvi guru
    Raizezesa nyika navaive mairi:
Raiti roti roringisa nyika'yi huru,
    Raiti: Ndinika tenzi wezviri kwairi!
Masango aya nemiti izere makomo,
    Nouswa uhwu hwangoti bibinu nesango,
Naiye Mwenje anoerera napagomo—
    Zvose zvaichive zvake, nouchi mumhango.

The Grave of Some Unknown Person

Here lies the body of some unknown person,
Beneath the shadow of a big rock refreshed.
    Even though gales may blow, this beloved one,
    Lies untouched in his deep sleep.
Here lie bones—once a living person,
One who breathed and sang songs to the *marimba's* music,[1]
    One who shared the anguish and our common mortality,
    And chanted war songs to enhance his courage.

His life ended, they placed an earthen dish,
    Broken vessel, upon his grave,
Not knowing when he perished—or how;
    No other grave sign or marker
Speak of his dying year.
    Nothing whatever! Only visible silence:
The mute earthen pot, sharded on the grave-site,
    Along with piled up stones facing a cave's mouth.

Beneath the flaking, flat boulder,
There his head was laid deep—
    Briars and weeds grown above him;
    Thick signs now—they tell of turning years.
What can we read from this simple pottery
Where there is no alphabet to spell our way?
    From this grave, what can we ever learn?
    Nothing! Grim quiet here gives no response.

Notice! There his head was laid;
    And the people grouped around his corpse.
Darkness closed in as his last sunset.
    Left alone, he lay in darkness, deep.
Indeed! Indeed! This earth beneath us
    Has swallowed up many who never had the chance
To open up like a flame lily of the plain,
    Nor ever to spread fragrance in the lovely air.

Perhaps on this hill lies a great hero
Who shook this land and its people:
    A hero who, wherever he looked out, over this great expanse,
    Could say, these are mine: I am the master!
These once open plains, and these forested hills
(Now sadly overgrown by strangling alien trees)
    And yea, even the *Mwenje*[2] flowing gently below the *kopje.* . .[3]
    All these were his, and the honey too, in the tree.

Zvino wasara mugomo a'a ega ega;
  Nyika'yi yaaifamba yose paimire
Isati yave nenhare idzo dzega dzega,
  Nhasi yave yomutorwa ndiye changamire.
Haichatorwa mapfihwa okukomba choto
  Okuti tande nemhuri kunze kuri kweru.
Haichatorwa masvinga okukuhwa moto
  Wokuitira tuzukuru ngano manheru.

Chii chinonzi upenyu kuzove mapfupa
  Anove ndiwo asara muguva arere?
Wabhururuka, chokwadi, koinga wapfuka
  Mweya, neshungu kusandura nyika waive.
Aendepiko maoko aibata zvombo?
  Aendepiko makumbo aibata nzendo?
Aendepiko maziso aive nerombo?
  Yaendepiko pfungwa yaive noruwando?

Semakore anokwidiba gombero rose,
  Zvinodaro nomuguva wangobeturira;
Hezvi wafukatira churu kwenguva yose,
  We'a nhengeni kumadziro ichatsvukira.
Upenyu chiiko? Mwenje here unodzima?
  Hezvi paguva ndimire neyangu shamwari,
Yedu mwoyo ichipungayira paruzima,
  Nepfungwa dzedu dzisiri kufunga kwaMwari.

Bereft of life he sleeps alone under his hill,
    High above the land his tread once quaked,
Long before these foreign fences estranged the land;
    There is a new master now.
No longer can the hero's folk harvest hearth stones,
    Nor around gather to talk of a quieter day,
No longer can the hero's folk collect wood
    And sit in the stinging smoke telling their son's sons
        the nation's stories.

What is our life, since all we have is bones
Left rotting in the forgotten grave?
Flown away, oh yes, his life has escaped,
This brawn and spirit once panting to change the world.
    Where have those strong hands gone which seized those weapons?
Where have those dark-sinewed legs gone which strode the miles?
Where those eyes which saw such wealth, the crowded villages?
    Where the brain and will which schemed out such lordly plans?

As the clouds cover the bright sky,
    So, the grave darkens this bright ghost,
Now, back turned to life, lifeless,
    In our minds you grope upward like
The wild plum clambering forgotten on the hut's back wall.

What is any life? Is it the light that flickers away?
    Here, on the sunken grave, with a friend, I stand,
Our hearts darkly searching within ourselves;
    Our earth-bound thoughts being far from God's.

---

1. *Marimba,* so-called African piano.
2. *Mwenje,* a tributary of Mazoe river flowing near Howard Institute.
3. *Kopje,* South African word for a stony, bare hill.

Nguva Yokufudza

Ndinoyeukwa nebani rokumusha kwedu,
   Rine maruva machena nouswa urefu,
Rinofudzira vafudzi vomunyika yedu,
   Rine mikute inokuva nenguva ndefu,
Rine madziva anonwiwa nemombe dzedu,
   Rine shiri dzinoimba mumiti mirefu.

Zvakwaichinge chirimo chichinge chasvika,
   Rose basa rokukohwa richinge rapera,
Mvura yokufa kwegore ichangoturuka,
   Hozi dzizere dzichinge dzisingazopera,
Taimuka mukanganyama kuchakasvipa,
   Huswa huchipenya dova risati rapera,

Njiva nenhengu dzichinokuimbira zuva
   Raipenzura pakati makore pazere;
Shaveshave rakarinda muhamba meruva,
   Jongwe richikukuridza kumutsa varere.
Taizarura zvipfuwo paneyiyi nguva
   Toenda nazvo mafuro manyoro kuzere.

Pasi pomuti mukuru—hunde yomukute,
   Waive pedyo nedziva raigara kondo,
Ndiyo nzvimbo yataida pataidya hute,
   Pataitamba nebishi rainge rehondo
Zuva rovheneka kutsi gombero makute,
   Shiri dzichinokuimba munyhasi merondo.

Mwoyo ichiri mitete kunge madzvanzvana,
   Kana nehwiza nemombe dzainge shamwari.
Kunyange mbada dzairura dziri muHaha,
   Dzainge shamwari kukunda shamwari vanhu.
Nharira, Haha, naChouchi dzainge tsvingo
   Dzaitidzivirira kune vane misara.

Asi parainge makomo rakwira zuva,
   Vafambi romanikidza kutiva mimvuri,
Wainzwa padziva iri pane yiyi nguva
   Tichituhwinha mudziva risinganyn'uri
Kwese kwese rakakombwa nehambakachere,
   Yaive pedyo nedziva'ri redu vapwere

Asi imwe nguva hatina yataidisa
   Sokuswera tichipopa majaram'chara
Tiri kuna Chipfururwi zuva richipisa,
   Nokuraura mudziva mhumbu raigara,
Nokuswera mumumvuri womuti muhombe,
   Nyenganyenga dzichinzvenga muhamba memombe.

Herding Time

I remember the wide plain at our home,
Spotted with white flowers and rippling grass, where
Slim shepherds guard their flocks,
Grazing the rich pastures where the fruit-bearing *mikute* trees
Bend over the insect scudded pools, swizzled by thirsty cows,
While joyous birds sing the summer through in the thick boughs.

Remember when spring had just come, the wind soft,
The hard work of harvest done,
The first patter of new rain touching our skins,
Our barns still packed as if we could never eat them up,
Rising up, early in the dawn, we shivered,
All a-shimmer the beaded bush and prairie grass.

Then the dove and the shrine sang the breakfast sun,
Clearing the tabled sky of clouds,
And the fasting butterfly still asleep in the dewy blossom,
Not so the noisy cock rousing the heavy heads—
Forcing us all to let out the urgent, penned beasts—
Hustling together we'd wet thighs in the tall pastures.

Later, beneath the giant bole of the solitary *mukute*,[1]
The home of the kingfisher and soft shade,
We'd lounge, munching the *hute* fruit,[2] spitting the pits,
Clacking and laughing, as noisy as boys playing war—
And all the while the brother sun burning the air.
Music sprouted from the birds as they drank
    in the puddled claypits.

The sapling bends easily and so our young hearts then,
When the grasshoppers and the cattle were like friends.
Even the leopards pad-padding the *Haha* hill,
Seemed friends, not ravenous furred terrors,
Nharira, Haha, and *Chouchi,*[3] green bulwarks,
Shielded us from the frivolous: they were solid truths.

Now, my mind calls back the high noon fire,
All blazing the bronzed sky, everyone fleeing to shadow,
Even afar they could have heard us at the pool,
Diving, splashing, skin-cooled in the clear water,
And all about us, the wild okra,
Choking the pool's edge, except for the boys, serene.

But nothing was more enjoyable
Than hunting large grasshoppers
In the burning grass along the *Chipfururwi* river,[4]
And afterwards poking at the mudsuckers in the bottom pools,
Then lazing back to grass-floating in the shade of a father tree,
Noting the swallows darting amongst the browsing beasts.

Heyoka, miseve yezuva riri kudoka,
	Yaiti yorebareba kumusha todzoka,
Mombe taikokorodza rongondo nenzira,
	Majongosi namadhonza achirongondoka;
Naidzo njuma nemhou dzine mhuru dzadzo,
	Dzaienda dzokuma dzichitungana zvadzo.

Dzaitiyeuchidza rurumbidzo rwakare,
	Naiwo meso achiona dziri munzira:
Chena, nenhema, netsvuku, nepfumbu zvakare,
	Naidzo dzine makamba nenzira dzorira,
Dzine matsaratsadzi noruvara rwembizi,
	Dzose-ka dziri mukumbu dzoyambuka rwizi.

Hedzoka, imwe neimwe yopinda karwizi,
	Imwe neimwe kunwa mvura ichisunama,
Imwe neimwe yoyambuka mhiri yorwizi,
	Dzimwe nedzimwe dzoedzesera kutungana,
Dzimwe dzofunhidza mhuru padanga dzirere,
	Sokunge kuda kuziva kuti ndidzo here.

Chiona, mhuru kumafuro dzanga dzasara:
	Imwe neimwe kumhou yayo yotizira,
Imwe neimwe yopumha muswe nokufara.
	Kana nemhou zvadzo mbikiti dzinomira
Dzichizeya—vamwe mukaka vave kukama,
	Kana naidzo hamiro dzatongoziyama.

Tarisa, upenyu uhwu hwafumuka zvino,
	Hapachina kuverenga upfumi nemombe.
Kana naiyowo yezviri mberi tariro,
	Hapachisina ruzivo tave semarombe.
Kana nairwo rutendo norwedu rupono,
	Zvanhasi zvave zvanhasi, mangwana amheno.

Asi makore kunyange ndogara mazhinji,
	Handizowana rufaro runokunda urwu,
Haruwanikwe nokuti wapfuma zvizhinji,
	Kana nokuti ruzivo wawana rukuru:
Ruri mukuzvidekadza kwepfungwa yomunhu
	Isina shungurudzo nebishi muupenyu.

Vapfumi, hamuna chikonzero kuzvikudza!
	Kutsakatika munongotya kwepfuma dzenyu.
Nemi vazivi iyi nyaya musaizvidze!
	Muri varanda vehana dzoukuru hwenyu
Ava vafudzi zviripi zvingavatambudze?
	Hwavo upfumi imombe dzinobova-mhoo!

Then, when the shadows of the setting sun
Began to hunt the marge of the plain and we thought of home,
We rounded up the horned bawlers, prodded them toward the village,
The unbroken yearling, the tamed bullock, plodding together,
The polled ones, the dripping uddered cows with the skipping calves,
Nuzzling, moo-ing, butting at each other.

They spoke to us of the ancient glories,
Their eyes coins to us, as we watched them treading
        the pathways,
The white, the black, the red, and oh, the lovely olive dun,
And the large spotted ones, all on the trailways,
And the spangled ones and the zebra-striped,
The rich lowing herd, plashing the ford.

There, coming up, one by one, stepping the bank,
One by one bending to steal a drink,
One by one swishing the water,
Some playful, mocking water fights, horns swinging,
Now at the kraal, nosing the baby calves, left behind,
The mamas hunting the private loved smell of their own.

Just see how the spindly new-borns, lonely all day,
Run toward the full-sacked females, eager to let down
        their milk
Each in time finding the home nipple, their tails flickering
        in expectation,
Chewing the cud, the cows stand still, sharing milk with calf and man,
The milk dinning the pails, frothing quickly over the rim.

Consider! This world and this reckoning of wealth is gone.
No longer do we joy in our cattle as signs of health,
We've given up the sure footed ones,
The milky whiskers of the hungry nuzzler calves—
And fool-foolish we invest our time in less knowable things,
Earning today, without meat and milk in the kraal,
What of tomorrow, will it feed us well, if at all?

Yes, the rich of today! What makes you so proud?
You are saddled with fears of loss, you live in unsafe tomorrows.
And you schooled ones, don't be too quick to dismiss the old days.
You carry heads full of what? your pockets full of holes.
Think back, see the shepherds, all the people, cattle-breeders,
Grass nourished, milk and meat and hide, living wealth, rich moos!

---

1. *Mukute,* water boom tree growing near water.
2. *Hute,* edible fruits of the *mukute* tree.
3. *Nharira, Haha, Chouchi,* names of residual hills in Mazoe District.
4. *Chipfururwi,* tributary of *Chirayire* river.

Dambiro RoHwangu Hwana Uduku

Mazoe! dambiro rangu dzvene rahwo hwangu hwana uduku,
Munyika tsvene ine hova dzinofadza huru nenduku;
Rondo iro kwandakaumbwa nechimiro chounhu hwangu,
Kana zvino ndichitarisa panguya yokumuka kwangu,
Zviri kunge sokunze kuri kujeka pamarirakwedza,
Pam'soro pawo makomo, rima rodzingwa nechiyedza;
Ndenge sendiri pabutiro rokutsi kwehope dzamare,
Nyamba rwuri rufaro rwuri kufugura zviye zvakare.

Nemi makomo eGunguhwe! Harahwa dzemhanza dzakare,
Pasi pamakatukunyudza, pasi pevu pasichigare;
Mumwe wenyu apo napapo—chimhukutu chinyararire,
Mhuri dzenyika muchiyeva dzakaita chifararire,
Rugare here, nhaimi'we! rwoupenyu husopimika
Hwavanhu hwezuva nezuva pane izvo zvinoitika;
Vanorima gore negore, havaverenge namakore?

Tarisa tukova kubvira rinhi twunongosarukira,
Twuchiserereka mujinga memakomo, twondundudzira
Zvinyoronyoro, twoyerera, chidekadzwa twunofukura,
Apo pane kamwe nakamwe, semadzukwa, twunotukura,
Kare nazvino twuchangopa kune venyika ino mvura.

Makomo, mvura, denga, pasi, hwangu unhu zvakakurisa
Namazhinji makomborero, chokwadi, zvikandipfumisa.

Pasi mujinga mechikomo chichimire chinyararire
Paive nomusha wavanhu waive pedyo neNharire.
Yaive nzanga yawo musha—rave dongo pasi pegomo.
Kwaiti chirimo chasvika—mabasa ave omuromo,
Vaitamba ari mapitse muzvivanze zvomuruzhowa;
Vaigobaya nenhindiri, vamwe vodzadzarika vowa,
Navamwe vachiita tsimba—nemiviri vamwe yadunda;
Naidzo nyimo dzichisikwa, dzichigochwa navo vakunda.
Kana kutamba mudambiro, aive mapitse chaiwo;
Makumbo achijakaidzwa, dakara kunze kwayedzawo,
Vatambi rukutu vaneta—mukundi osara munhanga.

Naidzo ngoma dzemitumba dzichidandaura kuridzwa,
Vakuru vachijakaira nemagavhu hosho dzoridzwa;
Naidzo ngoma dzobvundurwa kune chinyakare vaida,
Kana nembeyamwa dzarinzwa pasi nehuro vokaida,
Vachisvikirwa namashave—vamwe vakashonga nehomo:
Ndizvo zvazvaive zvichiri zvomusha mujinga megomo.

The Playground of My Youth

Mazoe—beautiful, ever-exciting playground of my youth!
Lovely land flowing with pleasant streams;
The clay-pit of my humanity, substance of my personality:
Now, when I look back at that time,
The sky first alight with the rising sun
Above the hill-tops, dispelling the darkness,
Dreaming, entranced, night-veiled,
Youth's joyous riches break out of sleep.

And you, *Gunguhwe Hills!*[1] Bald-headed omens,
Eroded, hard granitic, residual humps, eons old—
There, haunched all of you, quiet and looming,
Watching over the tribes that huddle about your feet:
Will we be rich? Will your people be happy?
These tillers, tireless, timeless, and each day follows a day—
Once a quiet circle of content.

Look at the ever-fresh streams, over-flowing in summer's rains;
Eternally, dropping, wetting down the flanks of the hills;
Smoothly flowing, nibbling their banks vernally.
Here and there, bouldered, they bubble, wildly dance;
All these years these waters have quenched the people's thirst.

Hills and water, space, earth and sky, have moulded me;
Have blessed me much, dowered me much!

Beneath remembered hill-side, massive silence,
Lived a village, and active people at the foothill of *Nharire*.[2]
Large then, now, all ruins 'neath the quiet slope.
Then, when spring came, festival, fields forgotten,
People contested, each with each in the open grounds,
Aiming sharp sticks at the rolling *nhindiri* wheels;[3]
Wrestling, falling, casting *nyimo*-peas[4] in the hollowed stone;
The victor roasting his toothsome spoils later.
Even dancing was a combat—
Feet treading against the drums' beat—the victor remaining,
Till all others dropped, sweaty and haggard at end of night.

And the tall *mitumba* drums[5] talking above the hubbub;
The old folks leaping to the clatter of the *magavhu*[6] and the
rattle of the *hosho*.[7]
And those ancestral drums thundering out the old stories;
All troubles forgotten by the loud-singing celebrants.
Some got into a trance when the dancing climaxed,
Swooning some in the ecstasy of the leaping.
This is what it was like in the village beneath the hill.

Kwaiti nomusi wakati, zviyo zvichiri pamatara,
Kwese kwese kwaikokerwa rokupura zviyo jakwara.
Kwaizoti zvaunganidzwa paruware pauya boka,
Vaigoungana'po vanhu pane yakakokerwa hoka.
Waigonzwa dzobuda huro kuna vaigona kuimba,
Pamwechete mhuro dzoti zhi! "wosiye ngoma!" vachiimba.
Kwaizoti pamasikati vanhu vaiti mboya mboya,
Hwahwa hwonwiwa navapuri, jee ari'wo matukiro,
Somusara zve nechibhende, pamimvuri yepaburiro.

Rukweza rwaiti rwachekwa rwaunganidzwa navakwambo,
Kwaichigokokerwa zvino wokurova guva mutambo;
Kamusumo, hako, kopirwa kumudzimu womushakabvu,
Vachiguwa: "Uyai, Baba! Musango mamuri chibvai!
Imba yenyu yazarurirwa, tauya kuzokutorai."

Hedzo nengoma dzemashave dzairidzwa hwose usiku,
Dzaigorarodandaura: Dandam! Dandam! Tiku ti-ti-ku!
Navamwe vaisveta ropa vachitamba—dzamara rusha,
Vachisveta ropa'ro mbishi raidzo huku dzomumusha,
Kana kudzingisa nembudzi dzichibvarurwa hurokuro.
Nengondo vachiyedzesera, hwai nembudzi dzichirinhwa,
Asvikirira emadzviti—naidzo mombe dzichitinhwa.
Nembira dzichidandaura dzichipembedza hombarume,
Dzechidzimba—dzemasivinda—dzichiridzwa navo varume,
Naidzo nyanzvi dzichipfupwa mumapitse ayo mitambo,
Mudandare rouyu musha wangove dongo pachikomo.

Nomumwe musi richidoka, dzokokorodzwa navafudzi—
Mombe dzainanzva gokoro—varisi vachiridza murudzi,
Varume vouyuyu musha, madekwana vaigarira
Pamatanda epamatanga vakamirira kufarira
Matanga emombe'dzo dzavo—hwaive upfumi hwakare.
Hedzo, dzichingoririmiswa, dzichitinhwa zhinji samare,
Ari pano oti: Tarisa! Tarisa yangu njuma hombe!
Ari papo oti: Ringisa! Ringisisaka yangu nzombe!
Ari papapo oti: Hona! dzanguwo ini zvangu rombe!
Ndidzo nguva dzaiverengwa upfumi nedanga remombe
Muupenyu hwouyu musha wave dongo rachiti nyengu,
Panguva dzemisi yakare, vari paguta'ri raDengu.

Nomumwedzi we Gumiguru zhizha nairo rosedera,
Kucharara mhuka musango kundovhima vaikokera.
Varume navo vakomana, zvoudzimba vaifarira,
Zvokundovimisa nezvombo vaienda vabungatira.
Tsvana, nemhembwe, negwarati mumambure dzaitinhirwa,
Navavhimi nehombarume, vaidzoka nezhinji nyama,
Mumasango omumakomo edongo'ri ravakatama.

On another day, the villagers
Invited everyone all about to the threshing of the fingermillet;
They laid down the unhusked grain on flat stone,
The people standing in a wide circle, waiting.
A high voice rises up—the other dropping into tune—
Flails the beat—all together in the song "Don't leave the party!"
Noonday came, everyone spreads out on the ground,
Swilling, jibing each other—a merry crowd,
Sitting, jabbering, tree shaded, by the threshing rock.

Again, at year's end, all grain gathered in,
The people joined in the celebration of "unveiling the grave";
On the old man's sunken plot they set a pot of beer,
Crying, "Come back, ancestor, wise father, leave this lonely place;
Your house stands empty, waiting for you, and we've come to fetch you."

All night long, tom-toms resounded—
The words moaning on to the drum's din, those voices of *mazenda*[8]
 and *mashave!*[9]
Fresh blood some drank—even the women guzzled,
Tearing at the throats of the squawking hens,
Or gashing the pulsing throats of the quaking goats,
Playing war, some, and driving "captured" cattle before them,
Feigning to be the *madzviti* dancing spirits;[10]
Dancing to the harmony of the *mbira*[11] and the rhythm
 of the *mitumba* drums;
Bo-oum the hunters' drums pounding taut cow-skinned praise,
Heaving, jostling the heroes, the prize-winning warriors dancing
So good were they in that village's heart-place,
The village now in ruins in the revisited night.

Another day draws to sunset, shepherds urge on
Their slow moving beasts, halting to lick the salty soil near the river,
The villagers, quiet and slow too, at eventide
Perch on the cattle kraal logs, like misers, gloating in the horned heads,
Their lowing beeves, wealth, brown footed in the old days, pushing,
Running, heads bobbing, hard driven by the herd-boys.
Each watching man says, "Look! Just look at my poll cow!"
And then another, "Behold! just see my bullock!"
A third cries, "Just watch my spotted one!"
Those days power, riches, walked on four legs—
Bellowing days they were—in the town of *Dengu*.[12]
The life of the hill-village, now flat in ruins.

Once, I remember, late October, the rains soon due,
A hunting party, to be out long, strode from the village.
Men and boys, barking dogs, putting the village behind them,
Jouncing at their shoulders, the sharp weapons of the chase,
Hungry the points for the fawn, the buck, the sable antelope
 terror-stricken heaving in the spread nets;
Rich with prey, hunters and heroes, shambling hounds, porter red meat
Out from the forests about *Dengu*—now in ruins.

Kwaizoti zhizha rasvika, nemichero yowa mujiri,
Vanhu vomumusha waDengu vaitibukira kwariri.
Hute, mabou, namazhanje, netswanda vaituta zvose,
Naidzo tsangidze, nehacha, namatufu, netsvanzva dzose;
Kwaive kusiri kufara kwomusha mujinga megomo
Waive pedyo nechisango—wangove dongo pachikomo.

Asi nguva dzazopinduka, kwakauya voruchengera,
Nyika yose ndokuibvuta, norufaro ndokutorera
Rwaive mumusha waDengu waive mujinga megomo.

Mukati meyeyo mizhanje, nemisasa iri chikomo,
Kwangoti dzu zimba rechechi kwarinoswera richiguwa
Zirume risogusa ndebvu, richiimbisa nokusuwa,
Nokutapatira maware edongo'ri raDengu rose,
Nemharidzo yaro inoti: Runyararo kwamuri mose!
Hakuchina nemheremhere yorufaro rwuya rwemhando.
Vana zuva rose pfumvuma, miviri papata nechando,
Vari muchikoro nechechi yamadzibaba akapika.
Kana nechizvarwo chepasi chopararira dzose nyika
Ruzivo rutsva kundotapa—zvinotishamisa muromo,
Zvaisambovepo pamusha wangove dongo pachikomo.

Zvino zvose zvakaparara, pachikomo penge seguva—
Kana naiwo mweya wavo waifemewa iyo nguva,
Sebute, wakanyangadika—wenge pfiro yakaruvinga.

O, musha uya waDengu, waive megomo mujinga!
Hakuchina nemheremhere—kana neinochema nhengu,
Asi zvino rangove dongo—dongo romusha'yo waDengu.

In the summer, with the fruits full ripe,
The people of *Dengu* flocked to the forest:
Wild plums and loquats, and the *mabou* fruit,[13]
    all they gathered up in wicker-baskets,
Plenty too were wild medlars, sour plums, *tsangidze*[14] and
  hacha[15] they were named,
      And happy the people, stain-lipped, in the village,
      God-gifted to be so near a forest—but now,
      Dengu is gone!

How times have changed; the crafty ones have come,
And have taken over the land, and also the happiness
Which once was in *Dengu*—that hill-village—
So that now, in the loquat grove, and the misasa yonder,
A large church house stands where cries out
The big, bearded man, chanting his own kind of anthems.
Often he climbs up the rocks near the ruins of *Dengu*,
And intones his sermon, preaching: "Peace be unto you!"
No more is heard the joyful ancestor songs of yesterday.
Today, the day entire, children sit—bodies freezing, shivering,
Gathered in schools and in the church of the alien fathers.
Now our youths travel far, they know the pathways of the world,
Seeking out new knowledge—new ways, bringing back—
Disharmonies, new tunes never heard of in the village near the hill.

    Now all the life of the hill-village is gone; it's finished!
    Even the spirit that breathed in and out of the huts then,
    Like a mist, is evaporated, is nowhere to be found.

    Oh, oh, lost men and beasts and huts—foot-hill village!
    No more joy quivers in your many hearts—not a breath of life:
    All abandoned, shattered hutments, rotted, wind-turned *Dengu*
      at the bottom of the hill.

---

1.   *Gunguhwe,* a hill in Mazoe District.
2.   *Nharire,* correct name is Nharira, a hill in Mazoe District; the "e" form is for
     rhyme with "chinyararire."
3.   *Nhindiri,* a large bulbous root of the wild lupin which when carved is used as
     target for practising throwing sharp-pointed sticks.
4.   *Nyimo,* black-eyed peas used in popular game.
5.   *Mitumba,* tall drums.
6.   *Magavhu,* dried squash filled with pebbles and tied to legs for dancing.
7.   *Hosho,* hand rattles.
8,9. *Mazenda* and *Mashave,* the dances of ancestors' spirits.
10.   *Madzviti,* literally, the greasy, non-flying, grasshopper, whose name was
     given the Ndebele—the northern branch of fugitive Zulus under Mzilikazi
     who arrived in Mambo's country in the 1830's during the reign of Rozvi
     Mambo, Dyembeu.
11.   *Mbira,* the so-called African hand-piano.
12.   *Dengu,* an old village, now in ruins.
13.   *Mabou,* wild plums, fruits of the water boom tree growing on drier land.
14.   *Tsangidze,* wild plums; tree grows on drier land, or at foot of hills.
15.   *Hacha*—alt. *chakata,* edible fruit of muhacha tree—*parinari curatellaefolia.*

Bembera Kushiri Yorushishe

Nhai iwe shiri yorushishe!
Uchidaro unodandaurei
Wakati zunye ugere saishe?
Pfumvu unodzipishinurirei
Dzepasi penyika pasichigare,
Uchidzibvongodza zvadzo dzirere:
   Ndiko! ndiko! wodandaura—dandaura!

Inzwa, razara murudzi renje;
Pahuro pako wopafetenura.
Zvichida nenhamo dzinenge hwenje,
Uri kujuja neshungu huru;
Nhamo netsambwa zvokupandutsa,
Wogungudzika wopupa nefuru:
   Ndiko! ndiko! wondaura—dandaura!

Ndiani angaatsanangure
Marere echipfuva chako,
Uri wega auri kupungura,
Aunobva washowerera zvako?
Zvichida nhorido dzaChaminuka,
Kana dzaDibora nedzaNehanda:
   Ndiko! ndiko! wodandaura—dandaura!

Kunyange ndisoziva nezvauri,
Ndiri murima rezve huro dzako,
Asi dandaura mwana'we shiri,
Urwo chigadza mwoyo rumbo rwako,
Kuziira madzerere rwandiri,
Ndiri muchisango cheGoromonzi:
   Ndiko! ndiko! wodandaura—dandaura!

Nomurugare, woimba karumbo
Nekazwi kasina kutambudzika;
Norwiyo rwako ruzere ruvimbo,
Wotura befu wakasununguka.
Kwangu kushure nemberi irima;
Zvandinoita zvinobva mukutya:
   Ndiko! ndiko! wodandaura—dandaura!

Iwe uri nyika dzine zambara,
Haumborohwa nehana yokutya;
Jecha kwese kwese rotambarara—
Munhamo dzangu ini ndinotya.
Ndiratidzewo matsime emvura
Eino nyika neniwo ndiimbe:
   Ndiko! ndiko! wodandaura—dandaura!

An Ode to a Bird of the Sand

Hello, bird of the sand!
   What are you chattering about to yourself,
   Quietly seated, royally?
   Why do you recall sad tales
   of the earth's long gone days
      by stirring them from their deep slumber?
Ndiko, ndiko—wildly chattering!

Listen! The open country fills with your whistling;
   Your throat, distended,
   Perhaps with distress as murky as a forest pool
   And blood-sore in your great anxiety;
   Are pain and calamity driving you mad
      as you peer around, your beak raging?
Ndiko, ndiko—wildly clattering!

Who can uncode
The mysteries of your music
Spilling from your song-chamber
Loudly chaunting?
   Perhaps it's the story of *Chaminuka,*[1]
   of Deborah, or of lost Nehanda?
Ndiko, ndiko—wildly blattering!

Though I know hardly what you say
   Puzzled greatly by your full-throated song,
   Still, sing on, young sand bird,
   Heart-felt, your plaint pours forth,
   Vaguely I feel I do understand
      as I pause here in the *Goromonzi*[2] plain:
Ndiko, ndiko—hearing your chattering!

Even when in seeming joy you trill your notes,
   Absent of pain, no longer foreboding;
   Chanting a song of hope,
   Letting fly your entire feathered nature,
   still, on your melody I superimpose my dark past
      and grey future—for what I do I do in fear:
Ndiko, ndiko—wildly clattering!

Though you live in a rock-strewn land,
You appear unafraid of ever going thirsty,
Even though the arid wastes stretch on all sides
My troubles you throbbing shout out.
   Don't you sense my need, Sand Bird, of pure springs?
   Not this desert of the Goromonzi Valley!
Ndiko, ndiko—wildly blathering.

171

Ndiratidzewo rwemwoyo rutsungo
Rwunokusimbaradza nomunjodzi;
Ndidziidzisewo kurasa nungo,
Nokuuchengeta mwoyo pangozi;
Naihwo ungwaru hwezvakadzama
Hunotisimutsa mukufumuka:
    Ndiko! ndiko! wodandaura—dandaura!

Tinoyemura iwe wegombero,
Uchitiyemurawo isu vepasi,
Usingayeukwe mazwi anoti:
"Kakara kakanuna hudya kamwe,"
Nesuwo tiri munhamo zvikuru,
Hatina musi usina makore:
    Ndiko! ndiko! wodandaura—dandaura!

Ndinodisa kuti dai ndiri'we
Nenhamo ndisingazvambarariswe,
Ndichingodandaura shiri sewe;
Misi nemisi ndisingazunguswe,
Ndisina nenhamo yezviri pasi,
Ndichiimba nziyo chigadzamwoyo:
    Ndiko! ndiko! wodandaura—dandaura!

Share, Bird, give me your heart's fortitude.
    Can't you strengthen me in face of danger?
    Teach me how to cast off false tranquillity,
    Sing me confident when I'm threatened,
    and help me find the way to find important things—
        and take us—all of us—out of shame—degradation:
Ndiko, ndiko—wildly chattering!

Listen, though we envy you the open sky,
    And (I imagine) you envy us the closed earth,
    We remember the old saying:
    "An animal is fat because he ate another,"
    meaning: each of us thrashes in agony
        and no day passes without a cloud.
So, it's *Ndiko, ndiko*—wildly shattering!

Obtuse, you impose your deafness to our cries,
Careless, you whistle past our constant cares,
Oh, how drunken we'd be in your song's potions
Free from all the humanoid cruel notions,
    Just singing a song to our heart's ease!
So, my vain hopes, *Ndiko, ndiko*—wildly flattering.

---

1.   *Chaminuka,* the celebrated MuRozvi Prophet of Chitungwiza, b. circa 1804, and killed by the Matebeles circa 1879.
2.   *Goromonzi,* a District 18 miles northeast of Salisbury.

Bembera Kujenaguru

(Rungano rwoMwedzi rwaKare, nerwaNhasi)

Rungano rwaKare:

Muka, jenaguru, m'koma wenjedzana,
Ufadzise hwanzvo hunonanaidzana,
Rigoti rozoti zuva ropatitsa
Isu, namakore roanyangaditsa,
Rigowana iwe wakamugumbata
Wako mudzimai wakamufungata.

Rungano Rutsva:

Wazove tariro, nhasi iwe mwedzi,
Unorondedzerwa navo vemarudzi.
Hapachina simba ringakudzivire
Kuungwaru hwavo, kana uchenjeri,
Iwe hunotsvaka kukurondedzera
Uhwo hwanzvo hwako nokukutorera.

Rwakare nerwaNhasi:

Hokoyo, iwe Mwedzi, zvino pari nhasi,
Wazove dambiro revanhu vepasi.
Wovanzepi hwanzvo hwataiyemura
Hune svinga risina anoyamudza?
Kunyangofumurwa navakasvikako,
Asi vavhevhani vachakuda chiko.

Iwe shiri chena isina mapapiro,
Unovaridzisa tsamwa dzemadiro,
Unovapandutsa vachiri madzukwa,
Vachangoputirwa norudo rwarukwa.
Vheneka nomwenje wako'yo mutete
Ufadzise rudo ruchiri rutete.

Nguva dzemauro mwedzi uri mutsva,
Unovadziidzisa varwo rudo rutsva
Kumonerwa kwadzo tsambo dzokudana,
Kusaka mauro pano kuwadzana
Pakati pemwoyo yavanovhevhana.
Vanoedzesera maitiro ako.

An Ode to the Full Moon
(Old Moon Legend, plus New Moon Legend)[1]

The Old Story:

Arise, full moon, elder brother of the crescent one,
Make glad the lovers that hand-in-hand do stroll.
When the rival sun's gleam breaks all sleep,
Melting away the clouds of night,
He will find you, Man-Moon, keeping close
Your sky-wife, embracing her.

The New Story:

Today, masculine moon, you make us look up—
All peoples, like the sea pushed and pulled by thee—
Seek you out, these flighty-wise ones,
These, oh-so-clever ones,
Steel-orbed, to steal your spatial bride.

Old and New:

Watch out, Man-moon, today
Your sky has become the fly-ground of earthly men.
Where now can you hide that sweetheart we once envied you,
She, so faithfully head-portering the sky-faggots for your fire?
You've been hunted out by these sky-goers—
Though we lovers, more earth-held, still admire your tattooed face.

You, eternal moon, white bird without wings,
You inspire lovers to make the "tchick"[2] sound of love,
You cause the young ones to be wild—
Those who are enmeshed in love at first sight,
So, shine forth your soft light
And gravitate lovers into each other's arms.

At twilight at the time of the new moon,
You teach those in love for the first time
How to put on round bracelets of love;
That is why there's so much passion
Between those who are courting each other;
They are merely doing what you do!

Muka jenaguru, nyanzvi yavavhevhi!
Vanhu vagonyara—venhema varevi—
Mwando ugomutsa unotonhorera
Unozovhuvhuta nokudzidzorera
Shiri dzomujese nokurara dzive—
Mweya wakapora vavhevhi vative.

Sail out then, full moon, the hero of lovers!
And put to shame those whose love is not true;
Call out the cool night's breeze
Which lulls the birds to sleep
Huddled close in the forest's darkness—
    And, give all lovers joy of the soft night.

1. The old moon legend is that there is visible on the moon a woman perpetually carrying a bundle of firewood on her head as a form of punishment from the Creator for having dared to fetch fuel on a day called *Chisi*—Sacred Day of Rest. The second story refers, of course, to the modern American Astronauts who landed on the Moon recently and, thus, "destroyed" the sanctity of the "Moon Lover."
2. "tchick" sound: sound expressing displeasure, but often with lovers, this is paradoxical and is a playful expression of pleasure.

NURSERY POEM

Nhaiwe, Taritari

Nhaiwe, Taritari!
Ho!
Mwana waTarimanguwa,
Ho!
Simudza chana ndisipo,
Ho!
V'eni vedziva varipi?
Ho!
Vakaenda kuUsiyo,
Ho!
Wane Usiyo hwapinda,
Ho!
Mbudzi isina muromo,
Ho!
Kuchema inoti chii?
Ho!
Inoti tununu dziva,
Ho!
Zvana zveguta zvirema,
Ho!
Zvakanzwa mhou kurira,
Ho!
Zvikatizira kumusha,
Ho!
Kuvasikana vatete,
Ho!
Vakanga vasine vhudzi,
Ho!
Nokuti vaichigara,
Ho!
Mudziva guru tununu,
Ho!
Simuka, huya tiende!
Ho!

Hey Taritari[1]

Hey, Taritari!
Ho!
Thou child of Tarimanguwa!
Ho!
Lift up the child in my absence.
Ho!
Where have the owners of the pool gone?
Ho!
They have gone to Usiyo.
Ho!
And there they found the Usiyo gone.
Ho!
How does it cry?
Ho!
It bubbles like a spring-fed pond.
Ho!
The children of the city are dumb-bunnies.
Ho!
They heard the mooing of the cow.
Ho!
And, scared, they fled homewards.
Ho!
To where lived thin-looking girls,
Ho!
Girls all bald-headed.
Ho!
Because they used to live,
Ho!
In a pool of deep water.
Ho!
Arise, let's go to the spring-pond.
Ho!

---

1.   A "nonsense" children's verse with secret sense from an ancient story.

LOVE

Mudikani Wangu

Mudikani wangu, kunyange uri kure,
    Asi ndiri wako.
Wakandipa mwoyo, wangu ndikakupa
    Kuti ive yedu.

Kunyange uri kure uchinge sezuva
    Riri kure neni,
Asi uri pedyo, sokudziya kwaro,
    Kunondifadzisa.

Mudikani wangu, unenge chipfeko
    Chino mwema mutsva,
Unenge sorumbo; unenge kudziya
    Komoto pachando.

Ndinoayeukwa mazuva ay'aye,
    Norufaro rwawo.
Handinai rumbo, handinai pfungwa,
    Asi yako chete.

Makomo eNyota m'nyika yaChiweshe
    Ine mvura zhinji,
Anondifungisa nenyika yauri,
    Iwe ruva rangu.

Pedyo neshamwari, pedyo navavengi,
    Hazvirevi chinhu;
Iwe uri zvose izvo zvandinoda,
    Ndinofadzwa newe.

Kunyange ndoputirwa nematambudziko
    Muno muMazoe,
Asi pfungwa yako inobengenura
    Bute rokusuwa.

Gara senyenyedzi! Gara ruva rangu!
    Rufaro rwemwoyo.
Ndinokupa rudo rwakapetwa zana,
    Kuti ruve rwako.

My Loved One

My loved one, though you may be far,
   still I'm yours.
You gave me your heart, and you mine I gave—
   So both are ours.

Though you are as far from me
   as is the sun,
Your distant light—how warm!
   yet kindles me.

My loved one, you're like a new garment
   upon my body, with its smell of newness;
You are like a fresh song that delights;
   the warm red tongue of the winter's fire.

My day-dreams bring back our green days—
   and their pleasures.
Even now, no song lifts, nor thought,
   but of you alone.

The hills of Nyota in Chiweshe's land,
   (how rain-misted they are!)
Remind me, tell me, where you're hidden,
   My beloved flower.

Close to friends, close to enemies—
   neither has any meaning;
You alone are my preoccupation;
   I am absorbed in you.

Though anguish round about me squats
   here in Mazoe,
Your image out-blots
   my lonely pain.

Oh, stay my bright star, my flower,
   my breast's delight!
A hundredfold I give my love over
   that you may burnish it bright.

Kumhandara Yangu

Handikumbire kupiwa kwemiromo kugunzvana,
Kana kuti ndigumbatwe naandinoda maoko,
Kana nokunyemwerera kwanhasi, kana mangwana,
Kana nokudziirirwa nezviri chipfuva chako.
Aiwa, mhandara yangu—izvi zvingandidadise,
Yangu shungu zvikapedza,rudo rukawa sedamba,
Nokuururutsa mwema unondikwezva kwauri,
Iwe unokutevera mugwara raunofamba—
Asi kuumbana kwoga kwemweya iri kwatiri.

Tarisa! mhandara yangu, somuti wakati kutsu,
Nokwauri zvinodaro nezviri chako chipfuva.
Mudiwa wangu, unenge sedzehwe rakati utsu
Pedyo nemvura yehova rine endudzi maruva;
Unenge zandakubaya iro randakakambira
Mujiri rine mazhanje kuti ndikukushe ndega.

Nokunge wakatsinzira, unenge mwedzi usiku
Norujeko rwakapfava, unovhenekera nyika.
Nokunge wonyemwerera, unenge chairo zuva
Rotsvuka kumavirira norunako rwegoride.
Nokunge usisaseke, unenge zuva'ro guru
Ravanzwa pasi penyika, kana kutsi kwemakore.

Asi ini ndinochema nokukuva kwemichero
Kwauri yakati kutsu ichazokuva nokufa.
Chirimo chinochemera pfumvudza ino neyeyo,
Gore rahwedza yomuka, gore rofa nayo yofa,
Asi iwe une pfiro inondizadza kusuwa.

Chaizvo, mhandara yangu, takautsara muganhu
Munyika dzisozi'ikanwa kuna ani—asi mwoyo—
Nairwo rudo rukuru rusingazivwe navanhu
Urwo rwatinopfundira chinyararire mumwoyo.

Kana uchitsigaira, zviye uchityokatyoka,
Unenge Kanemavara—mhou yasekuru wangu—
Inako kuzere simba kwetsinga kutyakatika.
Hezvi, uchadebudzika paruvara ruva rangu,
Namatama akazara, nezvaoo zvinopenya,
Nokuti dzinobve ropa ndodzauchiri kutemwa,
Kana naiwo maziso ako asinai jenya,
Hausati waremerwa neye makore mitoro.

To My Full Grown Girl

I do not ask for a kiss,
Or the embraces of the arms I love,
Or for your smile today or tomorrow,
Or the warm abundance of your breast—
No—my full grown girl, these would make me over-proud
And weaken my longing, my love;
And dissipate the fragrance that entices me,
The perfume that follows you wherever you go—
I long only for our souls to be caught tight.

 Behold, my beloved, like a fruit-laden tree
 So are you with the fullness of your strong breast.
 My dearly beloved, you are like a garden in the valley
 Thick with flowers near flowing streams;
 You are like a *zandakubaya*[1] preferred above all others,
 In the grove of the loquats that I alone may win you.

With eyes closed, you are like the soft moon at night
Giving shine to the earth with its borrowed light—
But, your open smile is as the full-day sun—
Then, bright-red in the west, or under the earth;
Your smile withdrawn, you are then as the setting globe
Obscured in the evening clouds, with golden flair.

 Now I mourn for the evanescence of fresh ripeness
 So evident in you, and the spring
 Grieving for the blooms of the new year, now dying.
 The immortal spring comes back after its wintry death,
 But I—I must sorrow, knowing, mortal, you can pass by only once.

So we agreed, my full grown girl, to live our separate lives
Safe from endings, in a world unknown to life.
Our secret love we hug to ourselves,
We hide our hearts in our hearts.

 Now, when in your walking, your hips sway to and fro,
 You make me see *Kanemavara*[2] my grandfather's languid-eyed heifer,
 Her sweet bones clicking—sign of a sound body.
 So, you sway, proudly, firm-footed, stepping the virgin land,
 With full-blown cheeks, and shining temples,
 And tattoo cuts still beaded with young blood,
 Oh, and your eyes, still bubbling in innocence,
 Your flesh, supple, not yet strained, coarsened by time.

Zvino nguva ichasvika yandiri kuchema nayo,
Yadzisisazobvi ropa, yaisisazoti kutsu,
Iri kwauri michero, zvose namashizha ayo,
Zvichauna nokuoma, sokweruswiswi kupera.
Kana nokubatwabatwa, matama achazosvava,
Kana nokusvipuriwa, muromo uchaputana,
Kana maziso mashava, nenguva obvuruvara,
Kana nezwi rakanaka, nairo richazhezhera,
Kana naiwo mazino, nokudyiswa achaguka,
Namaoko akasimba, naiwo achadedera,

Asi rudo rwechokwadi,
          harungazive magumo.

Takatanga nokudana tisoziva zvoutsvene,
Kana nedziri kudenga ngirozi dzikafadziswa;
Mwoyo yedu ikaimba nziyo dzikatinakira;
Narinhi dzichazogara dziripo, hadzingagume;
Ndidzoka dzandiri kunzwa dziri kure dzinorira.

Asi wakanaka zvako, mhandara kunge pfumvudza;
Wakasikirwa kuyevwa kufanana ruva dzvene—
Kwauri usosvikika, murefu segomo guru;
Zvibvuwo kunge goride,
          mudiwa sembiri huru.

Wangu mwoyo ndinodisa kwauri ndiuradzike,
Ndigodisa kuti rwangu rudo nerwako rugare
Kwatiri rurambe rwuri, asi rusingasvikike,
Sorudo runenge denga riripo nhasi nakare.
Kusvika kwopedza shungu, asi fungira-mumwoyo
Inorukurisa rudo, rwunoramba rwuri rutsva.
Mudiwa wepfungwa ndiye chaiye pane chaiye,
Anenge muti nokutemwa,
          ndizvo, wotungira patsva.

Nziyo dzokunzwa nenzeve, pakare dzokanganwikwa;
Asi dzokunzwa nepfungwa dzinoramba dzichifadza,
Dzinoramba dzichirira dakara kusingapere;
Hadzingazive nenguva, kana chinonzi makore.

Norujeko rwunobaka rwuri mumaziso ako,
Kwete, usandivheneke,
          handidi zvokutosvorwa.

Ndine tsitsi nokusikwa kwako kune nguva nduku;
Wakazvarirwa kuyevwa,
          hwedza neguva wotorwa.

But the day will come when I shall mourn—
When your blood no longer crimsons your tattoos
And your rich frame shall have dropped its summer leaves.
As the grass, in autumn, turns sere, so shall thee.
So, even with constant touching soft cheeks will wilt,
Even with much kissing, thy lips shall shrink,
Even your shining eyes, in time, will lose their lustre,
Even your firm voice, it, too, shall quiver,
Even your hard white teeth, too, with so much chewing, will crumble,
Even your strong arms, they, too, shall tremble,
   But, despite all this, our love will stay.

At first, we came to love each other, not even knowing it,
Though the heavens' angels took joy of our love.
Our hearts' singing, so pleasing to us
Forever whispers in our souls—
Over time and space I hear those songs still.
For you are beautiful, spring-like, my full grown girl,
Created to be admired, like a brilliant flower;
You, irreproachable, unapproachable as a great peak,
Though precious as gold, and wanted as wide fame.

I would deposit my heart in your breast
So that, your heart and mine together could beat
For this and every day—but this cannot be,
Though we draw back, the sky stretches on forever,
And so our love, endlessly is reaching,
For, fulfilled, love ends; yearning keeps us both ardent,
Finer, fresher, ever renewed.
Imagined bliss is more real than real.
Love is like a tree which waxes with much pruning.

The common songs we hear are soon forgotten,
But those we hear in our minds deeply please,
For they go on echoing for all eternity—
Having no paternity from time, they drag not with the years.

With that sparkle that beams from your eyes
I'm hit; please lower your lids in looking,
I can't bear the blaze.

I lament your so-quick passing glory
Born to seize my regard,
You, and I, looking, still must die.

Ndinovimba kuti sezvo uri muuya kudai,
Uchave anovimbika muzvikuru nezviduku;
Chiuya, mhandara yangu, rufu tirugadzirire.

Zvino imo mumakuva muchawanikwa mapfupa,
Yedu mweya isisimo, yavandutswa nokuvanzwa,
Yaumbana pamwechete, tiri musha wedu mutsva.

Pamapapiro erudo, seshiri huru, tokwidzwa,
Tonanga nzira yedenga inokwira nyika itsva;
Hatichazokurukura nenyaya dzemisi iye.

Pamwechete tichatunga kana muguva tomera,
Tenge Mufandichimuka, rufu usingaruzive:
Ndipo patichazoziva
      rudo rusingazopera.

I sincerely hope that you, alive and fine,
Stay pure and sweet-scented, in all you do,
So, prepared for death, together, we'll be.

Now, so I imagine, in our graves rest our bones,
Though our spirits rise out, elsewhere we are hiding,
Elsewhere, each with each, in our new home.

Bird-pinioned, light-boned, angel-feathered,
We fly up-ward-ly, aloof to our new land;
Our earth-cares below in the downward earth.

Together, we'll sprout from the grave
Like the Resurrection Plant[3] which knows no death.
We then, only then, shall our eternal love resolve.

---

1. *Zandakubaya,* an annual bulbous plant used in a popular game in gathering wild loquats *(mazhanje).*
2. *Kanemavara,* name of a cow, or person.
3. The Resurrection Plant *(Mufandichimuka),* a dying-and-resurrecting-plant, native to local hillsides, and often used medicinally. The plant has small leaves and, when the dry plant is placed in water, the leaves soon turn green again.

Ruva Rangu Shora

Ruva rangu shora rinenge nyenyedzi
Kana ichipenya mugombero guru;
Rinokunda zuva, rinokunda mwedzi
Kana wovheneka uri jenaguru.

Pasi pemakomo, pasi padzo shongwe
DzeNyota dzizere mweya wakapora,
Ndokwandakawana rinofadza shombwe
Richangovhurura nhengo dzaro shora.

Pandakariona, ndikasarishora,
Noutete hwaro, richangovhurura,
Ndikarida kwazvo, ruva rangu shora,
Ndokubva'po ndenge ndaniwa nembura.

Kana kovhuvhuta, noruwa rwazara
Unotonhorera mweya wemasora,
Unorinzwa bani nomwema razara
Worunako rwaro ruva rangu shora.

Ndichinoriona, iri ruva rangu,
Mazuva mazhinji ose akanaka,
Ndaiperekedzwa neshamwari yangu
Pakudoka kwaro zuva rakanaka.

Zvino wangu mwoyo wakafa neshungu
Kuti dai waro kuuna rarega;
Ndikadisa kuti ndiritanhe, hungu,
Ndigogara naro muupenyu hwangu.

Paye, iri ruva rangu ndichafunga,
Ndakangoziva kuti rudo ibenzi
Rinofamba kwese kwese richidzunga;
Kana kunge mwenzva unofamba tsenzi.

Ndudzi dzemaruva izhinji panyika,
Asi ini rangu ndiro rega shora
Pakati paose Mwari akasika,
Pane wangu mwoyo rakatema nyora.

Ndipe iri ruva muupenyu hwangu,
Kuti mwoyo wangu uve nokugutswa;
Handizonyunyuti napakufa kwangu,
Kunyange ndozofa mweya wopurutswa.

Chiyevo hapana panyika chikuru
Chingakunde iri ruva rangu shora,
(Musha worunako, ruyevo rukuru),
Rinokura zvaro riri mumasora.

My Yellow Flower

It is, it is my starry flower
Warming the eye in the sky
Far out-twinkling sun and moon
So bright it is—so light!

'Neath the hills—beneath the rocky slopes
Of the Nyota crags cooled by vagrant breezes,
That's where I came upon my lovely flower
In its first bloom, so yellow.

When I espied it, I knew its worth
Its fragile petals, newest blossom,
I loved it much—my golden petals
And left the hills whelmed over with love.

When the wind blows and fills the glades
With its mountain breezes soothing the veld,
Anyone, travelling through the land,
Will rejoice in the perfume of my saffron bloom.

As I went to visit my bright flower
During many happy days
A friend came with me, calm, happy, too,
At the sunset of a lovely day.

Now my love scalded my heart
I, hoping only it would not wilt,
Before I could pluck it—this flower,
And keep it mine all my life.

So, dreaming about my flower
I came to know that love is like a fool,
Who stumbles everywhere, not minding his feet,
Or, it's like the blind path of the cane rat.

There are many kinds of flowers on earth;
But mine is a once only yellow plant—
Of all that God created,
It marks my heart, indelibly.

Oh, given this flower of my life,
My heart can be put to ease,
I'll not grumble as I breathe my last,
Nor groan when I give up my ghost.

Earth has no greater "might" to show
Than my yellow flower—
A whole host of beauties, a wondrous sight
So shyly, this one, blooms in the veld.

Mufudzi Nomudiwa Wake

Uya, mudiwa wangu, muno mubani,
Mukati memikute musina ani,
Ndizokunekaidza muno mubundo
Tigosiya varimi vomuruundo.

Makomo aya isu akatikomba,
Achatidzivirira vanotinyn'omba;
Neshiri dzinoimba dziri mubinga,
Todzinzwa tisisina vanotivinga.

Ndozokuwaririra madangaruswa,
Namashizha matete — mutsago uswa;
Motsi dzevudzi rako uchazoruka
Woita dzove nhemba dzinosaruka.

Yetsvana nhembe huru ndokusukira,
Ndizvo, nhanda dzechuma worukirira;
Tsungare dzemindondo woruka zvako,
Nepfumba worukira m'maoko ako.

Ndichazokupopera hwiza mugan'a
Munoparutsa tsoka pachando man'a;
Nouchi hwomumhango ndokumorera,
Mazinyana eshire ndokutorera.

Uya uzoterera kuziriridza
Kwenyuchi mumaruva dzonyinyiridza;
Nenjiva muusanza dzichiyaruka,
Mbiri nembiri, hedzo, dzobhururuka.

Ndichazokuudza rungano rukuru
Rwaiye Mhembere mufudzi mukuru,
Achifudza mubani danga rehwai
Mvura kwese yamisa ichiti vai.

Ari mumukute, kuringisa boka,
Bazi romuti'yo ndokubva ratyoka,
Ndokutiwo tuzumu pasi rukushu.
Mhembere ndiye nomusana bukushu.

Hwai ndokuungana dzochemedzana,
Ndokumutakura dzomutembedzana,
Pasi zvinoyera dzonanga kumusha
Nomufudzi Mhembere achiti rusha.

Ndokurushaura dzichiri kure,
Dzemberi dzodairwa nedziri shure.
"Mhembere wawa! Mhembere wawa!
Tinofudzwa naniko, Mhembere wawa?"

The Shepherd and His Love

Come, my love, to this plain,
Amid the lonely *mikute* trees,
That I, with you, may stroll in the open *bundu*[1]
Leaving behind us the tillers of the land.

These all-encircling hills
Shall shield us from the intruding ones;
But, once safe, we shall listen
To the forest birds' lovely songs.

I'll find and spread out reed grasses,
And tender leaves—your pillow more bundled grass.
The curls of your hair you will put
Into circular coils, long, and lasting.

A large fawn buck apron I'll make you,
And, on it, you'll embroider patterns.
Tasselled band of beads you'll weave,
And grass bracelets wind around your arms.

For you I'll hunt grasshoppers in the plain
(Where morning cold breaks the skin of frozen feet);
And honey in the tree I'll fetch for you,
And fledgelings, too, I'll get you.

Come, and listen to the humming
Of the honey bee buzzing, buzzing in the flower;
And see dove nestlings fly out the nest,
In twos, we'll see them winging away.

I'll tell you a marvellous story
    Of *Mhembére*[2]—a great shepherd—
Herding his sheep over a wide field
    And the rain threatening everywhere.

While in a tree keeping an eye on his flock,
    Leopard-like he sprawled watchfully,
But the old branch cracked beneath his weight
    And Mhembére fell; broken-backed he writhed on the ground.

Around him the sheep gathered bleating;
    And together, somehow, they got him back—
Nuzzling him home, the marvel of the earth,
    Groaning, bleading, Mhembére, the sheep, oh, so slowly.

Then, they began to baaa—while yet afar;
    Those in front being supported by those behind, warning:
"It's Mhembére who has fallen! It's Mhembére who's hurt!
Ah, who will herd and guard us now that Mhembére has broken his back?"

Mufudzi wakanaka, chido chavose,
  Anochemwa navanhu venyika yose;
Mufudzi anoruny'a, munaki afa,
  Hwai hadzingachemi nokunge afa.

Uyaka, tizogara mune mipondo—
  Dzvukam'piriviri rayo minhondo
Richazokupfukira, mudiwa wangu,
  Wakapfunya chisero panyhasi pangu.

(Thus, we see) a good shepherd is loved by all,
    And is mourned throughout the land.
A peevish shepherd is only good when dead;
    No grief over him when he breaks his head.

Come, then, let's live here among the *mipondo*[3] trees—
And the crimson leaves of the *minhondo*[4]
Will entrance you, my loved one,
While you sit cross-legged by my side.

---

1.   *Bundu*, an untilled, natural plain of grass and light wooded forest.
2.   *Mhembere*, a legendary herdboy who fell from a tree and broke his back. The tragic story is related in A.S. Cripps' book: *CHAMINUKA*, The Sheldon Press, London, 1951, pp. 9-10.
3, 4. *Mipondo and Minhondo*, species of leguminous trees with edible legumes.

Kumwanasikana Dzukwa

"Kwaziwa mwana wamambo!
Unoendepi nechombo?"

"Ndafunga mhiri yaRuya
Kwandaigara na'mbuya."

"Koinga zuva radoka,
Chirega kuenda woga.
Yezhizha mvura yamisa,
Kunze kwasvipa, tarisa.
Ruya rukova rukuru,
Zambuko rake iguru;
Rinda ufume mangwana,
Zvinokuripa nezana.

"Kunyange mvura yamisa,
Handina chinondityisa,"
Ndokudaro munhukadzi
Pamusha waMunyaradzi.

Hautye rima rezhizha
Zvaunodai kushizha,
Nhai mwana iwe Soko?"
Harahwa'yi ndokubvunza.

Dzukwa'ro romusikana
(Kunge zuva romushana),
Rakademwedzeka zvaro
Ndokupindurawo roti,

"Ndichirumwa nei, Tembo?
Ndichifamba ndo'mba rumbo
Rwomudiwa Chamaringa
Uyo wandiri kuvinga.
Mazviita, ishe wangu!
Pokurinza mwoyo wangu
Ndapashaya kwazvo kwazvo,
Handingamborinda nazvo.

Ndokufamba mumafuro
Yave nguva yemauro;
Samusha ndokuti kapu
Dzukwa'ro rachiti shapu.

To A Young Woman

"Greetings, noble daughter!
Whither are you bound?"

"I'm thinking of the land beyond the *Ruya* river
Whence I used to live with my mother's mother."

"Look, the sun is set,
Dare you to go alone?
See, the summer rain storm builds up,
The thunder-heads blot out the sky—
Besides, *Ruya* is a mighty river,
And its ford is wide;
Stay for the night, you can leave in the morning,
It is better if you wait."

"Though the rain is threatening,
I have nothing to fear,"
So said the venturesome woman,
Being, then, at Munyaradzi's village.

"Do you not fear summer darkness,
Even as urged on as you seem to be,
You child of Soko?"
So questioned the old man
But,
The brave girl
(Beautiful as the great sun of spring time!)
Confidently hurried on,
Striding down the narrow path,
Flying away, she cried over her shoulder:
"What can harm me, Tembo?
As I go along, I'll sing a song
Of my loved one, Chamaringa,
He, whom I'm going to see
So, thank you, honoured grandfather!"

And to herself, "I cannot hang back more—
So hard beats my heart
No longer can I sleep apart."

So she walked on through the pastures,
Even though the night closed in faster.
Amazed, the village elder
Stared as she disappeared from view.

Zvino, hoyo, ndokudzika,
Pazambuko ndokusvika;
Kunze kukabva kwarema
Denga rikati rochema.
Chii chaimuyambutsa
Rukova runokungudza,
Mahape ongopunzira,
Nyika mvura yotandira?

Zvino wakati apinda,
Kukave ndiko kurinda,
Ndokuve hama yehove
Achinyn'ura mumurove
Denge richingoti vai

Ndizvozvo, nokuchimbidza,
Mumwando inohwihwidza,
Makore ndokumuchema
Nemisodzi yakarema.

But,

> We see her as down the hill she strides,
> Headed for the rushing ford,
> Darker yet, more lowering, the clouds barge the sky,
> And now, water weeps across the veld.
>> How now dare she step into the swollen Ruya
>>> Turbulent, lashing its banks,
> Waves now, where earlier only gleaming quiet?

> Still, passionate, she rushes into the wet wildness.
>> No lover this, she's tossed and swallowed.
>> Friend of the fishes, she swims, over-swooned,
> Floating in flood,
> Arched overhead, the bolt-flashing sky.

> And this way, so quickly,
> Amid the howling, wetsome winds,
> The mourning clouds, let us say,
> Let down their tears in the dark night

> Over her. . . .

Tichafa Dzikiti

Munochemeiko, verudzi rwedu?
Munomuchemeiko, Tichafa wedu?
Waifanira kutura upenyu,
Somufiri nduramo nechokwadi,
Nokuzarurira vanhu rugare.
   Nyenyedzi yaivheneka zviuya;
   Bangami raiwo ose matenda;
   Shamwari yavaduku navakuru:
   Aive shamwari yedu, Tichafa,
   Dakara pazuva rake rokufa.

Akaona upenyu hwouranda
Hwavanhu vagere mukufumuka;
Kana naiyo yenyika mirau
Ichiita vanhu uraurau,
Akashaya mwoyo pokuurinza.
   Akarwa, kwete somuparadzi ropa,
   Asi nepfungwa mafurusa mweya
   Dzavazhinji vasingadi kunzwana:
   Aive murwisi, uyu Dzikiti,
   Dakara pakuti kwake rikiti.

Tarisa ropa raidzo mbirimi
Rave mucheturo wavavirimi.
Rave kusununguka kwavasungwi,
Rinokudzama kunenge Manungwi;
Roita murove, upamhi gungwa,
   Hunovashayisa kana nepfungwa;
   Neropa rake, mudiwa Tichafa,
   Richavamukira ngozi yokufa.
Ngatihupembedze ushwindi hwake
Hunotiratidza kuti titsunge.

   Hezvika chokwadi chinouraya,
Varevi idi angove makuva.
Nhaiwo, chokwadi tovanza here
Nokutya kureva idi rizere
Nokuti tinotya kubeturira?
   Ingozi ipi yakapandukira
   Ruva renyatwa nokubwinya kwaro,
   Nokuridimura riri nhevana?
   Aive shamwari yedu, Tichafa,
   Dakara pazuva rake rokufa.

An Elegy for Tichafa Dzikiti (1926-1962)[1]

For whom, for what, are you weeping?
Ti-chàfa you mourn for so loudly?
He who manfully paid the cruel price,
Paid fully the price for truth and who did not barter;
He insisted the door of freedom swing wide.
Star-bright he shines in our funereal sky;
Physician, knowing the pain of each of us—
The frets and twists of body and of mind.
Friend of child and grey-hair,
Most strong this friend, Ti-chàfa.
He shelters us yet, even in his death.

Looking, he saw lost, out-looking eyes—
Faces, grim, tense-jawed.
He knew the legal chains that chaffed our arms—
That iron-spliced man from man, making them yoked "beasts."
Aware, so moved, his heart made him act,
Fighting, peacefully but valiantly,
Rallying the people against their despair—
Against those others, enemies of honest peace!
Indeed, he was a fighter, this Dzi-ki-ti,
Our support till he died, and still.

For we believe the blood of any brave man
Will poison drip in the feverish brain of the murderer.
Ghost-vengeance paying back the dark crime.
So, Dzikiti's blood, flooding as high as *Manungwi*[2] hills,
Will lap and swallow, flood-like, this blood of Tichafa—
Muddling their sickly days, for the aggrieved spirit
Haunts the cruel ones; therefore, we honour his courage.
He shows us yet how to be brave!

Though we know speaking truth kills
And honest ones go quickly to their graves—
Shall we be daunted from the right way
For fear of the burial pit in the rocky ground?
What ngozi-spectre blasted his fresh life,
Cutting the trim stem of his days,
Blighting the flower's bright petals?
Oh, he was our friend, this\Ti-chà-fa,
Till and even after his willed death.

203

Ndinokushuwa, mudiwa Tichafa,
Kana ndichafungidzira zvekare:
Nairwo rwako ruvimbo kwandiri,
Nomuupenyu vaduku tichiri.

Kana nehova dziri muZimbabwe—
    Nomutusipiti twuri mumabwe—
    Hazviikwanire misodzi yangu
    Yandinochemera Tichafa wangu.

Aive shamwari yangu, Tichafa,
Ndichamushuwa kudzamara ndafa.

Tears I drop for you, beloved Ti-chàfa,
Wet-eyed, remembering, our days together
You, trusting and confiding in me,
When our hearts beat with youthful blood.

Now, you're gone; all the waters of Zimbabwe, her
Bubbling springs, tearing rock-filled rivers,
Will not equal the rushing wetness of my tear-drops
Falling, eroding my face's landscape, tears for Ti-chàfa.

He was my friend, this Ti-chàfa,
I'll grieve for him till I die, too.

---

1. *Tichafa Dzikiti,* the late Dr. Samuel Tichafa Dzikiti Parirenyatwa.
2. *Manungwi,* hills in Mazoe District.

PERSONAL

Mimvuri

Shamwari dzemisi yakare,
   Idzo dzisisipo,
Dzine misodzi netsitsi,
   izvo zvisisipo,
Munzira mhamhi dzakare
   Madzakatizvuva —
Dza'a mimvuri yedunhu
   isisina mumhu.

Shamwari mhenyu dzakare
   dzinounhu hwedu;
Hwedu upenyu dzigere;
   dzine pfungwa dzedu;
Nesu kwavari tigere
   muupenyu hwavo,
Pfungwa dzichigungudzika
   tofunga nezvavo.

Murudo rwataivhevhana
   tichiri vatete,
Ndizvo tichibatsirana
   nomupfungwa nhete,
Munhamo toyambutsana
   tichiri vaduku:
Ndoshamwari dzakanaka,
   dzouduku hwedu.

Nzendo dzataichifamba
   tine tsoka ndefu;
Nzvimbo dzataichitamba
   pamimvuri mirefu,
Papfumvudza yemaruva
   achitipfukira—
Zvangove mimvuri
   yemisi yakare.

Maruva ataipwanya
   achiri matete,
Ano mukume kunyanya —
   sorudo rutete —
Kana tofunga zvakare
   madzukwa tichiri,
Uko kudana kwakare —
   kwangove mimvuri.

Shades

Friends of the long gone days,
Now no longer with us,
Whose tears and sympathy
    Are no longer here,
Who, in those days,
    Led us long ago—
Now, mere shades of the plains,
    They are invisible, unshaped.

Our old friends
Share our humanity—
Share our life,
    And our very thoughts
As we share all of theirs
    In their waking life.
When we are in trouble
    We turn to them.

When we courted our sweethearts,
    In our tender days,
By sharing our feelings,
    We had lighter burdens,
And so, we crossed together the river of sorrow
    In our young days!
These were the warm, good friends
    Who shared our innocent years.

The memories of journeys we took together
    To countries far away,
And the haunts of our youthful games
    In deep, tree-cast shadows,
All around us grew the flowers,
    Delicate, bee-bothered, fragrant,
All these are now mere shades
    Faded those buried days.

The petals we crushed
    In their tenderness,
Yellowing our hands their pollen
    Like golden love, fragile:
Oh, when we recall those days
    Of our "younghood"—
Those old loves and lovers—
    We are less, and they only cast shadows.

Pakudoka Kwezuva

Zvino zuva ravira,
Mimvuri yerima yopararira,
Uko nokokoko yofararira,
Hurekure dzorira.

Kutsi kwawo makore
Ari kuwoneka mwenje mukuru.
Asara ave matsvuku zvikuru,
Kumagumo enyika.

Inzwa ruzha mubinga!
Shiri mumiti ra'aserevende,
Mumatavi madzati ngerengende
Rima, nyika rovinga.

Zvino, hona muguta!
Ma'akuvheneka zvionioni,
Zvinotaima semadhaimoni,
Senyenyedzi kudenga

Vanhu vari muguta,
Muguta iri risingamborari,
Mavanoyera rugare nemari,
Kunyengedza, upenyu.

Inzwa, mhere muguta!
Vanhu nengoro re'asererere,
Mumigwagwa yakati ngwerevere,
Hakurarwi muguta.

Kana zuva ravira,
Pfungwa dzinogungudzika dzorinda,
Dzotura befu muhope dzopinda,
Kure nemhere yeguta.

At Sunset

Now, the sun goes down,
Night's shadows creep across the land,
Darkness spreads quickly on the earth,
    As cattle egrets cry out.

Beneath the last lighted clouds,
Blazing in the lost glaze of light,
The sky suffuses—bleeding a crimson spray,
    At the ends of the earth.

Listen, what's that stir in the bush?
A flutter, then the crowded birds chorus out,
Perched in branches, pierced by shafts of last sun,
    Just before night engulfs all things.

Now, let's turn to the city,
Brash street lights blaze (no need of sun)
Sparkling like blown-up diamonds—
    Light balloons, rivals of the stars above.

Beneath them, among the people of the city,
Never sleeping in all its parts,
Man and woman brighten their lives with money—
    Electric, golden, their earthly deceits.

Listen, hear the city's shouts and curses:
Manwomanchild and machines grind out a howl,
Dark streets, garish-streaked by neon,
    Fight the night, sleep is defeated.

When the country sun goes down,
Troubled minds find rest, get rest,
Their peace is dream their sleep unbroken,
    No city clamour; country man snores unwoken.

Usati Handikwanisi

Nokunge nhamo dzichikufudza,
Dzichikupedza nounhu hwako,
Usina ani waunoudza
Madanhaurwa enhamo dzako:
    Tarisa mberi! Tarisa mberi!
    Tarisa mberi penhamo dzako.

Nokunge kurwa kwotsviriridza,
Nemhandu dzenge dzasimba kwazvo,
Pesvera simba kushingirira;
Zvinorukudzo umire nazvo:
    Ramba uchirwa! Ramba uchirwa!
    Ramba uchirwa nemhandu dzako.

Rudadadziko rwuri kupiko
Rwaiye munhu asakayedza,
Asakatyora kana rwiriko?
Yedza utadze—zvakare yedza:
    Kunyange denga, nerino pasi,
    Hazvakasikwa nezuva rimwe.

Mushingiriri anokudziwa
Navanhu vose neravo simba;
Kunyange ari pakuzvidziwa
NaMwari wake anongovimba:
    Iye haati, Iye haati,
    Iye haati "Handikwanisi."

Pane rugare pane mavanga,
Pakadeurwa ropa negano.
Nyika izere namagandanga
Asina hanyn'a, kana nezano:
    Vano ruvimbo, vano ruvimbo
    Vano ruvimbo vachazokunda!

Kwese kwauri uri murwisi!
Hapana nguva inokodzera
Yokuti uti, "Handikwanisi."
Kunyange shure nokudzokera:
    Ramba uchiti, Ramba uchiti,
    Ramba uchiti, "Ndiri mukundi."

Never Say I Can't

When adversity dogs your steps,
   Gluttons down your manhood,
With no one to tell
   The story of your affliction,
      Keep your face to the sun, keep it up,
      Hold it to the light, your shoulder to the gloom.

When the battle is fiercest,
   And seems it the foe will win,
Put more force in your blow
   And seize your pride and honour,
      Keep fighting! Keep stabbing!
      Keep struggling with your foes!

Whence can come pride
   From a man who's never
Broken the spear in battle?
   Try, though failing the first time, try again!
      Even making heaven and earth
      Took God some time!

The battle-strong man commands respect,
   For all praise him with their lungs
Even though he be deep-embroiled,
   Yea, in his Battle-God he vaunts himself:
      He never groans, he never whines,
      He never even whispers: I can't!

Where comes victory, there will be wounds;
   Blood must gout out 'neath the battle-axe.
For the world-veld is full of wild men
   Who seize and trample;
      But the steadfast, but the loyal,
      But the faithful, will overcome!

Wherever you are, you are a *mu-rwi-si!*[1]
   Never shall there be a time
For you to cry: "I can't!"
   Or, even in retreat, to turn your back:
      Keep shouting, keep crying out.
      Keep screaming: "Victory!"

Nyangwe upenyu hwako hwazara
Nehambe huru yokufumuka
Negodo guru huro ragara,
Upenyu hwenge sehwarunduka:
    Asi yeukwa! Asi yeukwa!
    Nguva ndimupi wavanotsunga.

Kubudirira hakusi nyn'ore,
Ndiko kwavanhu vano unhinhi.
Shingira zuva, mwedzi negore:
Shingira nguva yose narinhi:
    Urambe kuti, Urambe kuti,
    Urambe kuti, "Handikwanisi!"

Even though shame has soured,
    Spilled over your life's lip,
And a lump sits in your throat-well,
    Your tongue dead to any taste,
      Remember! Remember!
      Time rewards he who waits!

Victory is no low fig for easy plucking
    But high and tight, you must strain for it!
Fight on, for this day, and month, yea—even the year!
    Forever and a day hold tight:
      For the steadfast, for the loyal,
      For the faithful, will overcome!

---

1.   *Murwisi,* a mighty fighter, a fearsome aggressor.

Kana Ndafa

Kana ndazofa, imi machinda,
    Pano mumvuri muzondirinza;
Apo ndowana bumhudzo nyn'ore.
    Miraraungu nawo makore
Zvichazoimba nokwakapfava:
    "Rinda mudiwa, rinda zorora!"

Ndipapo pasi ndovumbamirwa
    Ne'vu repasi ndodziirirwa;
Nhamo dzopera nokurunzirwa;
    Dzoimba shiri nenziyo dzadzo
Pasi ndirere ndorezvwa nadzo:
    "Rinda mushoma, rinda zorora!"

Kunyange uswa hwozotepuka,
    Handichazenge ndichapepuka.
Kana mashizha okuhumuka
    Orinda pasi oturumuka,
Achazoimba nezevezeve:
    "Rinda muroro, rinda zorora!"

Kana vatorwa vachasvika'po,
    Vomira kure napandiri'po.
Dzichandichema hama chaidzo,
    Dzichipungura neshungu dzadzo,
Dzichindidemba kusingapere,
    Muhope dzangu huru ndirere.

Ndifushirei pedyo nemvura
    Yakadekara, payakapora;
Kure nenzvimbo dzamadzimbahwe,
    Uko kusina rukangarahwe;
Dombo paguva—chiyeuchidzo—
    Rovanzarikwa sechiratidzo,

Vanopfuura voziva kuti
    Makandirinza pano mutepe
Una mazanhi anorembera
    Anozosara achipembera
Achindi'mbira nokwakapfava:
    "Rinda mufambi, rinda zorora!"

When I'm Dead

When I'm dead, my friends,
   In a broad tree's shade dig me down,
Deep down I'll find my long peace.
    Rainbows and clouds
     shall softly chant:
Sleep, tired traveller! Sleep and rest!

Once enclosed in the earth's dark embrace,
   Soil can warm my cold flesh,
And close up, cut off, my cares and faults.
    Birds shall trill their songs,
    Cradling me into deep-set quiet below:
Sleep, tired traveller! Sleep and rest!

Though the grass shall sideways sway,
   Never shall I awake again!
Though the leaves shall drop down,
    Strewing the earth feather-falling,
    Rustling, they shall faintly whisper:
Sleep, tired traveller! Sleep and rest.

Though strangers pause to enjoy my shade,
   Standing near (but far off in spirit),
My kin, near or far, shall closely grieve my going,
    Crying their familial woe,
    Mourning my out-voyage eternal:
While in my deep dream I rest.

So, dig me down, down by the water,
   By the quiet pool so still,
Far from the royal caves;
    No rounded pebbles here in this place!
    Merely a chipped boulder—as simple mark,
Please let be hefted down to my memory.

That way the passersby shall see
   You laid me beneath a *mutepe*[1]
Whose languid ground-pointing leaves
    Rub fingers green-softly in commemoration
    Syllabating, hushing me:
Sleep, tired traveller! Sleep and rest!

---

1.   The *mutepe* is an African willow most often found along streams and ponds.

TWO POEMS BY LUKE C. CHIDAVAENZI

Our Love Near the River
The Turtle Dove

Rudo Rwedu Pedyo Nerwizi

Zuva rechando rinotapira rave pakati penzira yaro,
Makura ose ave machena mashanga awo apfukudzika,
Mwoyo wako nomwoyo wangu yakasangana inorufaro,
Ikarangana kufambafamba pedyo nerwizi rwemvura zhinji.

Tiri vaviri, mudiwa wangu, takasimuka paimba yedu
Takatangisa karwendo kedu tine rufaro rwakarurama;
Pedyo nepedyo takasungana mumwoyo yedu norudo rwedu,
Tikasangana navanhu vaye vanorukudzo runoshamisa.

Nomurusango takapfuura tikayambuka notukoronga
Twusine mvura twakangooma munyika iye yeshapa chena;
Tichitaura zvinyoronyoro dakara rwizi rwemihoronga
Inobereka pamunhuruka mvura yonaya vanhu vorima.

Pedyo nerwizi, padziva guru rakati svii nemvura zhinji,
Rinoyambukwa neigwa guru nguva yezhizha mvura yawanda,
Rine mitepe inoyevedza mhiri nemhiri netsanga zhinji,
Takazorora tiri vaviri tigere pasi pedyo nepedyo.

Takataura zvinyoronyoro nemazwi edu anotapira
Munzeve dzedu, tichionana uso nouso hunonyemwerera,
Norudo rwedu runoerera mukati medu rwofashukira,
Rwangu kwauri, rwako kwandiri, tosanganiswa mukati marwo.

Panzvimbo yose takave toga kure nevanhu veguta redu,
Tichiyevedzwa nemvura zhinji inoerera zvinyoronyoro,
Inofanana norudo rwedu runoerera mukati medu;
Nezvinhu zvose zvataiona zvakatikomba—mabwe nemiti.

Nechinguvana, takasimuka tokwira narwo rwizi rukuru,
Tichipesana nemvura zhinji inoerera kumavirira.
Zvinyoronyoro, nepamatombo aka'yandara makurukuru,
Takadevana naye Mhanyami rwizi rukuru rwenyika yedu.

Panguva yose takataura nyaya dzorudo nedzorufaro,
Tichiyeuka misi yakare yokutangisa kworudo rwedu
Yataidisa nokuutsvaka musi wanhasi unorufaro
Watinogara tiri vaviri murudo rwedu rwusingapere.

Our Love Near the River

Moontime, sun yellows down—
There the field, stubbled, bare,
We two together, sharing joy,
Walking, smiling eyed, to the rushing river.

Leaving our home behind us
Sauntering, no rush, full of each other—
Close, we touch and touch, love kindled,
Passing us, our people, gently greeting.

Through the gaunt woods—
Across the drift-hills—
We murmur softly—nearing the
Mhanyami,[1] now violent, tree edged, with *horonga*[2] willows,
      wood and rushing water.

Hitting the wet bank,
Looking down into the pools so deep
There, where big boats ferry in summer,
Now, sweet-swaying willows, hanging
Over the foaming banks of reeds.

Talking, we talk, the words are sweet,
Our ears full of their honey, our eyes
Filling our faces, all love, and the water outside,
Inside all calm love, you and me, the easy cross-over.

In every place we are alone, but we want more
So we walk on, following the coursing waters,
Our own currents cutting the channels deeper,
Our own moss and rocks and trees our inner landscape.

Then, very secure, hand-holding, watching the outer stream,
Our eyes tugged by the rush and push,
We search out, then gingerly step on the flat stones
Moving over the white spray of the mighty Mhanyami.

All the while we recalled our first days of love,
Calling back the streams of flowing love,
Floating still on the water's back with love,
Conjuring up the future of love, joined forever.

Zuva rogara makomo aye makurukuru emavirira,
Njiva nedzimwe shiri dzesango dzonanga dzose kuruzororo,
Takarusiya rwizi rukuru tine rufaro nokuwirira
Munzira yedu yaititora kuguta redu rorunyararo.

Mazuva ose, mudiwa wangu, ndinorufunga rufaro rwedu,
Norudo rwedu pedyo nerwizi runoerera zvinyoronyoro;
Hazvichadzima kunyange rinhi, zvichasaruka mumwoyo yedu,
Tichazvifunga misi nemisi dakara zuva ratinoguma.

Sun was no friend, now eating the tree-tops,
Doves and water birds seek the thick boughs for rest,
Warned by the flutter, dimness on river, peacefully
We turn homewards, leaving the water for our own nest.

So, each day, my beloved, our shared love lives,
And our happy days on the river's edge flows in our hearts;
These moments permanent in our memory, engraved in our breasts,
Breathe like eternal flowers, spring and summer till our last fall.

---

1.   *Mhanyami,* (misnamed *Hunyani*), name of a river—a tributary of the
     Zambezi river.
2.   Species of tree similar to willow, growing near river banks, and bearing edible
     fruit.

Bvukutirwa

Kunze kwomunda wedu mukuru,
Pedyo nerwizi rwetsanga zhinji
Rwakakombwa nemitepe mikuru:
Bvukutirwa rakavaka usanza.

Mumin'ando yematombo makuru,
Seri kwezvuru zvouswa uzhinji
Zvakakombwa neminzwa youturu:
Bvukutirwa raisweroimba.

Varimi vose vairiterera,
Navafudzi vaigarorinzwa,
Kuti roimba newewo terera,
Rinogaroimba netsitsi muhana.

Muswero wose rinongoimba,
Pamasikati napamauro:
"Guku kutizwa nehama!
Guku ndosara ndoga!"

Parungwanani, mashambanzou,
Unorinzwa richingunoimba:
"Guku kutizwa nehama!
Guku ndosara ndoga!"

Navanorinzwa voedzesera
Kuimba kwaro kunopa mutsa:
"Guku mukadzi waJeke!
Guku wakatsva makumbo!

Roti raneta rotapatira
Mumhepo muye munozorodza;
Nechinguvana robhururukira
Pamun'ando uya uri panhyasi.

Usarirove iwe mufudzi,
Navana varo usavatore.
Ukazviita wave mukudzi
Wenhamo yaro yarinochema.

The Turtle-dove

Far from us across our broad field,
Along the reed-pronged river,
Shaded by giant willows,
The turtle-dove built her nest.

    Hunting here and there, stony outcroppings,
  Behind the anthills tufted with grass,
    Resting on poisonous thorny trees
  The dove sang all the day long.

All the farmers paused to listen:
Even the shepherds waited for the notes,
For when it coos, each soul must stop to hear—
His thoughts darkened with the doleful refrain.

    Sun up or sun down it sings!
  Bright day or shadowed evening!
  "Coo! to be deserted by one's kin!
  Coo! I'm left so alone!"

So early, before dawn,
Its doleful plaintive coo you can hear—
"Coo! to be deserted by one's kin!
Coo! I'm left all alone!"

    Even those who hear it imitate
  Its piteous melody, coo-coo!
  "Coo! Oh, the wife of you-know-who!
  Coo! She has burnt her legs!"

When it is tired the dove flutters up,
Brushing the grey sky with its wings—
To circle soon towards its nest
In the thicket close by.

    So, please, shepherd boy, try not to kill it,
  Or steal its downy fledgelings!
  For, if you do, you can but deepen
  All the sorrows its nature must coo!

THE HIGH PLACE OF CATTLE

BY DINTWENG KOUSU

Ndevo Yen'ombe Luvizho

Buu! Shava hulu kaNkwatalala;
Tendevuka tilinge kanyi, n'ombe yatate;
Kumakumbo konga kwebuka lidwa munyika,
Kunsholo konga kweshumbalume.
Inolila, iti: Mbuu!
Ngono vaKalanga vakaitutha, veti:
Thukutidza zvimilo, hukutu zeve nenyanga;
Ikata mbumba unagasva;
Thukutidza nzi, nthudze ukadzila n'umba.

Gwendo gwedu tiyenda Xauta;
Tikayenda tili vashayi,
Tikavuya tili majaxa anotakula n'ombe.
Chilume chafila n'ombe chonofila vanandogwana.

Ndiyo ishango; ndiyo gavi likapomba nyika;
Ndiyo mazvalile;
Ndiyo gomo, ndiyo tanda chinoleyela thema;
Ndiyo dengu lovunila huzvi;
Ndiyo vachibikebike, ndiyo gavo lenyuchi;
Ndiyo gomba lemonga, ndiyo datho lalu;
Ndiyo shuvo lenzi, ndiyo vanyanchava;
Ndiyo zvikomo zvinji;
Eyi yakatiambudza gwizi gulizhele;
Ikamwa nkaka, udugwa mushupa, kunuvugwa mafuta
Anozhogwa ngevalongo nevazvele nengawana;
Nkaka mmwe mwiwa ngevana, mmwe udigwa mumakukhwa,
Uvombekwa, ukavanga zvodyiwa zvimwe nezvimwe
Zvakafanilana nawo seshadza kene thopi,
Kudya valumetate nevakadzi, vomayi nevana.

Nyika yakavakwa ngen'ombe; inolila, iti:
Mbuu!

The High Place of Cattle[1]

Buu, Big brown one of N'k-wa-ta-la-la,
Turn round that we can move homewards, ox of my father.
The leg part is like that of a great, wild animal
                    coming out of the country;
And the head part is like that of a lion.

It cries out, saying: Mbuu!
Then the Kalanga people[2] praise it, saying: Just listen to it!
See, the glistening nose, the hard horns and erect ears,
It leaps up and away on stiff legs,
This beast gladdens the village, for even its dung,
                spread in the houses—
                hardens like stone—
                polished, it glistens warmly.

And we, the young Rozvi, go our journey to Johannesburg,
Going as poor men, and there we save our pennies and shillings,
Coming back as happy ones, driving our purchased cattle,
Each of us, a tough man who has worked hard for his beasts,
Now we can work harder yet for those with breasts,
                for now we can pay
                the roora love token[3]
                (start up our families).

Yes the cow is in the middle of everything; it is the belt
                of bark which encircles all,
The bovine fertile producer which is
The hill, the refuge, the thick trunk that blocks the rhino,
The reaping basket for *mhunga*,[4] the *mapfunde*.[5] Oh, oh, she is
The clever wife who can cook anything; oh, the cow is a swarm of
                honeybees;
The earth-hive of the honey-flies, the bridging walk-way.

This beast is the home's passion; the mother of all tribes;
She is the mothering, protecting range of mountains.
For, has not this bawler helped us ford the rivers in flood?
Have we not milked her, the white richness pouring into the calabash,
                soon turned into butter?
The spreading delight smeared on themselves by the young brides,
                and the nursing mothers their infants?
Some milk is drunk by children, some poured into bags—
Stored to thicken, and then we mix foods of one kind and another
That go with it, like mealie porridge, or melon pudding,
To be gobbled by men and women, and new mothers and their babes.

Oh, the whole country depends on this cow, lowing, calling:
                Mbuu!

1. Originally collected by Dintweng Kousu at Francistown, Botswana, in the late 1940's and edited by Professor George Fortune, the above, slightly altered translation-mutation by Mutswairo and Herdeck is intended to clarify certain passages of the original. Fortune's title, "An Account of the Livestock Proper," has also been replaced by one hopefully more indicative of the sentiments of the poet and of his people concerning cattle.
2. An offshoot of the Rozvi group of the Shona (Zimbabwen) people.
3. The bride love-token negotiated by the families concerned.
4. *Mhunga,* bulrush millet.
5. *Mapfunde,* grain, or head of sorghum.

THE TALE WITHOUT A HEAD

BY HERBERT CHITEPO

Soko Risina Musoro

I

CHINYAMATIMBI!
Chinyamatimbi musha une mbiri,
Musha wakanaka kupinda yose,
Une upfumi mumatura
Nesimba mumaoko evanhu.
Chinyamatimbi musha unokosha,
Musha usingakanganwiki.

Chirimo chakasvika noupenyu utsva,
Chichinongedza mberi kuzvishamiso
Zvinotevera nokuuya kwezhizha.

Mukadzi akatura svinga rokugumisira
Akamira achitarisa bakwa rake rehuni,
Akanyemwerera akati,
"Tinozotenda dzapfuudza zhizha,
Zvakanzi, 'Tendai maruva madya hacha.' "

Ndaigara pasi mumumvuri padare
Ndichiteerera ungwaru hwevakuru
Vaiswera vachivhutira mvuto,
Kugadzira miseve nematemo,
Kuveza tsvimbo nemipinyi.

Ndakateerera vakuru vachitonga mhosva,
Vachiranga vaparadzi vepasi nemisha.
Mukuru mushava aive nemhanza,
Samusha mutema ane ndebvu chena,
NaVachinzara vaive noungwaru hunoshamisa,
Vane maziso anoona nezviri mumwoyo womunhu.

Ndaiswerosika nyimo kujana
Ndikadyisa chibahwe chaMai Munyara
Ndikanyimwa kudya manheru
Ndikatizira kuna ambuya,
Vakandigashira kunge ndisina kutadza.

Makomba ose nemipata yemakomo,
Zvose ndaizivana nazvo kunge shamwari.
Ndaiziva miti yose yomudondo,
Ndaiziva michero yose yomusango
Patsika tsuro nepafamba nhoro,
Ndaizviziva seshamwari yazvo.

The Tale Without a Head

I

Chinyamatimbi!
Chinyamatimbi is a village of renown,
a village fairer than all (others),
it has riches in its granaries
and strength in the arms of its people.
Chinyamatimbi is a village held dear,
a village not to be forgotten.

Spring arrived with new life,
pointing onward to the wonders
which follow with the coming of summer.

The woman set down the last bundle of faggots
and stood gazing at her shelf of firewood, and smiled and said,
"We shall give thanks when summer has passed, for
it has been said, 'Believe the flowers when you have eaten the shakata
    fruit.' "

I used to sit on the ground in the shade in the court,
listening to the wisdom of the elders
who spent their time blowing the bellows,
to make arrows and axes,
to carve kerries and hoehandles.

I listened to the elders passing judgement on cases,
punishing the destroyers of earth and the homesteads.
The brown-faced elder was bald,
the village headman dark-skinned with a white beard,
and SaChin'ara had wondrous wisdom,
with eyes that see even what is in the heart of a man.

During my turn at herding I spent my time spinning peas
and let (the cattle) eat the mealies of Mai Munyara,
and in the evening I was refused food and ran to the grandmother,
and she received me as if I had done no wrong.

All the gullies and passes of the mountains,
I knew them all as friends.
I knew all the trees of the forest,
I knew all the fruits of the veld.
The path of the hare and the track of the kudu,
I knew them as my friends.

Gomo rokwaMubvuwiri
Rine makuva pamusoro paro,
Gomo reNgwena rine ninga parutivi,
Zvose ndaizviziva nokuti ndakabva mazviri.

Ndakaona maganzvo achibikwa,
Hari dzedoro dzichikwidzwa gomo,
Mvura ikanaya. Mwari wepasi
Akabudisa upenyu hwembesa.

Ndakaona mudzimai akamira mudoró,
Akakunya marokwe achidyara tsenza.
Maoko ake akanga azere matope
Asi aiziva kuti muvhu raaibata
Aibatana naNyadenga mubasa
Rokukudza mbesa dzinopa upenyu.

Imba yaMai Mugari, mukadzi mukuru
Wepaguta reChinyamatimbi,
Yaive imba yorufaro rukuru kwazvo.
Vapwere tose taiungana imomo,
Tichiimba ngano nokutamba zvipari,
Manhanga achinokuibva pachoto,
Isu tichinyenama kudya nyimo.

Mukaranga aive nevhudzi jena,
Achisimira rokwe dema.
Aive mukadzi mukobvu
Aine mwoyo usingazivi kunyima.

Vaeni vose vakasvika paguta
Vakachengetwa sevana vomusha.
MuSena akange arasa nzira yake
Akapiwa pokurara asina kukumbira.
Murungu akanga achinokuvhima
Akawaririrwa akapiwa bonde.

Uyu mukadzi aive chishamiso,
Mwoyo wake wakanga uzere mutsa,
Zvakafanira mwoyo wavahosi,
Mureri wemhuri yaNyadenga,
Mugoni wepasi pasina magumo.

The Mount of Mubvuwiri
with graves on its summit,
the Hill of the Crocodile with caves in its side,
I knew them all, for I came from within them.

I saw the rain-sacrifices brewed,
the pots of beer carried up the mountain,
and the rain fell. The God of the earth brought forth the life of the
    crops.

I saw the woman standing in the river-side garden,
her skirts tucked up, sowing the African potatoes.
Her hands were filled with mud,
but she knew that in the earth she held
she was joining with the Heavenly One in the task of raising the crops
    which give life.

The house of Mai Mugari, the chief wife
of the stronghold of Chinyamatimbi, was a house of great joy.
All we children used to gather there,
singing stories and playing riddles,
while the pumpkins cooked on the hearth
and we ate our peas with smiles.

The youngest wife had white hair
and wore a black dress.
She was a thick-set woman
with a heart that knew no meanness.

All strangers who came to the stronghold
were treated as children of the home.
The Sena who had lost his way
was given a place to sleep without asking.
The European out hunting
had a mat brought out and given to him.

This woman was a wonderful person,
her heart was full of kindness,
as befits the heart of the Queen,
the nurse of the family of the Heavenly One,
lord of the boundless earth.

Murume wake, ishe Matimbi,
Wakanga ari murume mukobvu,
Mushava ane masopo,
Pamusoro akanga aine mhanza
Yainge guyo renjera.
Aifamba nembwa dzake nhatu,
Chekufa—kufira muumambo,
Hwandida—kundidira urombo,
Kutu—kukutura manyepo.

II

Kwakanga kwakaoma kunze,
Zuva riri kubanda kunge moto.
Ndakamira pagomo rokwamambo
Ndikatarisa makwara ose
Anopinda muguta ramambo.
Pakati penzira varume vaviri
Vakasangana.

Gotsi. Masanga changamire masanga!
Mufambi. Masanga changamire,
Dzenyama yedu chirombowe!
Gotsi. Dzenyama yedu, mhuka huru,
Kana masiya ichivira uko kwamabva.
Mufambi. Aiwa, ichiri kuvira kana vachibuda kuno.
Gotsi. Munhu ndiani izvi zvandinenge ndinomuziva;
Mufambi. Ini here? Aiwa. Ndiri mufambi chete,
Musha wangu makwara nemakomo,
Hama dzangu imhuka dzousiku
Neshiri dzinochema mambakwedza.
Gotsi. Ko mabvepi?
Mufambi. Ini here? Aiwa. Handina kwandinobva,
Nokuti handina kwandinoenda.
Ndiri mufambi asina musha,
Ndizvo pasi pose ndiwo musha wangu.
Saka ndichiti handina kwandinoenda,
Handina kwandinobva, changamire, ndiri mufambi.
Ko imi, ndimi ani?
Ava vose vanotungamidzana,
Vanoendepiko? Ngoma iri kuchema, iri kuchemei?
Gotsi. Ndezvedi uri mufambi kana usingazivi.
Ini ndiri muchinda wamambo mutongi—
Kwete, nganditi ndaive muchinda,
Muchinda wamambo anotonga vanhu.
Vangu vanhu vasara mweya chete.
Uyu mudungwe mudungwe wavanhu
Vaive vanhu vangu kare.
Zvino vanoenda dzimbahwe ngoma.

238

Her husband, Chief Matimbi,
was a stout man
with light skin and a moustache.
He had a bald patch on his head like a grindstone for millet.
He used to go about with his three dogs,
Chekufa—to die in the kingship,
Hwandida—to love me for poverty,
Kutu—to overturn falsehoods.

II

Outside it was dry,
the sun burnt like fire.
I stood on the Hill of the King
and gazed at all the roads
leading to the royal court.
In the midst of the way two men
met together.

Councillor. Well met, sir, well met!
Wanderer. Well met, sir, *dzenyama yedu chirombowe!*
Councillor. Dzenyama yedu, great animal, if you have left it brewing
    whence you have come.
Wanderer. Yes, it is still brewing, if they come forth at your home.
Councillor. Who is the man, since I seem to know him?
Wanderer. I? No. I am but a wanderer, my home is the roads and
    mountains, my kindred the beasts of the night and the birds that
    cry in the dawning.
Councillor. Then whence have you come?
Wanderer. I? No. I come from nowhere,
    for I go nowhere.
    I am a homeless wanderer,
    therefore is all the earth my home.
    That is why I say I go nowhere,
    I come from nowhere, sir; I am a wanderer.
    And you, who are you?
    All these who walk in file,
    whither do they go? The drum which is crying, for what is it crying?
Councillor. Indeed you are a stranger if you do not know.
    I am a son of the King, the ruler—
    rather let me say I was a prince,
    son of the King who rules over the people.
    All that remains of my people is their spirit.
    This procession is one of people who were once my people.
    Now they go to the place of sacrifice, where the drum resounds.

Mufambi. Kuneiko?
Gotsi. Hapana chiriko nhasi, kare zvose zvaiveko.
Nokuti ndiko kwaisangana denga nepasi.
Makore ose taiungana ikoko,
Isu zvisikwa zvepasi naivo vakuru
Vakatungamira kuyambuka rwizi rwepakati
Runotsaura musiki nezvisikwa zvake.
Mufambi. Maiungana kundodini ikoko?
Gotsi. Mambo ndiye mugoni wepasi,
Ndiye anotaura mutauro mumwecheteyo
NaChaminuka nehanzvadzi yake, Nehanda.
Asi zvino maganzvo akabikwa kaviri nekatatu,
Pasi pari gwenga, denga rikachena.
Mufambi. Zvakanaka, muchinda,
Endai kwamunoenda.
Makakomborerwa imi
Nokuti munofamba rwendo,
Munoringisa mberi
Nokuti mune mhanza.
Kunesu vamwe zvakapfuura,
Tinofamba asi hatifambi rwendo,
Nokuti tiri vanhu vomurima.
Endai kwamunoenda, imi makakomborerwa,
Endai kwamunoenda, imi mune mhanza.
Gotsi. Kana uchitsvaka kwokuenda,
Uya nesu. Kwatinoenda
Hatina sadza rokukupa, kwete,
Pfuma yedu mutsa norudo chete.
Mufambi. Tungamirai mberi, changamire,
Mwoyo unotenda chirango.
Mazviita, mandidaidzawo.
Gotsi. Zvakanaka, mhuka huru,
Hakuna chokutenda.

Wanderer. What is there?
Councillor. I know not what is there today,
   in ancient days all things were there.
   For there it was that heaven and earth were wont to meet.
   Every year we used to gather there,
   we the creatures of earth and they, the elders
   who led the way over the river in between,
   which divides the creator from his creatures.
Wanderer. To what end did you assemble there?
Councillor. The King it is who is lord of the earth,
   he it is who speaks in the same tongue
   as Chaminuka and his sister, Nehanda.
   But now the rain-offerings have been brewed twice and thrice,
   while the earth is yet a desert and the sky still bare.
Wanderer. It is well, prince,
   go whither you go.
   You are fortunate,
   for you go on a journey,
   you look forward
   because you have hope.
   For us others it has passed;
   we travel but we go on no journey,
   for we are the people of darkness.
   Go on prince, you are fortunate,
   go whither you go, you who have hope.
Councillor. If you seek a place to go,
   come with us.
   Where we go we have no *sadza* to give you,
   our wealth is kindness and love alone.
Wanderer. Lead on, sir,
   my heart gives thanks for your counsel.
   You have done well, you have invited me also.
Councillor. It is well, great animal,
   there is no need for thanks.

(Gotsi rakapfuura rikaenda.)

Mufambi. Vakakomborerwa vane mhanza,
Nokuti vane kwokuenda,
Vakakomborerwa vane kwokuenda,
Nokuti vanowana simba.
Nhasi ndaonerera,
Ndaona chishamiso,
Ndaona mapfupa anofamba
Asina marunda nenyama.
Tamba hako ngoma yako murombo,
Vakuru vakakunyepera
Vakati,'Upenyu hune mutungamiri.'
Famba hako nedondo,
Iwe une musha uri kwese kwese,
Iwe usingatsvaki magumo erwendo.
Ko iwe unondisekerera uchabveko,
Ndiwe ani unofamba uchiseka,
Vamwe vose vari kusuwa?
Kwaziwa, muchinda, kwaziwa, munoendepi?
Nhawatawa. Hungu, masanga, sekuru,
Masanga, mhuka huru!
Mandibvunza zita rangu here?
E-hungu, mandibvunza.
Machemera kuziva kwandinoenda.
E-hungu, sekuru, mapisira!
Zvino chitangai kududza zvenyu.
Mufambi. Chaunoreva chiiko, muzukuru?
Unoda kududzirwa chiiko?
Ndapisira chiiko? Papi?
Nhawatawa. E-hungu, sekuru, mapisira.
Makambotamba zvipari here, sekuru?
Mufambi. E-hungu.
Nhawatawa. Heeedya! Kuseka kwavamai
Vari kupepetera varume pfende.
Zarurai nzeve, vasekuru,
Vakuru vakati, 'Munhu haabvunzi
Zvipari zviviri.' Mandibvunza zita,
Asi mandibvunzazve kwandinoenda.
Mapisira, zvino chidudzai zvenyu.
Mufambi. Ndidudzire chiiko?

242

(The Councillor passed on and departed.)

Wanderer. Fortunate are they who have hope,
    for they have a goal.
    Fortunate are they who have a goal,
    for they shall find strength.
    Today I looked about,
    I saw a wondrous thing,
    I saw bones which walk
    without sinews and flesh.
    Play on your drum, poor man,
    the elders lied to you who said,
    'Life has a pilot.'
    Make your way over the veld,
    you whose home is everywhere,
    you who seek no end to your journey.
    And you, who laugh at me while yet approaching,
    who are you who travel laughing,
    while others are mourning?
    Be greeted, prince, be greeted, whither do you go?
Rogue. Yes, well met, grandfather,
    well met, great animal!
    Did you ask me my name?
    Yes you did so.
    You were anxious to know whither I go.
    Yes grandfather, you have broken the rule!
    Now you first explain yourself.
Wanderer. What is it you say, grandson?
    What do you want explained to you?
    In what have I offended against the rule? Where?
Rogue. Yes, grandfather, you have so offended.
    Have you ever played riddles, grandfather?
Wanderer. Yes.
Rogue. He-he-he! The laughter of women
    sifting grass for the men.
    Open your ears, ancestors,
    the elders have said, 'No one may ask two riddles.'
    You asked me my name
    but you also asked me my destination.
    You have broken the rule, now explain yourself.
Wanderer. What should I explain?

Nhawatawa. Zita ramunozivikanwa naro,
Nokwamunoenda nembira dzenyu.
Mufambi. Zita handina.
Ndinoenda kwese kwese.
Nhawatawa. Munoda zvokungwarira nhai?
Zvakanaka, sekuru,
Masangana newezera renyu.
Mbira dzenyu dzinotamba here, sekuru?
Mufambi. Hungu, kazukuru.
Mhawatawa. Dombondiridziraiwozve, sekuru.
Mufambi. Terera:—
Tibvesu, tine upandure,
Vanosara vachidya uparire.
Tifambe tiende mberiko,
Kunogara vakabva Chitungwiza.
Nhawatawa. Sekuru, hamukwanisiki woye.
Muri rombe here, sekuru,
Kana kuti muri kutiza botso?
Mufambi. Aiwa, ndiri mufambi chete.
Ko iwe, hauendewo here kuri kuenda vamwe?
Nhawatawa. Ini! Kuenda kundozviviga kuita sei?
Urombo ndinahwo asi handizvichereri guva, kwete.
Havasi vanhu vari kuenda uko,
Mapfupa asina nyama,
Handidi kunhuhwa kwehari yakabikirwa nyama
Gore rakapera.
Mufambi. Ndianiko waunoenzanisa nehari
Yakabikirwa nyama gore rakapera?
Nhawatawa. Midzimuyi iri kupfuura pano?
Nhumbu dzavo hadzizivi sadza.
Asi ndava kuenda, sekuru,
Ndabva kwavari kuenda.
Mufambi. Zvakanaka, muzukuru,
Famba uende kwaunoenda.
Une mwoyo noungwaru,
Unoseka uchitakura
Mutoro wako uchienda.
Neniwo ndinotakura mutoro wangu,
Ndakasvipa mwoyo ndichienda kwandinoenda,
Ndiko kumira kwazvakaita.

III

Nyika yavo izere hosha nemhare,
Chaminuka haachisina makumbo,
Upfumi hwepasi hwarovera mudumbu,
Nehanda naye waramba kuyamwisa vana vake.

244

Rogue. The name by which you are known,
and where you go and your piano.
Wanderer. Name I have none.
I go everywhere.
Rogue. So you like being clever, do you?
Very well, grandfather,
you have met your match.
Does your piano play, grandfather?
Wanderer. Yes, little grandson.
Rogue. Then please play for me, too, grandfather.
Wanderer. Listen:
Let us go hence, we who cause dissension,
They who remain will then live in harmony.
Let us travel, let us go onward
To where dwell those who came from Chitungwiza.
Rogue. Hey, grandfather, you are good indeed!
Are you a travelling minstrel, grandfather,
or fleeing from an angry spirit?
Wanderer. No, I am only a wanderer.
And you, do you not go where the others are going?
Rogue. I! What does it profit to go and bury oneself?
I am poor, but I do not dig myself a grave.
They are not men who are going thither,
they are fleshless bones,
bodiless spirits.
I like not the smell of the pot
where meat was cooked last year.
Wanderer. Whom do you liken to a pot
where meat was cooked last year?
Rogue. These spectres who are passing by,
their bellies know no *sadza*.
But now I am going, grandfather,
I have come from the place where they are going.
Wanderer. Very well grandson,
go on to your destination.
You are courageous and wise,
you laugh, carrying your burden
as you go.
And I, too, carry my burden,
I have become sick at heart going whither I go,
that is how things stand.

III

Their land is filled with sickness and dry weather,
Chaminuka has feet no longer,
the wealth of the earth has vanished into its belly
and even Nehanda has refused to suckle her children.

Mazuva mana ngoma yakarira paguta ramambo;
Ndakamira pamusoro pegomo rokwamambo
Ndikaringisa midungwe yavanhu vaiungana muguta ramambo.
Magwanza ose akanga azere vanhu vaibva kwese kunobva mhepo
dzinopinda muguta ramambo.

Hakuna aitaura nomumwe, kwete. Kana nemwana
akange ari pamusana haasakachema. Chinyararire,
murume wakatungamidza mukadzi wake nemhuri,
vose, mwii, kunyarara kunge vari kuenda kundochema vakafa.

Ndakatarisa makwara ose ndigere padombo pagomo
rokwamambo. Zuva rakakwira, mimvuri ikapfupika,
asi midungwe yavanhu haina kupfupika, kwete.
Kubvira mangwanani, zuva richabuda, kudakara manheru,
zuva rodoka, makwara akaswera akazara nevanhu
vaienda kuguta ramambo.

Ngoma yakachema ikadairwa nedzimwe kutumidzira
mashoko echido chamambo kune vari seri kwemakomo.

Makotsi nemakurukota amambo
Akaungana paguta ramambo
Kundobatsirana kusimudza nyika
Mutsika yevakuru vakati,
'Runzwara rumwe harutswanyi inda.'

Munwe nomumwe akasvika achiombera
Somuitiro werudzi rwake.

'Mhanda midzi mambo,
Mhanda midzi.'

'Uchafa unonyepa,
Unonyepa uchafa.'

'Kwenje uri shumba.
Kwenje uri shumba.'

Makotsi nemakurukota amambo
Akaungana paguta ramambo.
Mhuri yose yakaungana pana mambo.

Four days long the drum cried at the court of the King;
I stood on the top of the Hill of the King
and gazed at the lines of men gathering at the court of the King.
All the roads were crowded with men from all quarters
whence come the winds which enter into the court of the King.

None spoke to another.
Even the child on his mother's back did not cry.
In silence, a man led his wife and household,
all deathly hushed,
as those who are going to mourn the departed.

I watched all the roads, seated on a rock on the Hill of the King.
The sun rose higher, the shadows lessened,
but the lines of men did not grow less.
From morning at sunrise till evening at sunset
the roads continued crowded with men
going to the court of the King.

The mournful drum cried and was answered by others,
sending the news of the King's will to those who are beyond the hills.

The councillors and ministers of the King
gathered at the court of the King,
to help each other to raise up the country
in the way of the elders who said,
'One finger-nail does not crush the louse.'

Each one arrived, clapping in greeting
according to the custom of his clan.

'Divider of roots, O King,
divider of roots.'

'You shall die, you lie,
you lie, you shall die.'

'*Kwenje*, you are the Lion,
Kwenje, you are the Lion.'

The councillors and ministers of the King
gathered at the court of the King.
Every household gathered where the King was.

Zuva rose ngoma yakaswera ichichema,
Vanhu vakatamba kutamba kusina rufaro.
Mambo akaswedza zuva ari mumba,
Haana kumbobuda kana kwenguva shoma zvayo.
Asi vahosi, mukadzi mukuru wamambo,
Ndivo vakabuda vakapembera nesimba,
Simba rinoshamisa izvo risakabva mukudya.
Churu mukuru wakaswera agere padare,
Achiridza ngoma kudaidzira vanhu vose
Kuti, 'Unganai imi mose vaManyika,
Zuva riya razosvika, zuva rokugumisira,
Nokuti Nyatene akafanira kutinzwa nhasi,
Kana achizotinzwa kana narinhi muneyi nhamo.'

Varume vazhinji vakanga vakapfeka
Machira nematehwe machena nematema,
Vakatamba vakaimba vakanamata.

Zuva rakanga rava kupota,
Vanhu vose vakanga vaneta,
Mazwi akanga ava kuenda.
Mambo akabuda kubva mumba,
Chima ichichema, ngoma ichirira,
Iye achizvitungamidza nomudonzvo.

Muponda. Imi vanhu vomuguta,
   Nemi vose vafambi, tarisai,
   Uyu ari kufamba pano
   Ndiye mubvakure wakare,
   Ndiye wakapa muteuro akaponisa vasekuru vedu.
   Takamuona achisvika

   Kubva mhiri kwaZambezi,
   Tikamuziva kuti akanga
   Ari murume ane simba,
   Ane rudo kune vanhu vose.

   Zvino, chiringisai, wakotama,
   Musoro wake wawira pasi,
   Mapfupa emuviri wake akotama,
   Simba raive mumaoko ake rapera,
   Ungwaru nokutonga kwake
   Zvasara mumwoyo chete, zvaguma.

Muchirahondo. Zuva roumambo rave kudoka,
   Mhepo iri kuvhuvhuta
   Iri kudaidza shoko rokufa.
   Nzwizi dzaoma, dzasara madziva chete
   Azere mitumbi yavakafa.

All day long the drum continued to cry
and the people danced a dance without joy.
The King spent the day in his house,
he did not come out even for a little while.
But the Queen, the chief wife of the King,
she it was who came forth and danced with might,
a strange might since it came not from food.
Churu, the elder, spent the day seated in the court,
beating the drum to summon all the people, saying
"Gather together, all you Manyika,
that day has come at last, the day of ending,
for Nyatene must hear us today,
If ever he will hear us in this distress."

Many of the men were wearing cloths
and skins of black and white,
they danced, they sang and they prayed.

Now the sun was setting
and all the people were tired,
their voices were going.
The King came forth from his house
while the mournful drum-beat cried and re-echoed,
and he supported himself on his staff.

Muponda. O you people of the court,
    and all you strangers, behold,
    he who is walking here
    is the Comer-from-afar of old;
    he it was who offered the sacrifice which saved our forefathers.

    We saw him coming from across the Zambezi,
    and knew him
    for a man of might,
    with love towards all men.

    Now, see, he is bent,
    the strength which was in his arms has vanished,
    his wisdom and authority
    stay in the heart alone, otherwise
    they are gone.

Muchirahondo. The sun of the kingship is setting,
    the rising wind is screaming
    a tale of death. The rivers have dried up,
    leaving only pools filled with corpses of the dead.

Aripiko magamba akare?
Aripiko Nehanda naChaminuka?
Iripiko midzimu yokwedu?
Kugurukuta kwedu neminamato
Zvatadza here kusvika kwamuri?
Guta redu rine kuparadzika kusina kuverenga,
Vana vari mumaoko avamai, ruponiso ruri kure,
Vamwe varere nenhivi mumakuva
Asina kuchenurwa nemisodzi.

Marombe, imbai muchiridza tsuri,
Imi vatambi vane utsanzi, tambai,
Vachiremba mose, unganai nemishonga,
Pasi parwara, panoda murapi
Anogona kutiudza zviri mberi.

Ridzai mhururu, vamai,
Kwidzai manja, vadzibaba,
Imi madzishe, ridzai chima,
Pfekai maretso muridze njari,
Vanhu mose, nyararai,
Inzwai zviri kurehwa nemhepo

Ngoma yakaridzwa,
Vanhu vakaterera kuimba
KwaChuru, murume mushava,
Ane vudzi jena.

'Mirandu kana yawanda pamunhu,
Munoona nehama dzomupe gotsi.
Nzanga dzangu dziripi, ndiende?
Turi pano tunozondiwandira.
Vakomana, musazoitewoba,
Kutura midziyo muna Nyan'ombe.'

Where are the heroes of old?
Where is Chaminuka and Nehanda?
Where are our tribal spirits?
Our complaining and our prayers,
have they failed to come where you are?
Our citadel has (been struck by) numberless afflictions,
the children in their mothers' arms, their relief is afar.
Some sleep on their sides in graves uncleansed by tears.

Minstrels, sing and play on the flute,
dance, you skilful dancers,
gather with medicines, you physicians,
the earth is sick, she needs a healer
who can tell us what is to come.

Wail, matrons,
clap your hands; fathers,
beat out a mournful tattoo;
you chieftains, put on your robes of state
and play your pianos;
be silent, all you people,
listen to what the wind is saying.

The drum was beaten
and the people listened to the singing of Churu,
the brown-skinned man with white hair.

   "When vices multiply upon a man,
you see even his kindred turn aside.
Where are my emblems of manhood? Let me go,
these present (troubles) will overwhelm me.
Boys, never do (as I did),
set down your goods in the river Nyan'ombe."

Churu. Imi vanhu vokuguta,
   Nemi mose mabvakure,
   Tarisai muchiterera;
   Uyu amire pano
   Ndiye Chifambausiku wamunoziva,
   Ndiye akatitungamidza pano
   Akatipa chikomborero chenyika.
   Takamuziva tichiri mhiriyo
   Kuti ane mwoyo weshumba.
   Vanhu vose vakamuona
   Vakashamiswa kwazvo kumuona,
   Vakatendeuka kumunangisa
   Kaviri, katatu nekana.
   Vanhu vose vakamutya,
   Vakaverenga zvikomborero zvake.
   Vakaziva kuti kana Mwari
   Akanga amusarudza.

   Asi zvino chionai, akotama,
   Chiremba chomumusoro
   Hachisisina ndarama.
   Chigaro chokutonga
   Chogoverwa nevamwe.
   Mbiri yesimba rake
   Yadzama kunge madora.
   Chasara mumvuri
   Woukuru norunako
   Zvakapfuura nenguva.

   Aripiko Chaminuka akaurayiwa noruoko rwomwana,
   Akakonera mapfumo emagamba aRubengura?
   Aripiko Chaminuka akatiudza zvinhu zvichauya,
   Akaenda nezvikomborero zvake?
   Aripiko Chaminuka?
   Aripiko Mwari musiki?
   Mvura yaoma munzwizi,
   Minda yachena kunge makwenga,
   Kana nemichero mudondo
   Zvofira mudumbu repasi.

   Tiringise kumadokero kwezuva,
   Tiringise uko kwarinobudira;
   Zuva redu kupota,
   Kubuda here, kudini?

Churu. O you people of the citadel,
  and all you who have come from afar,
  behold and listen.
He who stands here
is the Nightwalker whom you know,
he it was who led us here
and gave us the blessing of a country.
We knew him while we were yet across (the Zambezi),
that he had the heart of a lion.
All men who saw him
were astonished to see him,
they turned to look upon him
twice, thrice, and yet a fourth time.
All men feared him
and numbered his blessings.
They knew that even God
had made choice of him.

  But now, see, he is bowed,
the Crown on his head
is golden no longer.
The seat of his justice
is divided among others.
The glory of his might
has tumbled down like maggots.
There remains but the shadow
of his greatness and beauty
which have passed away with time.

Where is Chaminuka, slain by the hand of a child,
who vanquished the spears of Lobengula's warriors?[1]
Where is Chaminuka, who told us the things that were to come
and then departed with his blessings?
Where is Chaminuka?
Where is God the creator?
The water has dried up in the rivers,
the fields are bare as deserts,
even the wild fruits
die in the belly of the earth.

Let us look to the place of the sun's setting,
let us look to where it rises;
our sun, is it setting or rising,
or what is happening?

Gotsi rokutanga. Nyarara kutaura, iwe mwana wenyika.
Zvakasikwa zvikarongwa nowedenga.
Isu tose tiri mapofu,
Tinoona asi hationiba.
Isu tiri zvimumumu,
Tine ndimi, asi hatina
Mutauro.
Tiri mhatsi,
Tine nzeve, asi hatinzwi.
Mambo. Madaidza ini, ndini ndauya;
Kuchine nyaya here, nyaya inotongwa neni,
Ini Mambo Mutasa?
Churu. Musi watakakugadza umambo, Mutasa,
Paguta rako rino, mugore rakafa baba wako,
Tendai ane zita rinokosha mumwoyo yedu,
Musi watakakukwidza pachigaro, Mutasa,
Kuti utonge isu nokuchengeta nyika,
Wakatukwa, Mambo, wakatukwa, Mutasa.

'Usauraye mhuri yaNyadenga,
Vadye vachiguta vanhu vose.
Nzara ikauya munyika ino,
Tinokutema.
Uzive kuti tinoda mvura,
Uchiita rudo kune makotsi ako ese,
Usaite guhwa kune vanhu,
Upfuye varombo,
Kana ndiani naani,
Uite tsitsi kune zvose
Zvinopinda muguta rako rino.

Uri muranda, Mutasa, uri bandadzi raMwari.
Maoko ako akachena here?
Mwoyo wako wakareruka here?
Yatadza seiko minamato yako kukwira denga?
Makore akapfuura pasi paitinhira
Pakatsikwa negumbo raMambo Mutasa;
Mbesa dzepasi dzikabuda kundokuombera
Nokundogutsa mhuri yako.
Izwi romunamato wako rakatakurwa nemhepo
Rikateverwa nemakore emvura.
Aripiko Mwari? Varipiko varanda vake,
Nehanda naChaminuka, vaponisi vepasi?

'Denga rake rakatenderera,
Harina magumo.
Mweya wake unopepeta uchivhuvhuta,
Uchienda kwaunoenda,
Uchibva kwatisingazivi.'

1st Councillor. Silence your talk, you child of the land.
(Things) were created and ordered by the Heavenly One.
We are all blind men,
we see but we see not.
We are dumb,
we have tongues
but no speech.
We are deaf,
we have ears but hear not.
King. You have called me, I have come;
is there yet some case, a case to be judged
by me, King Mutasa?[2]
Churu. The day we placed you in kingship, Mutasa,
in this your citadel, the year your father died,
Tendai with the name precious to our hearts,
the day we raised you to the throne, Mutasa,
to rule over us and care for the land,
you were bound by a curse, O King, bound by a curse, Mutasa.

'Slay not the family of the Heavenly One,
let all men eat and be filled.
Should famine come upon this land,
we will strike off (your head).
Know then that we desire rain,
deal lovingly with all your councillors,
spread no slander about men.
Enrich the poor,
and whosoever it may be,
show mercy to all
who enter into this your citadel.'

You are a servant, Mutasa, you are the bondsman of God.
Are your hands clean?
Is your heart light?
How have your prayers failed to climb the heavens?
In years gone by the earth trembled
when trodden by the foot of King Mutasa,
and the crops of the earth came out to greet you
and to satisfy your family.
The voice of your prayer was carried by the wind
and was followed by rain-clouds.
Where is God? Where are his servants
Nehanda and Chaminuka, the saviors of the world?

'His heaven is round,
it has no limits.
His spirit blows gently, blows strongly,
going whither it goes,
coming whence we know not.'

Gotsi rechipiri. Wataura, iwe muzukuru waMuchirahondo,
Wakarwa hondo dzaMutasa akafa,
Akatiratidza kuti gwara nderipi murima.
Asi rima harina mutungamidzi,
Tinobva murima tichipinda mune rimwe,
Tirimo tinoona, asi hationiba.
Kuno kwatiri kure kwazvo
Kubva pagomo rokwaChin'ai
Pakafira mukono wokwaMuchirahondo.
Mazwi ake nomuenzaniso
Zvakawanirana nenguva yazvo.
Mazuva ano nenguva ino
Hazvina ruenzaniso
Naikoko kwatakabva.
Mambo. Ndiwe ani unotaura kudaro?
Izwi rako ndinenge ndinoriziva,
Asi maziso angu haachina kupenya.
Ndiwe ani unotaura negamba,
Gamba rangu rine mwoyo mukukutu?
Uri mwana womuguta rangu here?
Gotsi rechipiri. Tinokuchingamidza takapfugama,
Iwe davi romuti werudzi rwedu.
Uri Shumba, uri mhanga renyika,
Uri mukono mudanga redu rino.
Ndiwe une simba rokunamata
Kune vari mberi kusina zita.
Tiri vana vako, Mambo,
Tiri michero yenhengo
Dzomuti mukuru, muti weShumba.
Mambo. Taurai ndinzwe,
Mutsanangure nhuna dzemwoyo yenyu.
Vakuru havasakanyepa, kwete,
Vakati, 'Zano mbairi.'
Ini Mambo Mutasa,
Ndinomira nedare.
Gotsi. Mambo, nyika yako yapera,
Vanhu tafa nenzara nenyota.
Simudzazve minamato yako iya
Yakatiponisa mugore raGochainhehwe.
Mambo. Ndini ndakamira pano
Ndichiringisa shure nemberi.
Kwatakabva irima,
Kwatinoenda irima.
Uyai nomwenje, imi vakuru,
Mutitungamidze muneri rima.

256

2nd Councillor. You have spoken, grandson of Muchirahondo, you
    who fought the hosts of Mutasa and died,
    showing us the way into darkness.
    But the darkness has no guide,
    we come out of darkness and go into another,
    while we are there we see but we see not.
    Here where we are is far indeed
    from the Mount of Chin'ai
    where died the bull of Muchirahondo's.
    His words and example
    were sufficient for their time.
    Our day and age
    have no parallel
    with our past.
King. Who are you who speaks thus?
    Your voice I seem to know,
    but my eyes have light no longer.
    Who are you who speaks of my warrior,
    my warrior of the courageous heart?
    Are you a child of my citadel?
2nd Councillor. We greet you on bended knee,
    you the branch of the tree of our tribe.
    You are the Lion, you are the spear of the land,
    you are the bull in this kraal.
    You are the one who has power to pray
    to those who are ahead in the nameless place.
    We are your children, O King,
    we are the fruit of the stem of the great tree,
    the tree of the Lion.
King. Speak and let me hear,
    unburden your hearts of their afflictions.
    The elders did not lie who said,
    'A plan is two.'
    I, Mutasa the King,
    wait in the court.
A Councillor. King, your land is laid waste,
    we the people are dead from hunger and thirst.
    Lift up again those prayers of yours
    which saved us in the year of Gochainhehwe.
King. I stand here,
    looking behind and before.
    Whence we have come is darkness,
    whither we go is darkness.
    Bring light, you elders,
    and guide us in this darkness.

Maungana pano paguta,
Mauya nenyama nedoro here?
Mafambira chii, vamai?
Mafambira chii, madzishe?
Mauya neiko kuzoteudza
Kuna Mambo Mutasa, mugari wepasi?
Gotsi. Mambo, mugari wenyika,
Mbeu itsva yomuti weShumba,
Muti mukobvu unoradzika wakati 'tasa',
Tiri mhuri yaNyatene,
Asi tiri mhuri yako.
Nhasi tauya kunewe,
Asi hatisauya nezvipo.
Zvipo zvinobva muvhu nomudenga—
Denga rachena, ivhu rave kutsemuka.
Zvipo zvako ndiwe ungatipe,
Ndiwe mugashiri nomupi pamwe.
Changamire, mukono wesango,
Tauya, asi tauya takachena.
Mambo. Wareva, iwe muzukuru waZvimbi.
Pasi ndepangu, asi handi pangu, kwete.
Ndepababa wangu, asi kana iye handi pake.
Pasi ndepaMwari, Mwari musiki,
Anogara muvhu, mumhepo nomumvura.
Imi varapi, nemi mose vangwaru machinda,
Simba renyu riripiko panyika?
Ungwaru hwenyu huripiko?
Ini Mutasa ndinotonga,
Asi ndinotonga muungwaru hwemakotsi angu.
Yaivepo nguva kare
Apo ndakagara paichi chigaro,
Ndichitonga nyika yose.
Ndakatonga, asi ndakatonga
Nesimba rinobva kumadzibaba angu,
Simba risina mavambo, randaiti harina magumo.
Takarwa hondo tikakunda,
Tikadzoka kumusha nendarama nepfuma.

Nyararai, vanhu vangu,
Ringisai mudenga,
Muone rudo rwaMwari.
Isai nzeve pasi,
Munzwe mazwi eruvimbo,
Mazwi emutsa waMwari.

You have assembled here at the court,
have you come with meat and with beer?
For what have you travelled, matrons?
For what have you travelled, chieftains?
With what have you come for sacrifice
to King Mutasa, the lord of the earth?

A Councillor. O King, lord of the land,
the new seed of the tree of the Lion,
the stout tree that lies straight and still,
we are the family of Nyatene,
but we are (also) your family.
Today we have come to you,
but we have not come with gifts.
Gifts come from the earth and the heavens—
the heavens are bare and the earth is cracking.
Your gifts, it is you must give us them,
you are the receiver and giver together.
Sire, bull of the veld,
we have come but we have come empty-handed.

King. You have spoken, grandson of Zvimbi.
The earth is mine but it is not mine.
It is my father's, but it is not even his.
The earth is God's—God the creator,
who dwells in the earth, the wind and the rain.
You healers, and all you wise princes,
where is your might in the land?
Where is your wisdom?
I, Mutasa, rule,
but I rule in the wisdom of my councillors.
There was a time, long ago,
when I sat upon this throne
and ruled with the power
which comes from my forefathers,
the power without beginning, which I thought was endless.
We fought battles and were victorious,
and returned home with gold and riches.

Be silent, my people,
look into the sky
and behold the love of God.
Set your ears to the ground
and hear the words of hope,
the words of the mercy of God.

'Hakuna kufa, hakuna upenyu.
Isu zvisikwa tine ukama
Neivhu dzvuku rinokudza mbesa.
Hama dzedu ishiri,
Vakoma vedu imhuka,
Asi mai vedu nababa
Ivhu, miti nemvura.
Mwari chete ndiye vatateguru.
Kufa kuripiko?
Mumvuri womunhu
Mweya waNyakuenda,
Muviri wake noupenyu,
Zvose tinazvo—
Kufa kuripiko?'

Vanhu vakanyarara vakateerera kutaura kwamambo,
Mumwoyo mumwe nomumwe akazvivhunza akazvipindura.

'Wakaendepiko mwoyo wandaiti ndowangu?
Wako wakautorepiko, murombo mugashiri?
Rakaendepiko simba randaiti ndinaro?
Rako nderipiko, iwe unoputswa nemhepo?
Ungwaru huya huripiko hwandaiti isimba?
Chako ndechipiko, mwana mucheche murerwi?
Gwara rangu riripiko randaiti ndapfumbidza?
Une maziso here, iwe nyakuzvinyengedza?'

Mufambi uya akanga avatevera akagara pakati pavo,
Akafunga pfungwa dzakewo pakati pevafambi.

'Terera, mwanangu,
Shamwari yemapofu.
Tose tiri nhengo,
Tiri matavi omuti mumwe,
Muti wezvisikwa zvisina maziso.
Ane maziso ndiNyatene,
Ane simba ndiMwari,
Ane ungwaru ndiwedenga.
Mutongi wemwoyo ndiMwari,
Simba rake riri muna iye,
Sezvo iye achigara kwese kwese.
Usaringise kure, kwete,
Ari pedyo pauri,
Anomirira chete iwe
Kuti uzvipire kuna iye.'

"There is no death, there is no life.
We created beings have kinship
with the red earth which makes the crops to grow.
Our kindred are the birds,
our elder brothers the beasts,
but our father and mother
are the soil, the trees, and the rain.
God alone is the first ancestor.
Where is death?
The shade of a man
is the spirit of the deceased,
his body and his life,
we have them both—
where is death?"

The people were silent and listened to the King's speech,
and each one in his heart questioned and answered himself.

Where has it gone, the courage I thought was mine?
Yours? Where did you get it, poor receiver?
Where has it gone, the strength which I thought I had?
Yours? What is yours, you who are swept away by the wind?
Where is that wisdom I thought was strength?
Yours? What is yours, O child still wanting care?
Where is my path which I thought I had beaten out?
Have you no eyes, you self-deceiver?

The Wanderer, who had followed them, sat among them
and thought his own thoughts among the strangers.

Listen, my child,
friend of the blind.
We are all limbs,
we are branches of the same tree,
the tree of eyeless creatures.
He who has eyes is Nyatene,
he who has power is God,
he who has wisdom is the Heavenly One,
the judge of the heart is God.
His power is within himself,
since he dwells everywhere.
Look not far,
he is near to you,
he waits only for you
to give yourself to him.

Isu ngatiimbe titondere zvipo zvedu.
Nyika yakanaka ine makomo
Anopenya nokun'anikira muuma,
Nzwizi dzinodzika dzichipembera,
Kuenda kwadzakabva,
Minda yakati 'rare' pachirimo kunyarara
Inosvipirira pazhizha nembesa,
Nemasango azere miti mizhinji
Ine mhando zhinji dzemaruva nemashizha.
Ngatipembere, isu takakomborerwa,
Tine miviri ine simba,
Ine mapfupa akagwinya.
Ngatitende Mambo isu,
Timukudze nokuti ndiye—
Ndiye mupi woupenyu
Nomugashiri wezvitendo.

Ndipeiwo nzeve dzenyu, vakuru,
Ini ndiri mufambi pakati penyu,
Ndateerera nyaya dzenyu nenhuna,
Ndikasara ndiri murombo mumwoyo.
Ndinokushorai kuti "pthu" kupfira mate,
Ndichiti, muri zvirema, kukutii zvirema
Kutokukudzai zvakare.

Simudzai maziso mudenga mutarise
Hope yaNyatene iri mumakore.
Munotarisa asi hamuoni chinhu.
Mwoyo iri kudeketera kuda kuziva
Gore rino tinopona here nenzara?
Nhamo ikauya tinoendepi?
Kupi kwamunoziva, mapofu asina maziso?
Chenyu ndechipiko, varombo vasina zvifugo?

Mangwana izuva raNyatene,
Munoriziva masvika kwariri.
Vakuru vakatinyepera
Vakati, "Vanhu vanorayirwa:
Gore harizi pakazarimwe."
Tose tiri vafambi panyika,
Tinotevera gwara idzva
Risina muenzaniso
Unobva shure
Kune vakatanga.

Isu mapofu evafambi,
Mapofu ngatifambe,
Ngatifambe nokuzvirereka
Murima riri mberi kwatinoenda,
Rima riri shure kwatakabva,
Mwari chete ndiye ruvheneko.

Let us sing and be mindful of our gifts.
A fair land with mountains
which shine and shimmer in the haze;
rivers which run down dancing to the place
whence they came,
fields which lie bare and silent in the spring
and are dark with crops in the summer;
and the plains filled with countless trees,
many-coloured with flowers and leaves.
Let us dance, we who are blessed,
we have powerful bodies
with mighty bones.
Let us thank God,
let us praise him,
for He—He is the giver of life
and the receiver of gifts.

Give me your ears, elders,
I am a stranger in your midst.
I have heard your tale and your affliction
and have remained poor at heart.
I despise you, spitting on you, pah!
and I say you are fools, to call you fools
is moreover praise enough for you.

Raise your eyes to the heavens
and look upon the face of Nyatene in the clouds.
You look but you see nothing.
Your hearts are consumed with desire to know
whether we shall survive the famine this year.
If trouble comes, where shall we go?
Where do you know of, blind men without eyes?
What is yours, poor men without clothing?

Tomorrow is Nyatene's day,
you shall know it when you have come where it is.
The elders lied to you who said,
Children can be instructed:
One year does not come whence another came.
We are all wanderers in the land,
we follow a new road
which has no parallel
in the past
for them that go onwards.

We blind wanderers,
as blind men let us walk,
let us walk and be humble
in the darkness which is before us whither we go,
the darkness which is behind whence we have come.
God alone is the light.

1. King of the Matebeles.
2. Mutasa, Paramount Chief of the Manyika group around Umtali.

BIBLIOGRAPHIC NOTES

FESO by S. M. Mutswairo. Cape Town, Oxford University Press, 1957. The first edition of 1957 went into a second impression in 1959 and a second edition in 1963.

MURAMBIWA GOREDEMA by Mutswairo. Cape Town, Oxford University Press, 1959. This work, a modern novel, was written in 1953-54 while the author was a teacher at Goromonzi Secondary School and it first appeared in serial form in *The African Weekly* newspaper, Salisbury, in 1958. Sponsored by the then Southern Rhodesia African Literature Bureau it appeared in book form in 1959.

AMBUYAMUDERERE by Mutswairo. Longmans, Green and Co., Cape Town, 1967. Written at the University of Ottawa, Canada while the author was a graduate student, this small children's book consists of traditional prose-poems which can be sung while playing games. The poems reflect traditional children's verse but are original compositions. The volume, profusely illustrated, was sponsored by the Rhodesia Literature Bureau, Salisbury.

MADETEMBEDZO AKARE NAMATSVA. Cape Town, Green and Co., 1959. This collection of the works of three authors was sponsored and published for the Southern Rhodesia Literature Bureau. It contains both traditional prose-poetry, mainly designed for young people, and contemporary verse influenced by European poetry.

Mutswairo's contributions were the following seven poems: Ruva Rangu Shora, Dzose Shiri Ndedzangu, Mudikanwi Wangu, Makomo Enyota, Guva Raasozi 'kanwa, Nyenyedzi Yedenga, and Dandanda Kujena Guru. All had been composed or reworked at Howard, a Salvation Army Institute in Mazoe District, in 1958 and where the poet was then a teacher.

Wilson Chivaura contributed eight poems to this collection, one of which, "Ruva Rangu Shora," seems to have been greatly influenced by Mutswairo's poem of the same title and otherwise close to it in substance and treatment. Mutswairo's poem, originally composed in 1948, appeared first in the newspaper *The African Weekly* in 1948, in the original Zezuru.

Eleven of the twenty-six works in the anthology were traditional poems collected and edited by Musa Shamuyarira. Many of such oral poems consist of a soloist's part and the choral response. Typical is the pattern illustrated in this song sung during a country dance much like the American barn dance where partners duck and weave in a circle and move toward and away from each other in special dance steps:

Soloist: Poti! Poti!
Chorus: Zinyangarinyanga.
Soloist: Ndinotsvaka wangu.
Chorus: Zinyangarinyanga, etc.

Soloist: In and out! In and out!
Chorus: Grab the horns.
Soloist: I'm looking for my sweetheart.
Chorus: Grab the horns, etc.

SOKO RISINA MUSORO by Herbert W. Chitepo. London, Oxford University Press, 1958, and translated and edited with notes by Hazel Carter. With the permission of Chitepo, Mutswairo has modified the original text in a few places.

BVUKUTIRWA (partly traditional) and RUDO RWEDU PEDYO NERWIZI by Luke Chidavaenzi. Published here both in original and English translation for the first time.

NDEVO YENGOMBE LUVIZHO AND OTHER LILIMA TEXTS (in mimeograph) edited by George Fortune from the writings of Dintweng Kousu done in 1949 at Francistown, Botswana, where Kousu was an interpreter at the Magistrate's Court. S.M. Mutswairo selected various fragments of Kousu's work and organized them into the form they appear in the present volume and he and D. E. Herdeck made a new translation and assigned the new title, "The High Place of Cattle," so as to indicate more clearly the point or sentiment of Kousu's ideas than did Fortune's earlier translation and his title, "An Account of the Livestock Proper." Fortune's edition of Kousu's Lilima text and his English translation and notes (based on the assistance and work of Mutswairo) appeared as

No. 21, New Series, Communications from the School of African Studies, University of Cape Town, July 1949.

For critical analyses see: E. W. Krog's *African Literature in Rhodesia*. Gwelo, Rhodesia, Mambo Press, 1966:

1. Pp. 149-152 and 201-210.
2. Pp. 153-157.
3. Pp. 174-179.
4. Pp. 164-168.

GENEOLOGICAL CHART OF "FESO" KINGS

LINES OF DESCENT OF THE VAHOTA
AND THE VANYAI AS RELATED
IN FESO

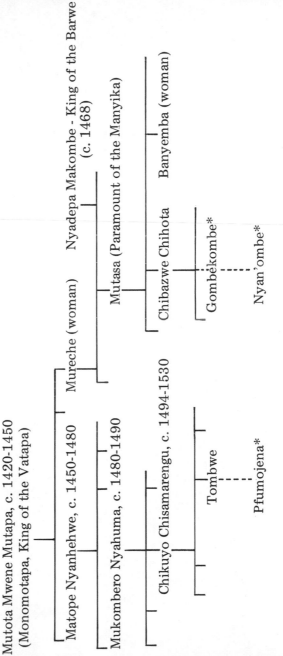

Mutota Mwene Mutapa, c. 1420-1450
(Monomotapa, King of the Vatapa)

Matope Nyanhehwe, c. 1450-1480

Mukombero Nyahuma, c. 1480-1490

Chikuyo Chisamarengu, c. 1494-1530

Tombwe

Pfumojena*

Mureche (woman)

Nyadepa Makombe - King of the Barwe
(c. 1468)

Mutasa (Paramount of the Manyika)

Chibazwe Chihota

Banyemba (woman)

Gombékombe*

Nyan'ombe*

*Fictitious

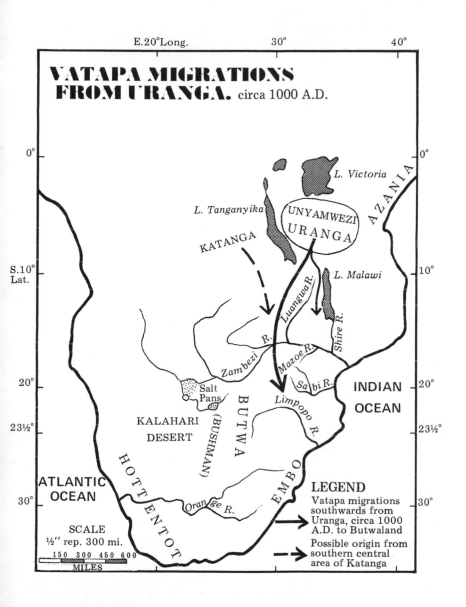

VATAPA MIGRATIONS FROM URANGA. circa 1000 A.D.

E.20°Long.   30°   40°

0°   0°

L. Victoria

AZANIA

L. Tanganyika

UNYAMWEZI
URANGA

KATANGA

S.10°
Lat.   10°

L. Malawi

Luangwa R.

Shire R.

Zambezi R.

Mazoe R.

20°   INDIAN   20°

Salt
Pans   Sabi R.

Limpopo R.

23½°   OCEAN   23½°

KALAHARI
DESERT

BUTWA
(BUSHMAN)

EMBO

ATLANTIC
OCEAN

30°   30°

HOTTENTOT

Orange R.

SCALE
½″ rep. 300 mi.

150 300 450 600
MILES

LEGEND

Vatapa migrations
southwards from
Uranga, circa 1000
A.D. to Butwaland

Possible origin from
southern central
area of Katanga

BIOGRAPHICAL NOTES ON AUTHORS

Solomon Mangwiro Mutswairo was born April 26, 1924, in Zawu, Mazoe District, Zimbabwe (Rhodesia). The eldest of the children of Christian parents, he grew up in present Zambia where his father and mother were both missionaries for The Salvation Army. After primary school at Ibwe Munyama in Zambia where he became proficient in Tonga, he received a teaching diploma from The Salvation Army School of Howard Institute in Rhodesia. He then studied at Adams College (1944-47) and after receiving a Rhodesian Government Scholarship he studied at The University College of Fort Hare (B.Sc., 1953, and University Education Diploma, 1958), at that time a branch of Rhodes University.

In 1953 he began to teach at Goromonzi Government Secondary School, and later became Headmaster at Sanyati Baptist Mission School. He helped found The Salvation Army Secondary School at Mazoe in 1958. He also organized branches of the African Teachers' Association of which he was District Chairman and also started the African Language Development Association, a forerunner of the Rhodesian Government Publication Bureau. Solomon arrived in the U.S. on a Fulbright Scholarship in 1960 for study at the University of Minnesota, but transferred to the University of Ottawa, Canada, to complete his M.A. in Geography in 1964. He is presently studying in the U.S.A. for a degree in Pharmacology.

He is married to Victoria, née Xaba, the first Rhodesian woman graduate of the University of South Africa, and daughter of the late Reverend Mdani Xaba, former moderator of the Bantu Presbyterian Church of South Africa and himself a B.A. and B.D., University of Edinburgh, Scotland. They have four sons and one daughter. His published works are *Feso*, the first Zezuru (Shona) language novel ever published (1957); *Murambiwa Goredema*, a novel published in 1959 and used in Rhodesian schools since; *Ambuyamuderere*, children's nursery rhymes (1967); and many poems in Zezuru in various local journals and in the Shona language anthology *Madetembedzo Akare naMatsva* (1959) and 1962). Awaiting publication is *The Zimbabwe*

Epic, a scholarly treatment of the Monomotapas and Mambos (Kings) of Zimbabwe; an autobiography; and many poems and stories.

Herbert Chitepo was born in 1923 in Rhodesia and after local schooling studied at Fort Hare for a B.A. degree, and in London at the Middle Temple, passing the bar in 1957. He was formerly the Director of Public Prosecution in Dar es Salaam and is now the Vice President of ZANU (The Zimbabwe African National Union). His epic poem, Soko Risina Musoro, was first published in English translation and its original Manyika (a dialect of Shona akin to Zezuru) in London in 1958.

Luke C. Chidavaenzi, born in 1923 in Mazoe District, Rhodesia, took a B.A. in 1953 at Fort Hare University College and has been a high school teacher all his life. He is now Headmaster of a high school in Harare-Salisbury.

Dintweng Kousu, born circa 1920, long served as a Court Interpreter at Magistrate's Court in Francistown. Botswana. His writings on the traditions of the Lilima people were utilized by George Fortune, an English scholar, in his own linguistic researches published in 1945 as *Ndevo Yen'ombe Luvizho.* Kousu's traditional poem, "The High Place of Cattle," appears in Fortune's study in prose fragments and has here for the first time been "assembled" as one poetic work by Mutswairo.